Hispanic/Latino American Families in the United States

An Introduction for Educators and Care Providers

Nancy Sebastian Maldonado
Lehman College of the
City University of New York, Bronx, New York
and
Lilia Lopez DiBello
Barry University, Miami Shores, Florida

Views expressed do not necessarily agree with positions taken by the Association for Childhood Education International.

Bruce Herzig, ACEI Editor
Anne Bauer, ACEI Editor/Design

17904 Georgia Ave., Ste. 215, Olney MD 20832

Library of Congress Cataloging-in-Publication Data

Maldonado, Nancy Sebastian.
Hispanic/Latino American families in the United States : an introduction for educators and care providers / Nancy Sebastian Maldonado and Lilia Lopez DiBello.
p. cm.
Includes bibliographical references.
ISBN 978-0-87173-179-1 (pbk.)
1. Hispanic American families--Social conditions. 2. Hispanic American families--Education. 3. Hispanic American families--Health and hygiene. 4. Hispanic American families--Religion. 5. Hispanic American families--Social life and customs. 6. Hispanic Americans--Social conditions. 7. Hispanic Americans--Education. 8. Hispanic Americans--Health and hygiene. 9. Hispanic Americans--Religion. 10. Hispanic Americans--Social life and customs. I. DiBello, Lilia Lopez. II. Association for Childhood Education International. III. Title.
E184.S75.M364 2012
305.868'073--dc23

2011049259

Table of Contents

Acknowledgments

This project would not have possible without the guidance, support, and patience of many individuals. First and foremost, we are indebted to Anne Bauer, editor extraordinaire, who was incredibly supportive and patient throughout this project. We would also like to thank the following individuals, experts in their fields, who provided their invaluable input through their willingness to review our raw manuscript: Alexandra Abreu, Ruth Ban, David Callejo Perez, Rebecca Harlin, Noemi Carrera-Herendeen, Susan Polirstok, and Lilliam Rosado. We are also appreciative to those who shared their voices in the Latino Reflections interwoven in this book. Gracias!

Dedications

This book is lovingly dedicated to my Latino family, my husband Peter and my children Amanda and Sebastian, and my grandchildren Joseph and Emma, who are the torchbearers of the wisdom and traditions of our families, the Maldonados, Sebastians, Rodriguezes, Santiagos, Lopezes, and Cabassas.

Nancy S. Maldonado

To my grandparents, Raul and Iraida Garcia, who were the inspiration for why I began thinking about the need to share my cultural identity with others. They lovingly instilled in all of us what it meant to be a Cuban American family. I am lucky to share this with my husband, Darin Di-Bello, and my children, Darin, Jr. and Dylan.

Lilia Lopez DiBello

Foreword

by Dr. David Callejo Perez
Saginaw Valley State University
University Center, Michigan
College of Education Carl A. Gerstacker Endowed Chair

I recently participated in a summit on Hispanic education in the United States. The speaker discussed how the federal government, for the first time, was going to actively pursue educational change for Hispanics. Members of the audience, many of whom were national leaders in education, posed interesting questions derived from personal experiences with discrimination, culture, and power. While the narratives were powerful, the solutions were simplistic and attempted to create narrowly defined goals. This meeting was a microcosm of Hispanic education in the United States—individuals speaking about the power of personal narratives and then creating consensus for a one-size-fits-all resolution. We need to see Hispanic education—and, more importantly, Hispanics—differently than we have; we need to listen to our own stories, and use those unique narratives to create diverse and multi-layered identities that will tap into our communities' rich artistic, literary, economic, political, and healthy environs, and create sustainability for our children.

When considering Hispanics in the U.S. education system, the typical discussion unfortunately usually relates to Hispanics' shortcomings and meeting a perceived "achievement gap." I hope readers will join me in exploring the idea of what happens when cultural choices run counter to ideas and habits put forth by schools and others involved in children's lives. In this book, Maldonado and DiBello explore the diversity of our families, beliefs, spirituality, child rearing, education, and cultural celebrations, guiding us through the varied and deep river that represents Hispanic culture in the United States.

As John Dewey (1916/1977) reminds us, renewing self and community best occurs in a democratic society where justice and caring are central. This is only possible in societies where central community figures shape, foster, and enrich young children's lives. By exposing children to a multitude of experiences that help shape their life stories, one day they will be able to enact those democratic ideals in everyday practice when they choose to vote, raise a child, and live within a neighborhood, and when they are asked to judge themselves as democratic citizens. Regardless of one's background or economic reality, the successful attainment of skills and fundamentals only occurs when the intellectual and emotional growth of that individual is respected, cared for, and enhanced—and this occurs only when the dedication, caring, talent, and intelligence of the child is allowed to flourish.

Minority students are just starting to make some progress in their struggle to compete in the classroom and workforce. Yet the simplistic notions of identity created by society could serve to nullify present progress in self-efficacy, and even place minority students at a greater disadvantage. Although research in the area of self-efficacy has been substantial over the past 30 years, and the process of labeling and evaluating race has been going on for some 40 years, little research has been done in an attempt to localize the cause of group identity for individuals or even subgroups. In other words, where do I belong as a Cuban within Hispanic culture? Hispanic students draw on various cultural and linguistic skills, knowledge, contacts, and abilities nurtured in their home communities that emphasize maintaining self-efficacy to maneuver through institutional barriers.

As I wrote this foreword, I wondered about the identity and future of my daughter as a Hispanic child in the United States. The authors of this text have considered the complex issue of Hispanic identity and offered the reader paths that can enlighten how we view, represent, and think about being Hispanic in the United States. Inspired by this approach to the study of identity, I want to tell the reader about my daughter, Icie Tru Callejo, who was born in November 2008 to a Cuban father and a Polish-Irish-German mother in Pittsburgh, Pennsylvania. I am not unique; most of my friends have married non-Hispanics and moved away from their homes. I hope Icie's story helps us appreciate who we are as Hispanics. Her *abuela* and *abuelo* were born in Cuba and came to the United States shortly before the Mariel Boat Lift in 1980, when my sister and I were very young. My mother had been a political prisoner in Cuba for nine years and instilled in her children the value of self-efficacy, being different while maintaining our Cuban roots. Icie's maternal grandmother and grandfather were both born in Western Pennsylvania, as was her mother. My wife, Emily, self-identifies as a Pittsburgher; many of her friends had similar backgrounds, a melting pot of generations of European immigration into industrialized Western Pennsylvania. Our daughter has tried picadillo and pirogues, and wore agua de violeta while enjoying the Pittsburgh Steelers' victory in Super Bowl XL.

Icie is being raised as a Cuban and a Pittsburgher—yes Pittsburgh is a culture unto itself—and is now living in Michigan. Although Spanish and Cuban culture is part of her life, in Michigan she is not likely to encounter many people like her. The majority of Hispanic persons she will meet will be Mexican, not Cubans (unlike my experience growing up in Miami). My wife and I are both Protestants (Baptist and nondenominational). We have been asked if we have thought about a church to baptize our child. Those who ask, both Hispanic and non-Hispanic, are bewildered to learn that we are not Catholic, which says a lot about the limited view of what being Hispanic means in the United States. Evangelicals are the fastest-growing religion among Hispanics. Based on such limited views, I believe that many people Icie will encounter will draw conclusions about her that will affect her for life.

As we begin to deal with the changing landscapes of the society in which we live, it is a requisite that issues of achieving sustained access to equitable education be explored. Parents and teachers have a responsibility to promote an authentic conversation that nurtures tools of success for individuals involved in the lives of our children. Discussions must include the words and lives of students, teachers, and community members; involve critical decision-making; and ultimately promote transformation. Our children's experiences must be included. What we find in many communities is that children's identities are ignored, dismissed, and perhaps not given a space to form.

The solution being proposed by reformers is that with higher standards, higher performance will come. Given the results from No Child Left Behind so far, we find that the places needing the most attention are classified as "failing" and have either been passed on to private corporations or have been closed while students are bused elsewhere. The argument put forth by the reformers is that teaching and learning should be solely based on scientific research. The human loss resulting from this ideological viewpoint may never be recovered.

McLaren and Hammer (1996) described how our sensibilities are bombarded with such a variety of media forms that our critical comprehension skills have fallen into rapid deterioration, leading, they argue, to a collective loss of reasoning and of history. These authors further posit that many American television viewers accept a distorted picture of the real world more readily than reality itself, a pervasive psychology of denial that has allowed a war against people of color to continue in U.S. cities. As we watch television shows like

Dora the Explorer and Handy Manny, I find myself questioning what we are teaching our children. In an attempt to be diverse, children's television has created caricatures of Hispanic culture. I hear non-Hispanics asking me about traditions they want to introduce into their homes in order to teach diversity (taco night or Hispanic Christmas—Los Reyes Magos), or telling me that they recently purchased a Dora doll because they want their children to be exposed to dolls from all cultures. Such shows provide these parents a safe space to acknowledge the largest minority in the United States without addressing such important questions as immigration, the Hispanic labor force, or the future of Hispanic education. Instead, everyone feels good when their child speaks two Spanish words and knows about *el Día de los Muertos* (the Day of the Dead, or, as a colleague at West Virginia University called it, "Mexican Halloween").

Parents have to carefully and continually teach the diversity that makes us uniquely Hispanic and American. In my own family, we have Jewish and Lebanese uncles on my mother's side. My two first cousins are biracial, living in Montreal and raising their children as Cuban and Quebecois. My nephew, who lives in Guadalajara, is married to a Mexican citizen and we often discuss the difficulties of bridging two cultures.

Hispanic/Latino American Families in the United States prompts readers to ask powerful questions, such as how does society shape our identity, how do we shape each others' identity, and how is our identity shaped by place. In *Pedagogy of Place* (2004), I wrote that the purposeful creation of spaces that constitute learning environments and the aesthetic dimensions of the created space of school all shape the ability of that public space to represent the needs and desires of the constituents it serves. Even with the Internet and the ease of communication across nations, we remain unique as Hispanics in the United States, affecting our world as it affects us. We are now in a world described by W.E.B. DuBois in *The Souls of Black Folk* (1903/2003) as straddling two cultures—in this case, Americaness and Hispanicism. This book before you is a multi-faceted account of insight, research, anecdotes, and resources, and is a testament to the richness of our culture and the possibilities for our future.

Introduction

We are thrilled to be able share our knowledge about and experiences in working with Latino families. Hispanic heritage is highly complex. Although we are grounded in the customs of Spain, much of our heritage and practice is derived from the indigenous people of the western hemisphere, Africa, and other European countries (including France, Ireland, and Holland). This book shares some information about the Hispanic communities in the United States, regarding child-rearing beliefs, values, education, health and wellness, and immigration issues. While it is impossible to generalize within this complex and varied community, this book provides some insight into practices and beliefs that may be characteristic of specific Hispanic families and, thus, may help educators and care providers build their understanding about the community and so better serve them.

The relevance of a book such as this one is that it gives parents, educators, political leaders, policymakers, and others an opportunity to share relevant information that will open doors of communication and allow for questions to be asked and answered. This process will lead to wonderful partnerships and help future generations to work in earnest toward excellence for all. "Partnerships, when developed with intentionality and critical consciousness, provide a vehicle for inviting the participation of all families" (Dotson-Blake, Foster, & Gressard, 2009).

The Authors' Histories and a Discussion of Terminology

Although our own backgrounds are similar, there *are* differences in our cultural practices and traditions. Nancy is Puerto Rican American and Lilia is Cuban American. As we prepared to write this book, we considered whether to use the term "Hispanic" or the term "Latino," and discovered that we identified ourselves differently in this respect. Upon consideration, we determined that a discussion about this difference would be a good introduction to the diversity within the Latino culture. By sharing our own personal cultural histories growing up, we hope to shed light on the complexities of our own "Hispanidad."

Lilia's Story

As we researched and gathered resources for this project, we realized that I was using the term "Hispanic" and that Nancy was primarily using the word "Latino" in our discussions. At first, I did not see the need to discuss the difference. In time, however, it became clear that some of the people we spoke to were very passionate about the choice of word to identify their ethnicity. We realized that the first step to take was identification of who belonged to this ethnic group we were exploring.

I began asking everyone around me—my mother, my father, my sister, my grandfather, my children, my cousins, my friends, my colleagues—what term they preferred. Some quickly gave me a preference without elaboration. Others halfheartedly asked me, "What's the difference?" and then went on to rationalize how the terms were pertinent to them within their own professional and personal experience. For others, the question clearly struck a nerve and I was surprised by how passionate they felt. I offer a brief synopsis of my findings.

Many of those who write about this issue agree that use of the term "Hispanic" became commonly used in the United States as a result of government efforts to quantify in 1980 how many Spanish-speaking households existed in the United States. Some of the initial government discussions about the terminology determined that the term "Latino" was too similar to "Ladino," a Spanish dialect spoken by Spanish Jews, and so was potentially confusing. Further concerns about the term "Latino" focused on ties the term might imply to Italy, Portugal, and France through an association with Latin and Mediterranean Europe. Discussions in favor of the term "Latino" noted that Spanish grammar rules allow for us to specify Latinos or Latinas. The word "Hispanic" does not allow us to specify gender.

By the 2000 Census survey, the criteria were distinguished even further to include Hispanics of all races. Also of interest is the fact that the government chose to recognize the popularity of the term "Latino" by using "Hispanic *or* Latino" in the 2000 Census glossary definition:

> Hispanic or Latino origin
>
> For Census 2000, American Community Survey: People who identify with the terms "Hispanic" or "Latino" are those who classify themselves in one of the specific Hispanic or Latino categories listed on the Census 2000 or ACS questionnaire—"Mexican," "Puerto Rican," or "Cuban"—as well as those who indicate that they are "other Spanish, Hispanic, or Latino." Origin can be viewed as the heritage, nationality group, lineage, or country of birth of the person or the person's parents or ancestors before their arrival in the United States. People who identify their origin as Spanish, Hispanic, or Latino may be of any race.
>
> 1990 Census of Population and Housing: A self-designated classification for people whose origins are from Spain, the Spanish-speaking countries of Central or South America, the Caribbean, or those identifying themselves generally as Spanish, Spanish-American, etc. Origin can be viewed as ancestry, nationality, or country of birth of the person or person's parents or ancestors prior to their arrival in the United States. (www.census.gov)

Clearly, the terms being used are meant to be inclusive and to acknowledge the identity most have with the language spoken. Great diversity exists, however, even in terms of language, because many different dialects of Spanish are spoken in the United States.

In fact, many of the people I spoke with did not wish to answer if they were Hispanic or Latino; rather, they wanted to identify with the specific country that they or their ancestors came from. So, I often heard "I am Cuban," ". . . Dominican," ". . . Nicaraguan," ". . . Honduran," ". . . Mexican," ". . . Puerto Rican," or ". . . Venezuelan." With a goal of bringing people together rather than promoting divisiveness, it would be a mistake to let ourselves get caught up in this argument.

Through dialogue, we can improve the way in which we communicate with Spanish-speakers in America. I have no doubt that I will soon be saying that I can relate to being "Latina," even though my preference usually lies in identifying with the term "Hispanic." Regardless of the term that one chooses to use, we can recognize the common goal of identifying with others who speak Spanish (either as a primary or a secondary language).

I was intrigued by this discussion of "Hispanic" vs. "Latino." Given that I was born in the United States, I have always considered myself American first; the fact that I spoke Spanish at home was a bonus. With each passing generation, I think it becomes even harder to maintain identification with certain cultures. I have never even been to the country where both of my parents were born (Cuba). I know that my children are even further removed, as English has become the dominant language in our household. As a result of working on this project, my family had conversations about cultural identity, expressing pride and sharing many stories. Furthermore, I am happy to share the story of my colleague, whose enthusiasm for the use of the term "Latina" can be engaging.

Nancy's Story

I grew up in Spanish Harlem, New York, in the 1950s, as a second-generation (mainland) American. My family considered itself to be American; indeed, Puerto Ricans have been Americans since Congress passed the *Jones Act* in 1917. My mother, who was born in Puerto Rico, referred to all Spanish-speaking people as "Latinos." She was proud to be a Latina and passed this feeling on to my sister and myself.

I attended school in Spanish Harlem from kindergarten until my graduation from the 8th grade. The school officials told my parents to speak only English at home, a common practice during this period. All Latino parents were told that eliminating Spanish at home would ensure success in school. At my house, my father, my sister, and I spoke English, while my mother spoke Spanish and we responded in English. That was the end of my experience speaking Spanish, as well as the end of my Latina self-identification until I graduated from college. I was then Puerto Rican American, or as my sister and I were coached to say by our dad, an "American of Puerto Rican descent."

The turbulent sixties re-opened the question of self-identity. Many Hispanic Americans went to the war in Vietnam, especially those from poverty-stricken areas. So many Puerto Rican Americans from Spanish Harlem came back to their families in coffins or came back ill from exposure to chemical warfare. I began to notice that each wake I attended had both the American and the Puerto Rican flags in displays of honor. I also noticed people in the community identifying themselves as Puerto Ricans, dropping the "American." I began identifying myself as Puerto Rican and "Latina" as a way of embracing my heritage.

When I entered college in 1970, I saw the category "Hispanic" on government forms. I found it interesting that the categories also included Puerto Rican. So I checked off Puerto Rican. College discussions during this period were filled with questions about the government, the Vietnam War, and heritage. Many interesting movements were conceptualized, such as bilingual/bicultural education, multicultural education, and a renewed understanding of the term "melting pot."

During those radical days of the 1970s, I was a Latina, a Puerto Rican, and a Boricua (derived from Boriquén, the indigenous name of Puerto Rico before the Spanish discovery). Throughout my studies in school, I learned that "Hispanic" related to the islands of the Caribbean, specifically the island of Española. So on a personal level, "Hispanic" became a term I associated with Latin American history, American history, and government-issued material.

In the ensuing 30 years, I married a Puerto Rican American and have raised two children as Latinos. We self-identify as Latinos because it has a lot of meaning for us. It is a Spanish word that means "of Latin origin," which encompasses a variety of groups. We prefer it to the English word "Hispanic," which means "of or relating to people of Spain, Portugal or Latin America" (Webster's New Collegiate Dictionary, 1995, p. 542). We do embrace the Spanish culture very much, but it is only a portion of who we are.

When asked the question "What do you prefer to call yourself? What is your self-identity?," I reply that I was born and raised in the United States and I am proud of my heritage as a Puerto Rican American. My childhood experiences, socialization, and emotions are grounded within a passionately charged cultural context, so I am Latina!

Concluding Thoughts About the Terminology From Both Authors

By sharing our own cultural identities and our preferences for identifying ourselves as either "Hispanic" or "Latino," we highlight personal choice in how individuals select what they wish to call themselves. We advise educators and care providers to listen to children and their families and not to hesitate to ask them about how they prefer to be identified.

Readers should expect to see each term, "Hispanic" and "Latino," used throughout this text. Moreover, the term "Latino" is used as a term inclusive of women. To get lost in an argument over whether we should be called Hispanics or Latinos would be a mistake. We can and should take pride in the use of both terms.

Organization of the Book

We took some time to decide how this book would be organized in order to best meet the needs of our audience, namely educators and care providers. We continuously returned to the notion that this project could only be a reflection of our own lived experiences. In other words, the lens through which we were processing and analyzing this information could, would, and should have an effect on the finished product. Therefore, we concluded that in order to truly represent the myriad voices within Hispanic culture, we would need to provide an opportunity for a group of Latinos to respond to our work. This group includes representatives from the media, religious settings, and educational institutions, as well as policymakers, artists, and health professionals. These reflections are integrated into our work in order to celebrate the diversity of our culture. We have interspersed excerpts from the reflections throughout the chapters. Placement of each particular reflection depends on the story that they told or is based on the insight that they provided. Appendix A, "Latino Reflections," includes all of the reflections shared throughout the book in their entirety. We hope that you enjoy these lived experiences as critical reflections that support the cultural identity of each "speaker."

Hispanic/Latino American Families in the United States is arranged in eight chapters. Upon identifying the topics we addressed, we often found it necessary to blend topics and related issues. The concept of cultural identity is very important to the premise of this book. We are pleased to share with you the foreword written by Dr. David Callejo Perez, which addresses this concept. His inspiring words shed light on an issue we feel to be of utmost importance and that is the ultimate reason we chose to undertake this project. Now is the time to think about future generations and now is the time to consider what we want the Hispanic/Latino legacy to be.

Chapter 1. Shifting Worlds: Changing Families, by Lilia C. DiBello, tells the story of Hispanic families and briefly highlights some of the immigration histories of particular groups—Mexicans, Puerto Ricans, Cubans, and Central/South Americans. Resources are provided for those who wish to read a more in-depth description of how and why these groups found their way to the United States. The major focus, however, of Chapter 1 is the concept of "familia."

Chapter 2. Health Practices and Cultural Beliefs, by Nancy S. Maldonado, highlights health and mental health issues of Hispanics in the United States, including sobering statistics about childhood obesity, asthma, diabetes, and oral health. Furthermore, we felt it was important to bring in the concept of spirituality and folk medicinal practices, as it ties into the overall well-being of Latinos. Many Latinos place great faith in homeopathic treatments.

Chapter 3. Spirituality: Care of the Soul, by Nancy S. Maldonado, provides a look at the multi-faceted beliefs of Latinos. She looks at the many religions practiced by Latinos, including Roman Catholicism, Pentecostal and Fundamentalism, Protestantism, Santeria, Islam, Judaism, and the Church of Jesus Christ of Latter-Day Saints.

Chapter 4. Child-Rearing Practices, by Nancy S. Maldonado, considers parenting styles in the Hispanic communities, including the struggle of disciplining children living in two cultures, and an examination of acceptable and unacceptable behaviors. Family value systems and how they relate to acculturation within American society also are discussed.

Chapter 5. Education Issues: The Latino/Hispanic Experience, by Lilia C. DiBello, discusses various issues in education affecting the Hispanic communities. It begins with a review of significant laws, court cases, and policies affecting school systems. This is followed by a brief summary of the different bilingual education programs and models of instruction. Successes and challenges of Hispanics in school systems are addressed, and the chapter also reviews the need to focus on higher education for this growing minority population.

Chapter 6. Special Needs: Disabilities and Interventions, by Nancy S. Maldonado, presents issues in special education regarding Latino children, particularly in light of the over-identification of Latino children for special services in education. Special attention is focused on how Hispanic families respond to their children with disabilities, and on coping mechanisms used when a child has been diagnosed with special needs.

Chapter 7. Images of Hispanic Families: Film, Television, and Children's Literature, by Nancy S. Maldonado, exposes the history of Hispanic stereotypes that have been present in media, politics, and children's literature. Special attention is placed on how Hispanic culture has influenced the current American way of life.

Chapter 8. Celebrations, Traditions, and Fiestas: Salsa y Sabor, by Lilia C. DiBello and Nancy S. Maldonado, reveals some typical customs and practices of Latinos, including birthday celebrations, *quinceañeras*, weddings, funerals, and sacramental celebrations.

Dichos and Supplementary Material

We also have included *dichos* (Latino proverbs) at the beginning of each chapter to set the tone. The *dichos* were selected from Cristina Pérez's *Living by Los Dichos: Advice From a Mother to a Daughter* (2006). Furthermore, each chapter includes a list of materials and resources and Appendix B provides supplementary reading suggestions and a list of videos. Appendix C provides music resources. The most comprehensive Appendix is Appendix A, which is a compilation of the reflections shared throughout this work, presented in their entirety. Appendix D provides some more in-depth information about legislation relating to bilingual education.

By intermixing our own cultural experiences and multi-faceted insights, as well as our professional experiences as teacher educators, this book provides a perspective on the bicultural experiences of Latino children and their families, whether they are recent immigrants or third-generation Americans. We hope that we have presented an authentic testament to both Hispanic/Latino Americans and the teachers and care providers who work with them.

Chapter 1
Shifting Worlds: Changing Families

Lilia C. DiBello

"En la tierra que fueras, haz lo que verás."
(Whatever land you go to, do what you see.)

"La familia es lo único que tenemos con toda certeza."
(With all certainty, family is the only thing we have.)

"Shifting Worlds: Changing Families" shares the story of Hispanic / Latino families by briefly highlighting some of the immigration histories of particular groups — Mexicans, Puerto Ricans, Cubans, and Central / South Americans. Through statistical data, the reader will receive a quick summary landscape of this rich and diverse cultural group. The context of this chapter is grounded in the concept of "familia."

Familia [fah-mee'-le-ah]—1. Family, the people who live in the same house together. 2. Family, those that descend from one common progenitor: a race, a generation, a house, a clan. (*The New Velazquez Spanish and English Dictionary*, 1999)

For most Hispanics, ties to family are of immense importance and permeate their lifestyles. For example, an *abuelo* (grandfather) and/or an *abuela* (grandmother) is an integral part of the family, and incredible respect is shown to the elders of the family. In all parts of the United States, the *abuelo* and/or *abuela* commonly live with their grandchildren and/or great-grandchildren. They may be the primary caregivers of the younger generation. The phenomenon of grandparents serving as primary caregivers is more common among blacks and Hispanics than among non-Hispanic whites, but the sharpest rise since the recession began has been among whites (Livingston & Parker, 2010).

At a recent family wedding, I introduced my youngest son to a cousin he had never met before. When we were driving home, he questioned why he had so many cousins and if it was possible that we just designated people *primos* (cousins), when they were only long-lost friends of the family. At first, I tried explaining that some were children of his grandmother's cousins, which technically made them third or fourth cousins. Then, I explained that his great-grandparents from Cuba each came from large families of seven children, which adds up to a lot of cousins over the years. After about 10 minutes of trying to understand the specific relationships, my son stopped the conversation to say, "You know, Mom, *primo* is just fine, and I don't need any more explanations!"

This exchange reminds me of what it means to come from a Hispanic family. A sense of belonging and a connectedness brings strength to everyone. If one person succeeds, the family celebrates; when someone is burdened, the family pulls together to help them through the difficulty. There is a peace in knowing that one is at home—a sense of belonging in Hispanic families.

So, what happens when families become blended with other cultures or when families immigrate to the United States, where they are surrounded by many other cultures? What sense of cultural identity is sustained or established when Hispanics become part of a new community? We must consider these questions as we see Hispanic families speaking Spanish in the home and English everywhere else, or what happens when the next generation of English-speakers marries and starts their own families? How strong are the family ties? What language(s) will they share with their own children? What culture will they identify with? Our world is definitely shifting; changes in families are inevitable and the implications for communities are great.

Structure of Family

To say that the structure of family has changed for Hispanic Americans is an understatement. Some changes in family structure may be attributed to the economic situations affecting families when they make their way to a new country. For second- or third-generation Latino families, changes to family structure may have more to do with social relationships they have developed within the community, changing dynamics of the family unit, or shifts in the educational opportunities of the family members.

What does the traditional Hispanic/Latino family look like? This is a difficult question to answer. Latinos live in homes with single mothers as the head of the household, they live in homes where married parents raise their children, they live in homes where the grandparents serve as the matriarch or patriarch of the family and help to cover expenses. Like the rest of America, you find a variety of family structures. The U.S. Census Bureau provides statistics that can help us learn a little more about Hispanics living in the United States. We discuss these findings with the understanding that all statistics are subject to some sampling error.

Multi-generational American family households are increasing as a result of immigration trends and economic trends that have caused a need for families to blend resources. "Hispanics (22%), blacks (23%) and Asians (25%) are all significantly more likely than white non-Hispanics (13%) to live in a multi-generational family household" (Taylor et al., 2010, p. 7). In fact, when looking at three-generation households (parents with adult children who have children of their own, who are all living under the same roof), Latinos have the highest percentage of families living in this model, with 48% indicating that this is their living arrangement (Taylor et al., 2010).

Statistics also indicate trends with respect to the marital status within Hispanic households. The data from the 2006-2008 American Community Survey show that for the population age 15 years and older, Hispanics were more likely than non-Hispanic whites never to have been married (37.6% compared to 26.4%, respectively) (U.S. Census Bureau, 2008). Due to the fact that just over a third of Hispanic households are led by single parents, the structure of the family unit continues to change. A study conducted by Landale and Oropesa (2001), which examined the involvement of fathers in the lives of mainland Puerto Rican children, noted that non-marital childbearing played a major role in why households came to be headed by single female family members. Although this study was not looking specifically at children living in the United States, it does shed light on the fact that households headed by single women are most likely not the result of divorce. While we cannot make any assumptions about the father's role in raising the children, the data do support the fact that a significant percentage of Hispanic children do not live in the traditional two-parent household.

Statistics do show that two-thirds of Hispanic families are still headed by married couples and the divorce rate for this group is one of the lowest, at only 8% (U.S. Census Bureau, 2008). Regardless of marital status, studies have shown that Hispanic mothers prefer close mother/child relationships. There is an emphasis on attachment and sharing cultural values with children (Escovar & Lazarus, 1982; Harwood & Miller, 1991), with a significant number of mothers indicating their desire for children to be respectful. It is quite common for Hispanic families to expect children to be very attached to the family unit. Although second- and third-generation Hispanic/Latino Americans are more likely to move away from home in pursuit of higher education, one can still find many families where sleepovers are forbidden, chaperones accompany daughters on dates, and children remain at home until they are ready to marry and begin their own nuclear families.

Diversity of Hispanic Population in the United States

A book dealing with the education of Hispanic/Latino Americans in the United States must address the immigration history of Hispanics in order to provide a framework from which educators and care providers can develop an understanding of these cultural groups. Immigration statistics show that Hispanics are a diverse group of individuals who live in many states across the nation. This section will explore what happens when families become blended with other cultures, or when families immigrate to the United States and move into neighborhoods filled with families from many other cultures.

A 2002 U.S. Census Bureau report revealed that more than one in eight people in the United States is of Hispanic origin (2003, p. 1). In fact, more recent reports indicate that although Smith remains the most common surname, two Hispanic surnames—Garcia and Rodriguez—are now among the top 10 most common in the United States, while Martinez nearly edged out Wilson for 10th place (Roberts, 2007). The American Community Survey in 2006 gathered information in reference to Hispanic population data. The data that was collected allowed for Hispanics to report their origins, and the survey revealed the demographic figures in 2006 to be from a total of a little under 45 million Hispanics/Latinos in the United States. Sixty-four percent of Hispanics reported to be of Mexican origin, 9% of Puerto Rican origin, 7.6% from Central American origin, 5.5% of South American origin, 3.4% of Cuban origin, and 2.8% of Dominican origin. Of importance to note was the fact that 7.7% chose "Other Hispanic," therefore not identifying with any of the groups presented by the survey.

Ask Latinos in any part of the United States about their cultural background and they are sure to tell you with great pride about their family's country of origin. For example, Nicaraguans wave their flags during Hispanic Heritage Month and do not wish to be confused with Hondurans, Guatemalans, Bolivians, or Peruvians. There most certainly is a difference, and this diversity within the Latino culture can be a source of great pride when discussing the accomplishments of an individual representing their country. For example, at any Florida Marlins baseball game, a multitude of Dominican Republic flags can be seen being waved by Dominicans coming to cheer for Hanley Ramirez. At the annual *Calle*

My Family Has a Proud History: Grace Ibanez Friedman

As I look back, I am grateful that I never lost my basic connection to my past, despite the years of living almost in an underground space, much like the main character in Ralph Ellison's *Invisible Man*. It is good to be one whole self all the time, visible and viable.

You can turn to the Appendix A for the complete reflection offered by Grace.

Ocho celebration (www.carnavalmiami.com/calle8/) in Miami, millions of people celebrate the music and food from their countries of origin, making it the largest Latino gathering in America.

Many cities in the United States have neighborhoods that are identified as "Little Italy" or "China Town," and certain cities have neighborhoods that celebrate a Latino heritage. In Miami, Little Havana has a large concentration of Cubans, while Sweetwater has a high concentration of Nicaraguans and parts of Doral are largely Venezuelan. Of course, Spanish Harlem in New York long has been associated with Puerto Ricans and is currently experiencing an increase in the Mexican population. These neighborhoods often have businesses, such as restaurants, bakeries, and food markets, and community centers and schools that reflect the various cultural groups.

The U.S. Census Bureau data reveal that Hispanics are more geographically concentrated than non-Hispanic whites. This statement is easy to verify in cities known for their high concentration of Latino families, such as New York, Miami, Los Angeles, and San Antonio. In 2006, the U.S. Census Bureau documented California, Texas, Florida, New York, and Illinois as having the largest Hispanic populations. Furthermore, studies (Pérez & McDonough, 2008; Swail et al., 2003) have shown that many students of Hispanic upbringing choose to stay close to home when considering their options for higher education, as reflected in the location of "Hispanic-serving institutions" in cities highly populated by Latinos.

Immigration

It is important for educators and care providers to have an understanding of how immigration may affect the families with whom they work. The 2000 Census allowed for Hispanics to identify themselves as Mexican, Puerto Rican, Cuban, or "Other Hispanic." Critics noted that the lack of opportunity to identify country of origin with more distinction might have led to a count that underrepresented certain groups (such as the South American or Dominican populations). Question number 8 on the 2010 Census form specifically asked, "Is person of Hispanic, Latino or Spanish origin?" If the response was "Yes," then the respondent had the opportunity to choose from four categories: Mexican, Mexican-American, Chicano as the first option; Puerto Rican as the second option; Cuban as the third option; and the fourth option was "Another Hispanic, Latino or Spanish origin" and the respondent was given the opportunity to fill in a box with the exact origin. Nevertheless, one must always consider that "since the number of undocumented immigrants from all Spanish-speaking Latin America who live in the U.S. has not been calculated, it is impossible to arrive at an accurate count of Latinos" (Novas, 2003, p. 7).

Mexican Families

For purposes of providing the reader with a background of who Latinos are in the United States, we will briefly discuss some figures from the 2010 Census. The Mexican-origin population increased by 54% between 2000 and 2010 and had the largest numeric change (11.2 million), growing from 20.6 million in 2000 to 31.8 million in 2010 (Ennis, Rios-Vargas, & Albert, 2010). Mexican Americans were found to be the largest subgroup of Hispanics in the United States, with the highest concentration living in California, Texas, Illinois, Arizona, and Colorado. Although a large percentage of Mexican Americans are second- or third-generation, the percentage of foreign-born Mexican Americans is still greater than 50%. This figure, of course, does not include a large number of undocumented immigrants. A discussion of the Mexican American experience would not be complete without a summary of why and when Mexicans chose to immigrate to the United States. Although it is evident that all families have their own story of "why," when large numbers emigrate from one country to another it is possible to identify some key motivations that will provide some understanding for educators or care providers.

Mexican American Families: A Brief Immigration History

There is a long history of migrant workers coming to the United States from Mexico. As workers in the fields, their primary goal was to make money to provide for their families back home. With the increase of fruit production in the state of California from 1850-80, Mexican workers played an important role in supporting that segment of American agriculture when Chinese laborers were no longer permitted to work, due to the passing of the Chinese Exclusion Act (1882). Furthermore, the Southwest areas of the United States previously belonging to Mexico needed a large number of field hands; it was natural to look south to Mexico for workers who were familiar with the land and climate to support commercial agriculture, the mining industry, and construction of the railroad that would connect the United States to Mexico.

After the Mexican Revolution in 1910, the Mexican government struggled with their economy and with meeting the most basic needs of citizens. As a result, between 1910 and the 1930s, many Mexicans had difficulty providing for their families and began looking north for opportunities where skilled labor was needed even more, as many Americans were fighting in World War I. Mexican workers signed contracts with U.S. ranchers (which became known as the first de facto Bracero Program) that stipulated rate of pay, work schedule, and place of employment, and was signed by an immigration official. Often, families were permitted to accompany a worker during the contract period. In 1924, the U.S. Border Patrol in 1924 was established and non-U.S. citizens working without required documentation were identified as "illegal aliens."

Mexican workers were efficient and hard-working and were willing to labor for very little pay. This caused conflict in some areas of the United States, where American laborers were fighting for improved working conditions and higher salaries to support their families. As a result, the United States began to regulate, quite stringently, the immigration of Mexicans and migrant workers.

Nevertheless, with the United States back at war in 1942, it became necessary to once again find laborers to help keep the U.S. economy stable. With the Bracero Program, millions of Mexican laborers crossed the border into the United States between 1942 and 1964 to work temporarily for farmers and ranchers. Families often traveled with the laborers in search of a better way of life. An estimated 4 million Mexican farm workers traveled north for work, and the Braceros (as many of these laborers came to be known) hailing from rural parts of Mexico sustained agricultural growth in the United States for a significant time. In 1947, with WWII over, efforts were made to reduce the workforce of migrant workers once again. By the 1960s, a large number of undocumented agricultural workers were still seeking employment, because their contracts had expired but they did not wish to return to rural Mexico. This led to conflict about immigration policy with respect to migrant workers, and ultimately to the formal termination of the Bracero Program in 1964. Although there was no formal need for the Emergency Farm Labor Service by the 1960s, many Mexicans still believed they could find greater prosperity for their families in the United States, even if it meant crossing the border without required documentation.

The Bracero Program legally existed for four decades, and it was difficult for American farmers to part with the supply of low-wage labor provided by migrant workers. In fact, in 1952, certain states (Texas, California, and parts of the Southwest) "persuaded Congress to adopt the so-called Texas Proviso, which specifically exempted the employers of undocumented workers from any penalty. It remained the law until 1986" (Suro, 1998, p. 82).

Many migrant farm workers (and their families) make their homes in the United States. The education of migrant children is a unique and challenging endeavor, as the transient nature of this population is a major challenge to school systems. Some of the resources available for working with this unique population are shared in Chapter 5, which focuses on education issues.

Puerto Rican Families

Puerto Ricans are the second largest sub-group of Latinos living in the mainland United States. Families with ties to Puerto Rico often travel back and forth for employment or to pursue educational opportunities. Puerto Rico has been a U.S. Commonwealth since July 25, 1952; therefore, Puerto Ricans are American citizens and there is technically no "immigration" to the mainland United States, but rather a migration from the U.S. Commonwealth island of Puerto Rico to the continental United States. The 2010 Census data revealed that high concentrations of Puerto Ricans live in New York, Florida, New Jersey, Pennsylvania, Massachusetts, and Connecticut (Ennis et al., 2010).

As would be expected, the research shows that Puerto Ricans migrate to the mainland United States in search of employment with higher wage-earning opportunities, to reunite with family, or perhaps to further their education. The relationship between Puerto Rico and the United States is a long one and, at times, a confusing one. At the end of the Spanish-American War in 1898, Puerto Rico became a U.S. protectorate. The United States needed to develop a relationship with Puerto Rico, but faced a language barrier and concerns about having a strong U.S. military presence on the island. It would take a little over 50 years and the strong political leadership of Luis Muñoz Marín to achieve a "free associated state" status (*estado libre asociado*) for the island of Puerto Rico. Puerto Ricans have voted repeatedly to keep their U.S. Commonwealth status. As a commonwealth, Puerto Rico is under the control of the U.S. Congress, and they send a non-voting member, an elected commissioner, to the House of Representatives to speak on behalf of the residents of Puerto Rico. All citizens of Puerto Rico may vote in election primaries for the President of the United States; however, they do not retain the constitutional right to vote in the general elections if they are living on the island. If living on the mainland, citizens do gain the right to vote in the general elections. Aside from the issue of voting privileges, issues of taxes and national identity (specifically with respect to language) would need to be resolved prior to statehood being an option that Puerto Ricans would seriously consider.

The special relationship between Puerto Rico and the United States has had a major impact on families. With younger generations speaking more English and having greater ties to the U.S. mainland, the question of which "culture" to identify with becomes complicated. For many, it becomes a goal of keeping ties to Puerto Rico alive through traditions and language, but assuming the role of an American citizen when on the mainland.

Cuban Families

People of Cuban descent are another representative group of Hispanics living in the United States. The greatest percentage of this group is located in the state of Florida, with the highest concentration in Miami-Dade County. Cuban Americans are also likely to live in

A Puerto Rican Daughter Reflects: Raquel Quesada

If one's life is molded by the experiences of our formative early years, then I am proof that what I have accomplished professionally, what I have emulated as a mother and as a friend, and what has driven my spiritual beliefs were profoundly shaped by my early experiences as a young Puerto Rican immigrant girl to the United States. From all the many remembrances that bombard my memories and spark around in my mind, the one that seems to stand out most is that of separating from my father when he came to New York to work and earn enough money to send to our family.

To share in more of Raquel's experiences and to read how her family life affected her upbringing, read her story in Appendix A.

New Jersey, California, New York, and Texas.

Prior to 1959, Cubans enjoyed a mutually beneficial relationship with the United States; residents traveled freely back and forth for business, pleasure, and to seek educational opportunities. After Fidel Castro took political power of Cuba in 1959, a large percentage of refugees began seeking political asylum in the United States, believing it would be only temporary and they soon would be able to return to their lives back in Cuba.

In the first few months of Cuba's transition into a Communist regime, many Cubans who did not want their children to be raised in a Communist nation were willing to risk separation from them in the hope that one day they would be reunited, either in the United States or in a non-Communist Cuba. Between 1960 and 1962, more than 14,000 unaccompanied minors made their way from Cuba to the United States; this exodus became known as Operation Pedro Pan (www.pedropan.org/). Under the leadership of Monsignor Bryan Walsh, the children were cared for in temporary shelters until they could be reunited with their families. The story of the children of Pedro Pan is a story of hope and trust and is a reminder of the kindness and generosity of a country willing to welcome neighbors from the south in need of shelter from a political crisis.

This group of immigrants features in several significant events. Not long after Castro took office, Cuban refugees living in America began lobbying for the United States to take a stand against the Communist government. By early 1961, just before President Dwight Eisenhower officially left office, he broke off official diplomatic relations with Cuba. This set into motion the opportunity for the CIA to work with Cuban refugees in Miami to plan for an invasion of Cuba by the U.S. Brigade 2506 (the Cuban Brigada), which was prepared to seek the ousting of Castro, upon the approval of the new U.S. President, John F. Kennedy. The designated landing site was on the south coast of Cuba, known as *Bahía de Cochinos* (the Bay of Pigs). The invasion would rely on over 1,400 Cuban exiles to lead the strike. With President Kennedy's approval, the strike occurred on April 17, 1961, in an area that was heavily guarded and against a Cuban Brigade that was fully armed and ready to defend itself. While President Kennedy approved the plan, he was not prepared to provide military backup for fear of retribution from other Communist countries and the possibility of starting another world war.

At the Bay of Pigs, 114 Cuban exiles lost their lives in the attempted coup and over 1,100 were taken prisoner. Exiles in Miami worked hard to secure the release of the prisoners by offering cash to Castro for their release. The U.S. government also provided food and rations to Cuba in exchange for the release of the political prisoners. It is said that the incident led many Cuban exiles to take a political stance as refugees in their newfound homeland. Cuban families were greatly affected by this turn of events and the realization set in that they would need to establish themselves in the United States for a significant period of time. Novas (2003, p. 189) noted that

> In later years, once their U.S. citizenship papers were in order, the overwhelming majority of Cuban Americans of the first wave registered Republican. Their preference for the Republican Party was founded on the belief that the Republicans were more effective at combating communism and dictatorships in Cuba and around the globe. They were also unwilling to forget the Kennedy betrayal. (p. 189)

Weeks turned into months and months turned into years. In 1966, Congress passed Public Law 89-732—the *Cuban Adjustment Act*—in order to process the large numbers of political refugees who were making their way from Cuba to the United States. This Act grants Cubans special status as political refugees, which allows them to apply for a green card after being in the United States for one year. Applications for permanent residence for Cubans may be approved due to political circumstances in their home country, even if they do not meet the typical criteria for immigrant eligibility under the Immigration and

Nationality Act (INA).

By 1980, with Castro still in power, the social and economic circumstances had deteriorated to the point of despair for many citizens of Cuba. In the spring of 1980, a small group of Cubans demanding political asylum from the Peruvian Embassy in Havana caused a riot in the city by crashing through the embassy gates. In response to this outcry for political freedom, Castro announced that all those seeking to leave the island would be free to leave from the port in Mariel, Cuba. Over 10,000 Cubans chose to seek asylum in the United States, the second-biggest immigration wave ever from Cuba to the United States. Castro then opened the doors of his prisons; in a six-month period, over 125,000 refugees, who became known as "Marielitos," made their way to the United States, with the help of many Cuban Americans who launched the "Freedom Flotilla" to help bring them to safety. While many of those set free were political prisoners, it is well-documented that a significant percentage of Marielitos were said to have had criminal records (Martinez, Nielsen, & Lee, 2003). Recent pieces published in reference to the Mariel boatlift emphasize the fact that the criminal records were tied to island political protests, religious dissent, or mental illness. It took years to get a handle on the flow of refugees and to reach a consensus about Cubans seeking to immigrate to the United States.

Cubans are still seeking opportunities for a better life. Fidel Castro, his health failing, did relinquish power in 2009, but only to transfer the Communist torch to his brother. As Cuba's economy continues to deteriorate, many Cuban Americans living in the United States with family ties still on the island struggle to reconcile recommendations for a continued embargo against Cuba with the humanitarian issues of families in need.

The typical Cuban immigrant family has now been in exile for a long time; children, grandchildren, and great-grandchildren born in the United States have no memory of a life "back home." Many learn to speak English as a primary language, perhaps with only one parent speaking Spanish with elders out of respect. You hear a mix of both languages at family gatherings, but the younger generations often identify more with their American ties than with the memories of Cuba. This is especially true when the younger generations marry into other cultures, and blended families evolve.

Central/South American and Dominican Families

Many who research the immigration patterns into the United States claim that the fastest growing immigrant population is from Central/South America and the Dominican Republic. Central American immigrants include individuals from El Salvador, Guatemala,

A Cuban Refugee's Story: Maria Elena Buria

I was 8 years old when the plane landed at Miami International Airport. Almost 50 years have elapsed since that eventful day, yet I can still feel and visualize the whole experience as if it had occurred just yesterday. It is hard to comprehend how a 30-minute flight, covering a distance of only 90 miles, could have such a profound and life-changing impact—but it did. Life would never again be the same for me or my family. It was on that day when we said goodbye to the land where we had first met life—the island paradise that would forever texture and color our life's canvas—and placed all our hopes, dreams and uncertainties on the promise of a new land—a land that we would, from that day forth, call "home."

Read the entire story shared by Maria Elena of her life experiences as a Cuban refugee in Appendix A.

Nicaragua, Honduras, Panama, and Costa Rica. While their reasons for immigration vary, economic hardship is often the primary motivation (Passel, 2006). A number of countries in Central America have experienced political upheaval, leading to government instability, guerilla insurgencies, and a general climate of violence and fear. The Pew Hispanic Center has published several research reports aimed at summarizing the migrant population, and found that the typical Central American is seeking a better life for his family. One might think that the undocumented migrant is a young male with a wife or children back in the home country, yet . . .

> In fact, the full portrait of the unauthorized migrant population is more varied. Unauthorized migrants also live as couples (sometimes with a spouse who is a U.S. citizen or legal immigrant), and many of these couples have children. Some children are U.S. citizens and some are unauthorized, and sometimes there are both U.S. citizen and unauthorized children in the same family. (Passel, 2006)

Once a family makes the transition to a new homeland, particularly if children are involved, it becomes that much more difficult to transition back, even when political situations might have leveled off.

South American immigrants are Colombians, Ecuadorans, Peruvians, Argentineans, Chileans, Venezuelans, Bolivians, Uruguayans, and Paraguayans. Immigration studies show that immigrants from these countries have been arriving in greater numbers since the 1980s, when they began searching for greater economic opportunities and unemployment drove them to seek a more stable economy. More recent immigrants have left their countries because of civil unrest and political turmoil.

The Dominican Republic occupies half of the island of Hispaniola (Haiti occupies the other half) in the Caribbean. Prior to the 1960s, it was uncommon for Dominicans to seek immigration to the United States because of strict government regulations. During the 1960s and 1970s, however, civil war drove many Dominicans to the United States in search of a more stable political landscape and better economic opportunity. Dominicans are still seeking asylum in large numbers and this particular sub-group of Latino immigrants is among the fastest-growing group. Meanwhile, the situation in Haiti has deteriorated economically since the devastating earthquake in January 2010, adding to the strain on the already fragile economy of neighboring Dominican Republic.

Undocumented Immigrant Families

Immigration has been a topic of controversy in America in recent years. The federal and state governments and various nongovernmental entities debate how to best protect the U.S. border and ensure an orderly process to immigration.

> About four-in-five of the nation's estimated 11.1 million unauthorized immigrants are of Hispanic origin. A new national survey by the Pew Hispanic Center, a project of the Pew Research Center, finds that Latinos are divided over what to do with these immigrants. (Lopez, Taylor, & Morin, 2010)

Native- versus foreign-born Hispanics/Latinos are at odds on such issues as the right to higher education for unauthorized immigrants, the legality of workplace raids, border patrols, the building of a border wall, proposals to require use of a national identity card, or state laws giving law enforcement officers the right to request identification from any person (such as Senate Bill 1070, passed in Arizona in April 2010). Hispanics who arrive without authorization in the United States face difficult challenges, including the psychological stress of dealing with the unknown in a new country and incredible economic stress.

The issue of unauthorized immigration is often complicated for educators and care providers. Public education systems and health services feel the impact of unauthorized immigration; states struggle to meet the needs of these undocumented families. Proposition 187 in California is an example of how quickly this issue can become divisive within a community. On November 8, 1994, California residents voted in favor of Proposition 187, which states that undocumented aliens are not permitted to enter the state's public education system, all the way from kindergarten through the university level. In addition, the proposition dealt with four other provisions, with the restriction of health care to undocumented immigrants being the next most contentious point. Proposition 187 eventually was overturned by a federal judge. Other states have cut back on some services, saying they burden the public service systems. In Florida, for example, children whose parents are undocumented immigrants may have graduated from public high school, only to discover they cannot attain higher education because of laws limiting their ability to seek financial assistance. Bipartisan legislation known as the Dream Act (http://dreamact.info/) has been proposed to address this issue.

Of greater concern are the large numbers of children being left in the United States after a parent or both parents are asked to return to their homeland. Deportation has increased in recent years, and one unintended consequence of this move toward stricter immigration laws is the separation of families. More and more families choose to leave younger family members behind to allow them to continue benefiting from the American way of life. The "Families for Freedom" organization, based in New York, argues that

> Every year, nearly 200,000 non-citizens—many with kids who are U.S. citizens—are deported and torn away from their families . . . resulting in more single parent households and psychological and financial hardship, or forcing their U.S. citizen children into deportation with them. These American children may have to start over in a country with a new language, fewer resources and an uncertain future. America's immigration laws force American children to lose their parent, or their country. Mandatory deportation is a life sentence of exile. Such a severe "one size fits all" punishment cannot be the basis of our immigration system. (www.familiesforfreedom.org)

Our work in preparing this introduction for educators and care providers will not provide answers for these dilemmas, because there is no simple solution. Yet, it is our intention to raise awareness of these issues so that educators and care providers can make informed decisions regarding how they might meet the needs of children and their families within their communities.

Economic Levels of Hispanic/Latino Families

While recognizing that Hispanics certainly cannot be categorized as being from any one particular socioeconomic background, it nevertheless is helpful to study the socioeconomic data available on Latino families. "Many Hispanic children are likely to be from lower socioeconomic backgrounds, particularly those whose families have recently arrived and are depending on minimum-wage jobs or are part of the 'shadow economy' " (Holman, 1997). Data collected for the Bureau of Labor Statistics (2010) reveals that Hispanics are much more likely than non-Hispanic whites to be unemployed. In October 2010, 8.8% of non-Hispanic whites were unemployed, as compared to 12.6% of Hispanics. When discussing Hispanics/Latinos and unemployment, a confounding variable is always language. This is particularly true for recent immigrants who are struggling to acclimate themselves to a new country, a new economic system, and a community that may not be supportive of those who do not speak English. From the perspective of the family, the ability or inability to be gainfully employed is a critical issue of survival.

DeNavas-Walt, Proctor, and Smith (2010) note that the poverty rate for Hispanics increased from 24.7% to 25.8% between 2008 and 2009; in comparison, the poverty rate of non-Hispanic whites increased from 8.6% to 9.4%. The statistics are sobering and if the root causes are not addressed, the gap will continue to increase. The Hispanic Scholarship Fund (HSF) works with many corporate sponsors to offer students hope for continuing their education, thus providing some change in the cycle of poverty. HSF studies reveal that if focus is not placed on reversing this trend now, it will be difficult in the future to make a difference.

> This situation won't get better on its own. Two factors associated with low educational attainment among children are 1) Living in a family where neither parent has a High School diploma, and 2) Living in a poor family. Today, two out of every three Hispanic children live in a family where neither parent has a High School diploma and one out of every two lives in a family in the lowest income percentile. If trends continue unabated, these numbers are projected to grow by more than 20 percent and 10 percent over the next decade, respectively. (The 2000 HSF Hispanic Education Study, www.hsf.net)

As a result of such findings, the HSF's recent mission statement focused specifically on doubling the rate at which Hispanics complete their college degrees, from 9% to 18%. Achieving this goal will depend on ensuring that Hispanic youth receive the necessary support to stay in school.

The dropout rate is a significant contributing factor to the declining economic levels of Hispanics in the United States. "Education is one of the fastest and most efficient means of social mobility; and yet Hispanics lag far behind other sectors of the population in educational outcomes" (Tashakkori & Ochoa, 1999). If Hispanics do not stay in school, they have less of a chance to move ahead economically. The trends clearly show that students from low socioeconomic backgrounds are 10% more likely to drop out and not finish high school, and the data show that a high percentage of children living in poverty are Hispanics. Between 2006 and 2007, the high school dropout rate, when measuring a single group of students over a one-year period, was 2.2% for whites, compared to 6% for Hispanics (USDOE, 2009).

These statistics come as no surprise for educators and care providers working with Hispanic families who are living in poverty. What is needed in these communities are strategies to help break the cycle of poverty. On a federal level, this crisis has caught the attention of policymakers. In October 2010, President Obama signed an executive order

Cuban Immigrant's Reflection: Ingrid

I explained that I had come from Cuba and was worried because I had never worked here before and was concerned that it would put me at a disadvantage, but nevertheless I began to fill out the application. . . . That was the end of my day. I needed so many negative moments in order for something really good to happen. . . . Before, I was a little shy; now, it's not that I stand taller, but that my bones seem heavier, stronger. I have had to live in three months all that I was not able to live before. I have been here for three months today. Sometimes, I ask myself why I have to live all of these changes. I appreciate the growth that has provoked so much adversity. Yes . . . I have so much more to say.

Turn to Appendix A to read Ingrid's full message written (in Spanish) to a family friend who was helping her transition to a new life in Miami.

renewing the White House Initiative on Educational Excellence for Hispanic Americans. The order requires the formation of a Federal Interagency Working Group to exchange resources and address issues affecting the lives of Hispanics nationwide, including housing, health, finance, employment, and education. The prosperity of Latino families ultimately will impact the entire nation.

The Emergence of a New Hispanic/Latino Family Construct: Summary

Evidence points to a change with each passing generation. The children of Hispanic immigrants identify strongly as being Hispanic Americans, and the grandchildren of immigrants have even stronger ties to the United States and identify even less with the familial country of origin. As educators, we must consider the role of the family unit and remember how strong family ties might bring cultural conflict to a family eager to retain ties to their "home." I recently heard a song sung by two daughters of a Cuban immigrant family; I recognized the passion in the lyrics because the story could have been my own. As they sang "Los Hijos de los Hijos" (we are the children of the "immigrant" children), I understood their struggle to comprehend their parents' and grandparents' angst. Younger generations find it difficult to consider the country of origin as "home"—a home we have never traveled to, never experienced. This modern life is built around a new blended family, in which the great-grandchildren of immigrants may have become so accustomed to living an American way of life that any other life does not seem authentic to consider. Educators will need to be sensitive to countries of origin in order to help families cross generational boundaries and navigate the shift to more blended cultures, those in which parents from very distinct backgrounds begin sharing the responsibility of building cultural bridges.

Questions To Ponder

- Given the strong ties to specific cultural groups, is it important to move beyond just general "Hispanic Heritage Celebrations" in order to allow students the opportunity to identify more specifically with a country of origin?
- As an educator or care provider and a community leader, how might you handle working with a Latino family who is living without authorization in the United States? What kind of conflict might that bring to your workplace?

Chapter 1 Web-Based Resources

2010 U.S. Census Bureau Data on America's Families and Living Arrangements
 www.census.gov/population/www/socdemo/hh-fam/cps2010.html
U.S. Census Bureau PowerPoint on Hispanics in the United States
 www.census.gov/population/www/socdemo/hispanic/files/Internet_Hispanic_in_US_2006.pdf
Hispanic Border Leadership Institute
 www.asu.edu/educ/hbli/
Pew Hispanic Center
 http://pewhispanic.org/
Pew Hispanic Center report on *The Size and Characteristics of the Unauthorized Migrant Population in the U.S.* (Estimates Based on the March 2005 Current Population Survey)
 http://pewhispanic.org/files/reports/61.pdf
Arizona Immigration Law -- Senate Bill 1070
 www.azleg.gov/legtext/49leg/2r/bills/sb1070s.pdf
Proposition 187 in California
 http://migration.ucdavis.edu/mn/more.php?id=492_0_2_0

The Dream Act
http://dreamact.info/
Hispanic Scholarship Fund
www.hsf.net
White House Initiative on Educational Excellence for Hispanic Americans
www2.ed.gov/about/inits/list/hispanic-initiative/index.html
Los Hijos de los Hijos sung by the Chirino sisters
www.youtube.com/watch?v=drISvoF0gVI
Immigration Website
www.nytimes.com/interactive/2009/03/10/us/20090310-immigration-explorer.html

Chapter 2
Health Practices and Cultural Beliefs

Nancy S. Maldonado

"De mi vida para tu vida."
(From my life to your life.)

Certain health practices and beliefs among Central American, South American, Mexican, and Caribbean Hispanics are of note for educators and care providers. Several of these groups base their cultural beliefs and practices solely on religious and indigenous ancestry, while others embrace those myriad customs, traditions, and beliefs as well as the European influence. Hispanic families may face a choice between modern medicine and folk medicine, curanderos/as (healers), shamans, and herbal medications and treatments. The quandary they face is exacerbated by the lack of adequate health care among Hispanics and its impact on the Hispanic family and community health care. This chapter provides some insight into physical, mental, and oral health issues in Hispanic and Latino communities, along with issues concerning health literacy and cultural beliefs that affect health and spiritual perceptions.

Health care is a serious issue currently being examined and politically debated in the United States. Inadequate or lack of health insurance can greatly affect the health, status, and stability of all families. Latino families are significantly affected by this crisis, and children represent 33% of the estimated 31 million uninsured Latinos currently living in the United States (Perez, 2000). Restricted access to health care is a critical issue for Hispanics with lower income status. It is estimated that "almost 60% of Hispanic adults with diabetes have an annual income below $20,000 compared with approximately 28% of non-Hispanic whites with diabetes" (Gary, Venkat Narayan, Gregg, Beckles, & Saaddine, 2003, p. 47). Environmental conditions, health beliefs, "health literacy" (being able to understand and process basic health services needed to make good health decisions), and health care access present significant challenges to disease prevention (Hispanic Health Council, 2006, p. 3).

Continuous health care and prevention are essential for children's healthy growth and development. It is estimated that 1.1 million poor Latino children in the United States are uninsured, compared with 806,000 white, 703,000 African American, and 95,000 Asian children (Kaiser Daily Health Policy Report, 2002). Flores, Abreu, Chaisson, et al. (2005) posit that uninsured children are vulnerable to illnesses and poor health and "are less likely to have primary care, visit a regular physician or other medical provider, to be immunized adequately, to experience adverse hospital outcomes as newborns and to have higher mortality rates associated with trauma and coarctation of the aorta" (p. 1433). In the state of Connecticut alone, Latino children are more likely to be uninsured (21%) compared to non-Hispanic white children (7%) and African American children (14%) (Hispanic Health Council, 2006, p. 6). These statistics reflect similar patterns in the rest of the nation. In Baltimore, Maryland, 70% of Latino families have no health insurance (Carter-Pokras, 2006, p. 6). Studies also show that Hispanic children are more likely to suffer from obesity, childhood diabetes, and asthma (Kaiser Daily Health Policy Report, 2002). Limited English proficiency may contribute to the fact that many Latinos experience difficulties obtaining health care, specifically health insurance coverage.

Latino children's health is vulnerable on all levels—physical and mental. In New York City, Puerto Rican children have the highest asthma occurrences of all Hispanic groups, 140% more than white children (National Center for Health Statistics: National Health Interview Survey, 2004, as cited in www.lungusa.org/site/apps/s/). The American Lung Association (2007) reports that "Hispanics are at risk for developing acute and chronic responses to exposure to air pollution since a disproportionate number live in areas failing to meet one or more national standards for pollution." Aside from respiratory illnesses, greater numbers of Latino children display symptoms of depression, phobias and fears, anxiety and panic, and other behavioral disturbances, when compared to African American children. Children of Latino migrant farm workers suffer from infectious diseases, nutritional maladies, obesity, and diabetes. They meet the criteria for public health insurance and other support programs, but are not enrolled due to their high mobility. Dental cavities and poor oral hygiene are prevalent among Mexican American children, but only 40% receive care and treatment. Mental health issues are also of concern. Hispanics from Central and South America often suffer from posttraumatic stress disorder as a result of distress endured in their home countries.

Perceptions of Physical, Mental, and Spiritual Health

Physical Health

Research shows that child poverty is associated with poor health, school failure, drug use, and teenage pregnancy, as well as other social risks (Perez, 2000). Poverty, juxtaposed with cultural and language differences, greatly affects health practices and outcomes. Hispanic children from low-income families are more likely to have poor dietary practices than their non-Hispanic peers (Perez, 2000). Lower-income families not only have fewer resources to buy food, they also often find it challenging to identify nutritious food among the thousands of unfamiliar food items in a typical supermarket. The wide variety at supermarkets can be confusing when language is a barrier to communication and appropriate selection (Hispanic Health Council, 2006).

The Centers for Disease Control and Prevention (CDC) reports that heart disease is the leading cause of death in Hispanics (24%), followed by cancer (20%), cerebrovascular disease (6%), and diabetes (5%) (cited in Rios-Ellis, 2005, p. 5). The Latino population also has a high rate of HIV/AIDS, with recent data indicating that HIV is rising faster among Latinos than for any other group. New infections increased by 26.2% from 1999 to 2002 (Centers for Disease Control and Prevention, 2003). Consequently, the probability of children losing a parent or a significant family member increases.

Mental Health

Latinos, similar to the general population, "suffer from depression early in life with its onset prior to age 25" (Rios-Ellis, 2005, p. 6). Most recently, Hispanics have been identified as a high-risk group for such mental health problems as depression, anxiety, and substance abuse (National Alliance for Hispanic Health, 2001, as cited in NCLR, 2005, p.

6). Depression among Hispanic immigrants is prevalent, as many experience feelings of isolation and alienation in a new country. Suro (1999) posits that the cultural distance and the loss of connection to the homeland is a serious problem faced by the immigrant parents of children born in the United States. "Depression is a serious challenge that many Latinos suffer from through physical manifestations; e.g., bodily aches, pain, back aches, or headaches" (Rios-Ellis, 2005, p. 6). Unfortunately, several studies indicate that Hispanics often do not seek the aid of professional health care providers and instead rely on family to support them in times of illness. If they do seek the care of a mental health provider, many do not follow up with further visits once medication has been prescribed. Part of the problem is the lack of psychologists, therapists, and psychiatrists who are sensitive to Hispanic cultural and linguistic diversity. In addition, many Latinos are not comfortable sharing their family's mental health problems and/or other related problems with health care workers. The *dicho "no se lava la ropa afuera de la casa"* (don't air your dirty laundry outside of your home) reflects this attitude.

Recent immigrants acculturating to a new environment in the United States face many stresses that affect their psychological well-being, impairing their decision-making, occupational functioning, and overall physical and mental health (Smart & Smart, 1995). Some face the stress associated with an undocumented status; fear of deportation is added to the isolation and lack of family support.

Coping in a strange land, not understanding the culture or language, affects Hispanics in different ways. Some succumb to substance abuse, which can contribute to physical and mental illnesses. Alcohol-related diseases are higher among Latinos in comparison to African Americans, whites, and Asian Americans (CDC, 2003). Drug use has risen sharply among Latinos, particularly Mexicans (Rios-Ellis, 2005, p. 12). High levels of substance abuse often result in high rates of domestic violence. According to Martinez (1997), domestic violence in the family is a serious and widespread social problem with mental health consequences for all victims involved. Latina immigrants suffer more due to their undocumented status (as they are reluctant to contact the authorities); in 2000, 48% reported that spousal violence had increased since immigration to the United States (Dutton, Orloff, & Aguilar Hass, 2000).

Spiritual Health

Hispanics are diverse in their many viewpoints and cultural practices. For many, spiritual and religious beliefs greatly influence their health and well-being. Despite some similar cultural values and health beliefs, unique indigenous and religious backgrounds affect their personal well-being. Many of their beliefs can be traced back to pre-Columbian times, specifically to the Mayans and a complex medicine system (Murguia, Peterson, & Zea, 2003). During pre-Columbian times, illness, health, and well-being were attributed to humans' relationship with nature, astronomy, and society (Garcia, Sierra, & Balam, 1999). Although some health practices among Hispanics may be well-rooted in historical medicinal systems dating back over hundreds of years, these healing systems are not the

Amanda's Reflection

My parents stressed the importance of being strong and educated in the American way, but to also respect the culture. When I was sick, they relied on the expertise of my pediatrician. But my grandparents believed in the natural remedies from Puerto Rico, of course.

You can turn to Appendix A to see the complete reflection offered by Amanda.

first choice among modern-day acculturated Latino families.

Many Hispanics rely on a traditional complex healing system of *curanderismo,* particularly "elderly Mexican Americans, who maintain strong attachments to these indigenous values, including those about healthcare" (Applewhite, 1995, p. 247). *Curanderismo* is an intricate healing tradition found in Mexican American communities throughout the United States, and shared with other Latin American cultures (Trotter, 2001). The aim of this holistic system is to promote a balance between the patient and his/her environment and, in so doing, uphold good health. Illness occurs when the patient is out of balance with one of the elements in the environment. Archetypical *curanderismo* follows three healing levels:

1. Material Level: material approaches to healing (physical treatments and supernatural healing practices)
2. Spiritual Level: spiritual healing and spiritualism
3. Mental Level: psychic healing. (Trotter, 2001, p. 130)

These levels reflect a mixture of folkloric medicine and Judeo-Christian traditions, interwoven with Hippocrates' Doctrine of the Four Temperaments (involving the four humors of blood, black bile, yellow bile, and phlegm) and the influence of hot and cold on the body (Trotter, 2001). Murguia et al. (2003) posit that a balance exists between the forces of nature and sickness and that a "break in this equilibrium could bring negative effects on the individual, the family and the community" (p. 44). An integral component of the *curanderismo* health belief system is loyalty to shamans and spiritual healers (*curanderas / curanderos*). Native healers share the religious values, morals, symbol systems, and language with the communities they serve. Thus, folk medicine and treatments provide a comfort level for many Latinos because of their familiarity and tradition. Curanderos (male healers)/curanderas (female healers) are respected in Latino culture for their gift of healing and a mystical ability to acquire guidance and assistance from unearthly powers. They are regarded as maintainers of life, health, and death.

Applewhite's (1995) study of elderly Mexican Americans showed that they "first learned about folk medicine in early childhood, adolescence and early adulthood. About 84% of the participants had received folk treatments from family members, neighbors or local *curanderos*" (p. 249). Bearison, Minian, and Granowetter (2002) found a similar reliance on folk healers and home remedies in their study of asthma and folk medicine. Dominican American mothers in this study substituted *remedios caseros* (home remedies) known as "zumos" instead of prescribed medicines. The mothers felt that "because asthma is a 'cold' disease in Latino folk medicine, the appropriate zumos are believed to have hot qualities . . . to restore balance" (p. 389). Mothers used such ingredients as cod liver oil, whale oil, garlic, castor oil, lemon juice, and aloe vera juice as therapies.

It should be noted that specific Latino cultural groups refer to their folk healers differently: Central Americans describe them as *curanderos, sobadores, parcheeros,* and *heribistas,* while Puerto Ricans and Cubans use the terms *espiritistas* and *santeros* (Murphy,

Elena's Reflection

As a young child, I recall the extensive use of Vick's Vapor Rub in our household. My abuela (grandmother) used Vick's for headaches by placing a layer of Vick's on her forehead, covered by a bandana, until her headache disappeared. My mother also applied Vick's on her abdomen for bad menstrual cramps and my father inserted globs of Vick's into his nostrils to clear his congestion.

1993). To treat ailments, many Hispanics turn first to herbs and folk treatments passed down from prior generations. Mexican Americans believe that herbs can be used for treating mild ailments (e.g., headaches, insomnia, etc.) and more serious illnesses (e.g., high blood pressure, nervous tension, etc.) (Applewhite, 1995). Prayer is the foundation of *curanderismo*. Curanderos/curanderas have strong religious faith and believe that they are given the gift of healing from God and so pray to the spirits, saints, and God for help in healing their patients.

Research has shown that many Hispanics prefer spiritual healers to physicians, as they believe that physicians do not have the knowledge or understanding to treat their medical ailments (Murguia et al., 2003). Moreover, they feel that physicians and health providers have no knowledge of such culture-bound syndromes as "*empacho* (stomach ailment), *susto* (fright), *caida de mollera* (fallen fontanel), *mal de ojo* (evil eye), *bilongo / hechizo* (hex), *ataque de nervios* (attack of the nerves) and *envidia* (envy)" (Murguia et al., 2003, p. 46). Curanderos/as are some of the most respected individuals in Hispanic communities, because of their knowledge and expertise in curing and treating the aforementioned culture-bound syndromes and other various medical conditions.

Health Literacy and Cultural Beliefs

Health literacy is an important issue that greatly affects Hispanic children and their families, specifically those who have just recently arrived in the United States. Health literacy defines individuals' ability to obtain, process, and comprehend the basic health information and services needed to make appropriate health decisions about themselves or their families. Latinos who have limited knowledge of the English languages and are newly arrived in the United States are at a disadvantage when it comes to health literacy. "Clear and effective communication regarding healthcare problems is difficult enough between consumers and providers who speak the same language" (Johnson, 2006, p. 853). Communication is crucial in understanding a doctor's instructions, when taking medications, and for following treatment. Campos (2007) found that "missed appointments, poor shared decision making about treatment and poor patient satisfaction can be attributed to miscommunication" (p. 813). Campos also found that poor health literacy was prevalent among diabetic Hispanic patients who had difficulty following written instructions for taking medicine or understanding the literature that came with medication. He stressed the importance of a sound patient-provider relationship to ensure that medication and treatment could be monitored properly. Campos defines key cultural values that support Hispanic cultures and that should be upheld in the Latino patient/provider relationship:

Terminology	Cultural Meaning
Simpathia	kindness, politeness, pleasantness, avoidance of hostile confrontation
Personalismo	formal friendliness; warm, personal relationships, characterized by interactions that occur at close distances (e.g., handshake, placing hand on shoulder)
Respeto	respect, including targeted communication based on age, gender, social position, economic status
Familismo	collective loyalty to extended family that supersedes the needs of the individual
Fatalismo	fatalism, belief that individuals can do little to alter their fate

(Campos, p. 814)

Lilliam's Reflection: "Que Dios quiera"

My parents watched over my colds carefully in the winter as they often turned into congestion, wheezing, and then asthma. Difficult nights would bring my grandmother from her house to my bed. She would intervene with rubbing alcohol, oregano herb tea, and prayers. Getting well was only possible with the help of God. All her prayers ended in "Que Dios quiera"—only through God's will.

Campos stresses the importance of respecting these cultural values with Latino patients, suggesting that bilingual providers and medical personnel converse in the patient's native language. They should show consideration for cultural values by being well-mannered; showing genuine interest in the patient's life (e.g., ask about their home life and families); using respectful terms when addressing patients ("*usted*" [formal "you"] rather than "*tu*" [the informal "you"]); inviting the patient to bring family members for support and to be another "pair of ears" for joint decision-making; and being sensitive to the patient's beliefs and values (Campos, 2007). A detailed discussion of *familismo, simpathia, respeto,* and *personalismo* is provided in Chapter 4, in relation to child-rearing practices.

Johnson (2006) also addresses the need for hospital translators who truly understand cultural beliefs and provide a complete translation between physician and patient. Using family members, which, in some cases, are children, as translators may not be the appropriate solution to the translation problem. "We would consider it malpractice to turn over the job of patient care and education to an untrained volunteer, yet this is exactly what we do when we are faced with a patient whose command of the English language is 'hello' and 'thank you' " (p. 853). Johnson makes the following recommendations:

- The health care provider must avoid using medical jargon.
- Someone who understands the words and concepts the health care professional uses must be present to translate that information accurately and make sure the person receiving the information understands it.
- The patient's questions and answers to questions must be accurately translated back to the health care professional. The volunteer translator should avoid answering questions for the patient.
- The health care provider should remember that it is customary in many Hispanic families for males to make important decisions for the family.

Johnson's statement that much information is "lost in translation" is valid. Flores et al. (2003), in examining the relationships between medical personnel and patients with limited English, emphasized the critical role of the medical interpreter to help avoid errors. Their study provides examples of mothers' misinterpreting information provided during pediatric exams. The mistakes include wrong calculations and frequencies for medicine doses. The Flores et al. study shows that 31% of the clinical visits with patients and medical personnel had evidence of errors in medical interpretation. Trained interpreters made fewer errors, but still made some miscalculations that "could result in potential consequences" (p. 9). Flores et al. suggest that more regulated training of medical interpreters would reduce the amount of errors in clinical encounters. Serious outcomes that could occur include "increased risk of intubation among children with asthma, drug complications, longer medical visits, impaired patient understanding of diagnoses, lower likelihood of keeping follow-up visits and impaired health status" (Flores et al., 2003, p.

8.). Another significant finding of the Flores et al. study is that "1 out of 17 [Hispanic] parents reported not bringing their child in for needed medical care because of these language issues" (p. 12).

Pharmacists also face many challenges when issuing prescription medications to Hispanic patients. March and Gong (2005) stress the importance of cultural sensitivity as an essential part of the pharmacist and patient relationship when assisting Hispanics. To provide the best care, they recommend that pharmacists acknowledge cultural beliefs and consider asking the following questions when communicating with Latino patients:

- How do you describe the problem?
- What do you think caused the problem?
- Why do you think the problem started when it did?
- What do you think the illness does?
- How severe do you think the illness is?
- What are the chief problems the illness has caused for you?
- What do you fear most about the illness?
- Whom do you turn to for help?
- Who should be involved in decisions about treatment?

(March & Gong, 2005, p. 211).

Quality health care among many Latinos is lacking. Barriers to wellness and appropriate care are reflective of poverty, lack of transportation, problematic environmental conditions, language barriers, and, for some, a fear of deportation. These variables reflect what several studies have shown—many Latino children receive a lower quality of health care with respect to diagnoses, treatment, and therapy (Kaiser Daily Health Policy Report, 2006).

Summary and Recommendations for Educators and Care Providers

Restricted access to health care, the high cost of medications, the stresses of assimilating to a new country, cultural and language barriers, and limited or nonexistent health insurance have an enormous impact on the well-being of certain Hispanics. The effect on family stability must be taken seriously. Teachers and care providers should consider the following:

- Pay particular attention when dealing with Hispanic children and their families in reference to health issues. For example, learn about health care resources in your community so that you can make sound recommendations.
- Respect and be sensitive to the cultural values of Latino families and address their health care needs by providing access to information and support in the families' native language (Campos, 2007).
- Interview families about their folkloric healing practices in order to understand particular "zumos" and remedies for common ailments.

Chapter 2 Questions To Ponder

- The National Diabetes Education Program (part of the National Institutes of Health) documents that approximately 10% of Hispanics/Latinos age 20 and older are diagnosed with diabetes. What steps could be taken at your center or school site to educate parents about this disease?
- Hispanics/Latinos are known to practice folk medicine, preparing home remedies to deal with an ailment. Consider something an elder in your family may have shared with you to "cure" an illness—how would traditional medical attention be different?

- As an educator or care provider, one strives for cultural sensitivity when addressing issues of diet and exercise. If the trend toward obesity in this country does not change, a national epidemic will ensue. What curricular recommendations could you make for all students that would benefit Hispanic/Latino families regarding diet and exercise?

Chapter 2 Web-Based Resources

National Alliance for Hispanic Health
www.hispanichealth.org/

Hispanics/Latinos and Diabetes – from the National Diabetes Information Clearinghouse
http://diabetes.niddk.nih.gov/dm/pubs/hispanicamerican/

U.S. Department of Health and Human Services—The Office of Minority Health
http://minorityhealth.hhs.gov/templates/browse.aspx?lvl=2&lvlID=54

Hispanic Health Course offered by the Department of Community Medicine, Baylor College of Medicine
www.rice.edu/projects/HispanicHealth/excourse.html

My Latino Voice – Health Wise – Timely Health Care News and Assistance
www.mylatinovoice.com/healthwise

Chapter 3
Spirituality: Care of the Soul

Nancy S. Maldonado

"Una buena acción es la mejor oración."
(A good deed is the best prayer.)

Spirituality is the root of life for many Latinos, influencing all aspects of day-to-day living. Multifaceted belief systems impact self-identity and interactions with one another. Many Latinos are deeply spiritual people who intensely value their devout traditions and rituals. This chapter reviews some of the religious beliefs and practices that may be part of Hispanic families' lives, including Catholicism, Protestantism, Santeria, Islam, and the Church of Latter Day Saints, without any intent toward judgmental application. It is strongly recommended that educators and care providers consider each and every Hispanic / Latino American in context.

Hispanics belong to various religions and so follow an assortment of faith practices. Catholics, for example, honor patron saints, holy days, and the sacraments. Others (e.g., Cubans and Puerto Ricans) may practice the rituals of Santeria (a religion grounded in African gods incorporated into the Catholic belief system). Some may worship *La Virgen de Guadalupe*, the brown virgin associated with the Indian-Mestizo population in Mexico. In recent years, many Latinos have turned to evangelical Protestantism.

Historical Perspective

McIntosh (2005) notes that Latinos from a New World background have a naturally spiritual heritage. The Meso-Americans whom Columbus met impressed him as "*una gente que vive en Dios*" (a people who live in God) (p. 12). In fact, McIntosh suggests that Columbus did not use the term "*Indios*" (Indians) because he thought he had arrived in India, but rather because he believed the natives were "en Dios," or naturally spiritual (p. 13). The temples, pyramids, and artifacts built to numerous gods, spirits, and divine powers by the Incas, Aztecs, and Mayans indicate that, indeed, they were a spiritual people. Aztecs, in particular, paid homage to hundreds of gods and spirits through religious ceremonies conducted over many hours during the day (Novas, 2003). Incas worshiped the sun as the father of all Incan emperors—creator and source of all life and protector of the earth (De la Vega, 1871). Their universal god was worshipped during "Yntip Raymi" (solemn festival of the sun), in which human and animal sacrifices and the best crops of the harvests were offered. Mayans were known for their architecture, mathematics, astronomy, and for religious rituals involving over 100 deities.

Some of the religious practices of the Meso-Americans were clearly violent, such as human sacrifice. When the Spaniards brought Catholicism to the New World, violent religious wars were occurring. In the 15th century, the Spanish Inquisition was responsible for torturing and killing "tens of thousands of Jews, Muslims, Protestants and heretics to purify Spanish Christianity" (McIntosh, 2005, p. 14). Eventually, this "purification" was aimed at the Native Americans in the New World and an overwhelming effort was made to convert them to Catholicism.

The introduction of slavery into the New World also played a part in the complex belief systems of Latinos. Most of the slaves brought to the Spanish territories were taken from Africa, namely Nigeria and the Gold Coast. They brought their own religious customs—spiritual rituals and traditions—that they preserved under the guise of the Spanish Catholic practices. They devised a way to worship their gods by associating them with the Catholic saints (Perez y Mena, 1998).

Thus, contemporary Hispanic culture is saturated with virtues and morals that can be traced back to Meso-American religions, African spiritual beliefs, and Spanish Catholicism. Modern Latinos embrace their spirituality via many religions. The following presents a brief description of some of these faiths and their influence on Hispanic daily life.

Roman Catholic Hispanics/Latinos

The majority of Latinos in the United States are Roman Catholics (Pew Hispanic Center, Forum on Religion and Public Life, 2007). The religion plays an important role for these Latino families, serving as the adhesive that keeps the family together. Faith is a valued virtue: "Faith in God, faith in miracles, in the ongoingness of life and faith that God will provide . . . faith is manifested through the deep-rooted Catholicism that took hold in Latin countries during the 15th century following the Spanish conquest" (Navas, 2000, p. 109).

Hispanic families practicing Catholicism uphold the traditions and rituals of the Catholic faith via family participation in services, and in celebrations of the saints. It is very common to find a crucifix or a picture of the Virgin Mary in Latino Catholic households. Shrines to saints and the Virgin Mary are common. In the southwestern United States, in particular, the Mexican tradition of reverence for the Virgin of Guadalupe is evident everywhere—in street murals, medical centers, and shopping areas, etc.

The Virgin of Guadalupe is extremely important for members of the indigenous New World cultures. According to the story, the Virgin Mary appeared in 1531 to an indigenous man, Juan Diego Cuauhtlatoatzin, as he was walking to church in Mexico City. "The Virgin identified herself as 'Coatlaxopeuh' (Quatla-soo-pay) in the Aztec language, which means one who crushes serpents" (McIntosh, 2005, p. 47), and promised consolation and

Jennifer's Reflection

I thought I would never leave Bolivia. I love my country, its geography, multiculturalism, and uniqueness in many ways. However, God had different plans for my life. . . . I wanted to serve God and He wanted to surprise me, and He sure did. In January of 2007, I met my husband in a divine way. God united us in the same place. Six months after we met, we said "I do" and promised to one another before God that we would be together for the rest of our lives. Miguel, my husband, is from Spain. Although we speak the same language, we had to get to know each other's cultures. He had an advantage since he served in Bolivia for two years as a missionary. It has been the most wonderful time in my life.

Jennifer's complete reflection on the importance of God in her life's journey can be found in Appendix A.

comfort to anyone who would pray to her. She appeared three times to Juan Diego and her image appeared in Juan Diego's cloak as proof to the bishop. A church was built on the spot where she appeared and Juan Diego's cloak is currently displayed in the Basilica of Guadalupe in Mexico City. In Latino Catholic practices, Guadalupe is the Virgin of illness and misfortune and the "Protectress of children not yet born" (McIntosh, 2005, p. 52). Mexican Americans are proud of their Virgin of Guadalupe and continue to worship her.

Traditional Practices

Catholic traditions that have been practiced for decades by many Latinos include festivals, visiting sacred places, and creating shrines to particular saints. Several Hispanic groups have their own patron saints or Madonnas. For example, Cubans honor St. Lazarus and *Nuestra Virgen de la Caridad* (Our Lady of Charity); Puerto Rican towns each have a patron saint, such as St. Anthony of Padua for the town of Dorado and *la Virgen de la Candelaria* (Virgin of Light) for Mayaguez; and many Latin Americans honor St. Miguel (St. Michael) as the saint who fights against evil. The saints are revered as intermediaries to God; Catholic Hispanics pray to particular saints for particular interventions (e.g., when something is lost and cannot be found, a prayer to St. Anthony is believed to help find the article; when selling a property, owners may bury a statue of St. Joseph on the grounds to help ensure a quick sale).

Important festivals and feast days include *Semana Santa* (Holy Week), when traditional processions, prayers, and vigils to observe the death and resurrection of Christ are observed. *La Navidad* (Christmas) celebrates the birth of Christ and many Latinos embrace the symbolism of the Virgin Mother, Baby Jesus, and Joseph as poor and outcast from their home. *El Día de Los Reyes Magos* (Three Kings Day, Epiphany) marks the end of the Christmas season, the 12th day of Christmas when the Three Kings followed a bright star to find the infant Jesus and shower him with gifts. Children prepare for *El Día de los Reyes Magos* by placing grass in a box for the kings' camels and a letter requesting gifts in their shoes. Cities with high concentrations of Latinos (e.g., Miami and Spanish Harlem) celebrate *El Día de los Reyes Magos* with a parade. Other traditional observances include *Día de los Muertos* (Day of the Dead, All Souls Day), a Mexican observance involving tokens, flowers, and foods as offerings to honor the dead (McIntosh, 2005). While traditional Roman Catholics deem this to be a solemn holy day, Mexicans celebrate it with special treats, parades, music, and fireworks as a reminder that death is unavoidable and that loved ones continue to be a part of their lives on a spiritual level (MacIntosh, 2005).

Transitions From Catholicism

The "Charismatic" movement within the Catholic church is gaining membership from the Latino population. This movement has belief structures that are similar to those of Pentecostalism. Believers hold onto traditional Catholic practices and teachings and see the Holy Spirit as evident in their being. They believe in divine healing and direct revelations from God (Pew Hispanic Center, 2007). The growth of this movement among Latinos can be attributed to the population's assimilation into mainstream culture. Studies have shown that first-generation, foreign-born Hispanics are primarily Catholic, whereas second- and third-generation Hispanics are more likely than their parents and grandparents to identify themselves as Evangelists, Protestants, or from another branch of Christianity (Murray, 2006; Pew Hispanic Center, 2007).

Santeria—Worship of the Saints

The slaves who were brought from Africa in the 1500s merged the beliefs, traditions, music, and practices of the Yoruba Tribe of Nigeria and the Gold Coast with the beliefs and practices of Catholicism. The slaves wished to honor the deities (*Orishas*) of the Yoruba religion, but were not allowed to practice their traditional religion. Therefore, they began associating their traditional gods with certain Roman Catholic saints. Each *Orisha* was connected with a corresponding saint, and with special colors, numbers, offerings, and intentions, as in the following examples:

Changó/Santa Barbara
  Colors: red, white
  Intentions: power, virility, overcoming one's enemies
La Caridad del Cobre/Our Lady of Charity
  Colors: coral, aquamarine, yellow
  Intentions: love, sensuality, money, arts, and human pleasures.
(Cortez, 2000, pp. 79-82)

Scholars define the merger of the Catholic and Yoruba religions as "syncretism" (Perez y Mena, 1998). Many Cubans, Puerto Ricans, and Dominicans in the United States practice Santeria—research indicates the religion has close to 1 million followers (McIntosh, 2005). Santeria is primarily practiced privately in the home; followers rely on oral tradition and do not go to specific houses of worship.

Santeria involves much secrecy as a result of its origins among the oppressed slaves, and researchers have experienced difficulty studying and researching the religion. Some of the Santeria practices are in direct conflict with accepted practices of the Catholic Church.

Grounded in folk medicine and practices, Santeria upholds the notion of sound mind, spirit, and body. Illness is considered a destructive supernatural force that requires remedies from the deities to restore balance of the three aforementioned elements. Various ailments can be cured or prevented by praying to a specific *Orisha* (Saint). San Lazarus/Babalu-Aye is the patron saint of illness; prayers, candles, and drumming are offered to him when illness occurs in a family.

Latinos who follow Santeria can find remedies and folk medicine at the neighborhood "botánica," which may serve as the neighborhood's pharmacy, health station, psychiatrist's office, and counseling center. They can buy candles, medicinal herbs, amulets, statues, talismans, oils, incense perfumes, and other materials used in the prevention of illness, healing, and treatment associated with *curanderismo* and other spiritual practices. Latinos with limited access to health care and expensive prescription medicine rely on the botánica for diagnosis and treatment.

Mainline Protestants

About 25 million Hispanics identify themselves as Protestants, including Baptists, Methodists, Presbyterians, and Lutherans (Miranda & Carrasco, 1994). "Mainline" Protestants believe in Bible study and spreading Christianity to the world, with varying specific practices and traditions.

For example, Baptists believe in salvation by grace alone through faith in God, without the aid of intermediaries (e.g., Pope, saints, etc.), and consider Christ to be the one and only mediator between God and man. The Baptist Church environment is often sparse, without the statues or paintings commonly found in Catholic churches. The Baptist Ministry has been reaching out to the Hispanic community. Several congregations in the northwestern United States are inviting Latinos to join, offering ESL programs and Bible study classes (Frerichs, 2003).

Lutherans also believe in interpretation of Biblical texts without the intermediation of a head of the church, such as the Pope. Methodists have a long history of advocacy for social issues in their communities and the world. Many Latinos are attracted by this engagement of the Methodist Church with global issues (Green, 2003). Presbyterians believe in baptizing their babies as a way of acknowledging God in their lives and have faith in their church community when seeking counsel and guidance from the Bible and the church constitution ("What Presbyterians Believe," 2009). They strongly believe that God speaks to them through the Holy Spirit via the church community and are committed to ministries throughout the world. They commit to a life's vocation (through career or volunteerism) as a lasting response to God.

Pentecostalism—Evangelical Protestants

According to the Pew Hispanic Center (2007), Hispanics' religious beliefs are changing. For example, the move toward evangelical belief systems, especially Pentecostalism, is increasing among Latinos. Pentecostalists base their faith on the belief that the Holy Spirit descended upon the apostles, filling them with the Holy Spirit and enabling them to speak in various languages and thus bring Christianity to people from all different cultures and languages. The Pentecostal Church's mission is to praise God and provide service to the expansion of the faith.

McIntosh (2005) notes the role of the Azusa Street Apostolic Faith Mission, in Los Angeles, as a significant contributor to the spread of Pentecostalism in southern California. In the early 1900s, from this mission, Abundio and Rosa Lopez spread Christianity and Baptism of the Holy Spirit ("speaking in tongues") within the Latino community. Two major groups were formed—*Asambles de Dios* (Assemblies of God) and Apostolic churches—and they continue to grow in Central and Latin America. Pentecostals believe in the power of healing and God's support in meeting all of their needs—health, economic, etc. Pentecostal practices include reading and studying the Bible for answers and solace, praying to God directly without intervention from saints or virgins, and spreading the faith through conversions. Pentecostal services, full of music and dynamic preaching, occur more than once a week, and frequent Bible study is held throughout the week.

Pentecostals are very involved in their communities, spreading the faith and providing aid and support to troubled persons, especially young people. Faith-based programs provide a place of refuge and sobriety for teenagers experiencing problems with drugs, alcohol, and gangs and/or social issues. Outreach efforts include Victory Outreach, a Pentecostal religious-based drug-prevention program, with worldwide services in Texas, Mexico, Central America, and Amsterdam, among other locations.

The Church of Jesus Christ of Latter-Day Saints (Mormons)

As the Hispanic population increases, various religions have seen a corresponding increase in their congregations. The beliefs of the Church of Jesus Christ of Latter-Day Saints are appealing to many Latinos. The Mormon faith encourages all individuals to live their lives with a deep sense of honesty, simplicity, humility, and devotion to the Lord. Mormons also believe in the importance of "family as the most basic, essential unit on earth" ("What Mormons Believe," 2007). Many Hispanic immigrants value this tenet, and it is the driving force behind their conversion into the Mormon religion. Immigrants can relate to the values of hard work, humility, and family as a way to explore new venues of spirituality in their newly adopted home (Ventura, 2005).

As in other Christian denominations, Mormons perform a significant amount of missionary work, such as community outreach via English language classes, and they provide free health clinics and legal aid for immigrant Latinos. These efforts help to make the Latino community feel welcome. The Mormon religion is increasing in the United States (60% of its membership is in Colorado and Utah) and is also rapidly growing in Central and South America, with over 2.8 million members (Ramirez, 2005).

Jehovah's Witnesses

Another denomination with increasing Hispanic membership is Jehovah's Witnesses. Latino immigrants are drawn to this faith because of its strong ties to the Bible, its main principle of family unity, and the religion's conservative nature. Jehovah's Witnesses believe in preaching and spreading their word door-to-door. They follow the New World Translation of the Holy Scriptures and believe in the second coming of Christ to bring justice to the whole world. They are known for not celebrating holidays, but do enjoy family gatherings, picnics, and other events. The Jehovah's Witnesses religion is the only religion in the United States in which the majority of their members are minorities; 52% of its members are black or Hispanic (Pew Hispanic Center/Pew Forum on Religion, 2007). Outreach to immigrant populations is strong.

Branching Out in Other Faiths

"Almost one in five Latinos have changed their religious affiliation or have ceased identifying with religion at all" (Pew Hispanic Center, 2007, p. 39). In recent years, more Hispanics are seeking spiritual fulfillment in religions outside of Christianity. The following section sheds light on the increasing number of Latinos who have opted for non-Christian faiths.

Hispanic Jews

Latinos have a rich heritage in Judaism. Jews were persecuted in Spain during the 1500s and in the 1800s; consequently, many migrated to South America, namely Argentina, Chile, Uruguay, and Mexico. During the Spanish Inquisition, many Jews left Spain for the Canary Islands, Latin America, and the Caribbean. Traces of this migration are evident in cemeteries and other sites, where the Star of David can be found carved into monuments and buildings.

Presently, most Latino Jews come from Argentina, Ecuador, and other South American countries—some are escaping anti-Semitism. Many have settled in Florida, but Spanish-speaking Jews also live in Texas, New Mexico, and Mexico. Many are descendants of the Spanish Jews who fled from the Inquisition. Some synagogues in these states hold services in both Spanish and Hebrew.

Hispanic Muslims

More and more Latinos are seeking connections with Islam because of its simple relationship with Allah without need for intermediaries: "There is no God but Allah and his prophet Mohammed" (www.islam-guide.com/frm-ch3-14.htm). Recent reports show that Islam is the fastest-growing religion in the world, and 60% of its converts are Latinos (Viscidi, 2003).

Latinos are attracted to the traditional values espoused in Islamic communities, such as reverence for the family and a quest for spiritual harmony. Muslims pray five times a day for inner peace, happiness, and comfort, and they fast during the holy month of Ramadan

Raul Pimental's Reflection

I went to public school because Catholic schools were so expensive and my mother could not afford them. I worked at my uncle's bodega, where I found many of the religious artifacts used for Santeria. I felt comfortable and uncomfortable at the same time. Needless to say, after being exposed to both spiritual worlds, I still felt like I was lacking something. I went to college for two years, [where I] took a course in Far Eastern Religions with a professor who really opened my eyes to true spiritualism. Today, I am 54 years old, a Buddhist, and very content in my third spiritual world!

For the full reflection, see Appendix A.

to achieve spiritual self-purification. Latino Muslims do face a few challenges, as there is little Islamic literature in Spanish and they are not always accepted by other Latinos or other Muslims (Bowen, 2010).

Hispanic Buddhists

Buddhism is a course of spiritual development and practice leading, followers say, to the true nature of life. The basic tenets of Buddhist teaching are simple and practical: nothing is predetermined or permanent, actions have consequences, and change is possible. Buddhism addresses itself to all people regardless of race, nationality, or gender. It professes practical methods (such as meditation) that enable its followers to comprehend and make use of its teachings in order to transform their experiences, to be fully responsible for their lives, and to develop the qualities of wisdom and compassion ("What Is Buddhism?," n.d.).

In recent decades, Buddhist centers have emerged in many Central and South American countries, namely Brazil, Colombia, Guatemala, and Mexico ("Buddhism in Latin America," 2006). In 2006, the Dalai Lama visited Brazil, Argentina, Chile, Peru, and Colombia. Many Latinos find Buddhism appealing, as it embraces diversity and encourages Hispanic followers to "renew connections to our language, childhood experiences, ethnic communities and countries of origin" (Zubizarreta, 2003, p. 18). Hilda Guitiérrez Baldoquín, of Afro-Cuban descent, writes that "part of my journey in Buddhism has been connected with my journey as an immigrant. I have always felt like an 'outsider.' The experience of 'looking in' and being 'kept out' has been a great gift, for it has allowed me to learn how to move in and out of multiple worlds" (Zubizarreta, 2003, p. 25).

Summary and Recommendations for Educators and Care Providers

Faith and spirituality are integral to the day-to-day lives of many Hispanics living in the United States. Whether they are Protestants, Roman Catholics, Jews, Mormons, Jehovah's Witnesses, Buddhists, or Muslims, they believe in God and family and seek richer insights through their faith. Therefore, teachers and care providers should strive to:

- Be aware of the religions represented by the children in their classroom or care.
- Understand that religion and family life are sharply aligned.
- Recognize and respect that family members may seek the help of religious clergy or shamans when making school- or health-related decisions.
- Maintain open communication by dialoging with parents (in their native language, if possible) about religious beliefs and restrictions and be sensitive to the child's role in the family's religious experiences. For example, respect the idea that children from families who are Jehovah's Witnesses do not celebrate holidays or birthdays, and that children from Islamic families do not eat pork.

Chapter 3 Questions To Ponder

- Hispanics/Latinos, traditionally associated with Catholicism, may be participating in many other religions and thus are transforming the religious landscape in America. In your community, how have places of worship been affected? Have you noticed a trend toward services being offered in Spanish to meet the needs of an emerging community in search of a new faith?
- Given the strong connection between family and religious faith, it is important to communicate with families regarding their beliefs and any dietary restrictions that a child in your classroom may have. If a child does not celebrate certain secular holidays, regardless of their ethnic background, how would you show sensitivity to their situation?

Chapter 3 Web-Based Resources

Hispanic Culture Online
www.hispanic-culture-online.com/hispanic-religion.html
The Pew Hispanic Center
Changing Faiths: Latinos and the Transformation of American Religion
http://pewhispanic.org/files/reports/75.pdf
The Academy of Catholic Hispanic Theologians of the United States
www.achtus.org/
Latino American Dawah Organization
www.latinodawah.org/
An Online Handbook of Hispanic Protestant Denominations, Institutions and Ministries in the USA
www.hispanicchurchesusa.net/
The Association of Crypto-Jews -- Hispanic Sephardi Crypto Jews
www.cryptojew.org/main_page.html
WikiLatino
www.wikilatino.com

Chapter 4
Child-Rearing Practices

Nancy S. Maldonado

"A los hijos se les tiene que criar con mano de hierro
y guantes de seda y hay que criarlos con
mucho amor, si no, no les enseñamos nada."
(Raise your children with an iron hand and silk
gloves and you must raise them with love;
without love, you will teach them nothing.)

This chapter discusses the role of children within the Latino family structure, focusing particularly on parenting styles and the effects of acculturation to American culture. This chapter highlights the importance of family and child rearing within the Latino community, and sheds light on cultural principles, caregiving practices and patterns, feeding practices, parent-child communication, gender roles, disciplinary practices, and guiding proverbs. Issues of individuality, family history, geographic foundation, migration, social class, religion, values, and traditions create unique experiences for each Hispanic family.

Certainly, Hispanic families should each be approached on an individual basis. Specific family situations and levels of assimilation greatly affect child-rearing practices. The information that follows highlights certain traditional practices that some families may continue to follow.

La Vida de Nuestros Niños (Our Children's Lives)

As generations of Hispanics grow up in the United States, numerous issues associated with child rearing arise as parents try to hold onto traditional parenting practices in a new culture that is diverse and considered permissive by many. How do Hispanic parents follow child-rearing practices that pay respect to their ancestors' values while existing in conjunction with conflicting views of "how to raise a child" in U.S. society?

Educators and care providers need to be aware of traditional attitudes, beliefs, and values embedded in the child-rearing traditions honored by many Hispanics, while avoiding creating or perpetuating stereotypes about Latino parenting. Inherent in traditional Hispanic child-rearing practices are the cultural principles of *familismo, simpathía, respeto,* and *personalismo.*

The Solidarity of Hispanic Families: Parent and Child Relationships

In Hispanic cultures throughout the world, family is the core of existence. *La familia* is the most valued aspect of Hispanic life, culture, and pride. From the birth of a new family member to the passing of an elder, Latinos honor family as they celebrate, sacrifice, endure loss and pain, and cope with day-to-day life. Rodriguez (1999) notes that the Hispanic family culture is "rich and vibrant, full of traditions, celebrations and strong relationships" (p. 20).

Latino families nurture and care for each other, creating lifelong bonds. Hispanic values are grounded in self-identity through family (Halgunseth, Ispa, & Rudy, 2006). Children from the same family ancestry socialize with one another, often eliminating the need to seek friendships outside of the family. Brothers, sisters, cousins, distant cousins, and children of godparents are often children's first and best friends.

Hispanic families make serious efforts to gather together at least once or twice a month for meals, to celebrate birthdays and sacraments, attend church services, and socialize by participating in group games. These family gatherings strengthen the Hispanic cultural identity, building pride in the Hispanic way of life (Cuevas De Caissie, 2006; Rodriguez, 1999). The emphasis is on generating strong family bonds to support alliances and cooperation, rather than rivalry and competition (DeBord & Ferrer, 2000). Family is always available to help with the children, caring for them and supporting their interests and needs.

In the Hispanic family tapestry, children are considered blessings, gifts from God, who are to be cared for and adored. It is not unusual to have over 15 members of a Latino family awaiting the birth of a new member at the hospital. Children bring pleasure, comic relief, and much pride (*orgullo*), as well as promise for the future (Cuevas De Caissie, 2006).

Child Rearing and the Four Cultural Principles

Familismo

Within the diversity of Hispanic culture and heritage (e.g., Dominican, Puerto Rican, Peruvian, Mexican, etc.), some cultural generalizations may be found. The value placed on family unity, respect, and loyalty is one of the most dominant cultural concepts characterizing Latino child rearing. Family loyalty is powerful and is the vehicle for passing cultural traditions and knowledge from one generation to the other (DeBord & Ferrer, 2000; Vazquez, 2004). "*Familismo,* a cultural principle, (centrality of family) is a force for Latinos that permeates every aspect of life" (Vazquez, 2004, p. 61).

Latinos have a strong respect for families formed beyond blood relations, as well. Close friends (*compadres*) become godparents for children and for couples getting married (i.e., best man or *padrino*/godfather, and maid/matron of honor or *madrina*/godmother). These roles are serious ones; godparents are responsible for providing guidance, support, and counsel on critical issues, including children's moral and spiritual upbringing, marital issues, and financial concerns.

Familismo requires that family come first, before anything else. Within the construct of *familismo*, the family hierarchy is highly regarded. Elders (grandparents, uncles and aunts, godparents, etc.) have a lot of influence in the family when decisions need to be made regarding any issue, from marriage proposals, children's discipline, and health care. Latino elders are esteemed and respected individuals, and babies and young children are cosseted and pampered (Guilamo-Ramos et al., 2007; Queralt, 1984).

In several of the Latino cultural groups, gender may play a significant role in how particular decisions are made within content-specific situations. For example, in some cultural groups, male children may be allowed greater opportunities to make their own decisions than female children. Gender preference as a cultural belief may be carried out by individuals who are newly arrived in the United States or have maintained this practice as a unique attitude in their family experience. To avoid stereotyping, we must affirm that this cultural practice is not supported by all Hispanic groups.

Vazquez (2004) found that Latinos are considered to be part of the family first before they are considered as separate individuals, which is in contrast to American cultural value placed on the individual as of utmost importance. This disconnect proposes a quandary for many family members, especially the first generation of children who have grown up with mainstream American values and have to live in parallel worlds.

Simpathía

Simpathía is a cultural principle that, loosely translated, means the development of well-educated, well-mannered, respectful, and polite children. Vazquez (2004) proposes that *simpathía* is a highly respected cultural principle signifying the traditional values of Hispanic culture. Much emphasis is placed on Hispanic children developing this cultural principle over many others. Latino parents prefer a *simpático,* well-educated child to a popular child (p. 87). *Simpathía* also accentuates the positive, promotes harmony, and defuses conflict (Guilamo-Ramos et al., 2007). Avoidance of controversy is key. Vazquez (2004) also proposes a contemporary version of *simpathía* in order to avoid any disconnect in the meaning and application of this cultural principle among Hispanic generations. She suggests that in a new approach to *simpathía*, parents allow children opportunities to make mistakes and be responsible for their own actions. Moreover, she encourages Hispanic parents to help their children develop their own individuality and decision-making abilities (p. 109).

Respeto

The cultural principle of *respeto* is also valued. Children as young as age 4 are taught to address *los ancianos* (elders) politely, and not to interrupt or interject their views in adult conversation or question elders' points of view (Halgunseth et al., 2006; Nava, 2000). A study of Puerto Rican mothers conducted by Tacon and Caldera (2001) found that the mothers focused more on their child's demeanor or respectfulness within a public context (p. 73). *Respeto* addresses the need for children to respect authority, with particular emphasis on age and social position (Guilamo-Ramos et al., 2007). Grandparents, godparents, and family elders hold social positions within the family that merit high levels of *respeto*.

Puerto Rican children are taught early to show respect for their elders by asking for *la bendición (blessing)*, a tradition that many Puerto Rican families follow every morning. When a child asks for *la bendición*, parents respond by saying "May God and the virgin keep you," and then kiss the child on the cheek. Requests for *la bendición* are made quite frequently throughout the day, as well—as children leave for or arrive from school and before going to bed. Children ask for *la bendición* from all family elders—grandparents, uncles, and aunts. Not to do so would be considered disrespectful.

Respeto also requires children to demonstrate responsibility and concern for family elders (Rodriguez, 1999; Vazquez, 2004). For example, adolescent grandchildren are expected to maintain a close watch on their grandparents and be available to them when needed. Children must not speak in loud voices or whine when addressing grandparents and family elders. They must always address elders by *"Señor"* and *"Señora"* or *"Don"* and *"Doña,"* never by their first names (Nava, 2000). Children are also taught that in order be respected themselves, they need to show respect to all members of their family, including older siblings. Older siblings are given respect, since they assume responsibility in the absence of adults. *Falta de respeto* (not respecting) an elder or sibling is a serious offense warranting consequences. Children who violate this principle must work to re-establish their dignity. Another potential *"falta de respeto"* can occur if sisters display affection toward their husbands and/or boyfriends in the presence of their brothers (Halgunseth et al., 2006).

Personalismo

Guilamo-Ramos et al. (2007) explain that *personalismo*, consistent with *familismo* and *simpathía* (p. 19), awards great importance to personal dispositions, inner qualities, warmth, trust, and respect. It can be further defined as warm and interpersonal relationships that generate closeness, harmony, responsiveness, and mutual respect (p. 25). *Personalismo* highlights familiarity and closeness, by touching and gestures that promote warmth and acceptance. Children are taught to be cordial, polite, warm, and friendly with family members and close family friends (Vazquez, 2005). It is not unusual for children to refer to close family friends as *tíos y tías* (uncles and aunts).

It should be noted that it is customary for Latinos to greet each other with a hug and/or kiss. "A hug and a light kiss on a cheek are also common greeting practices among women, and men and women who are close friends or family" (Clutter & Zubieta, 2009). This practice may at times conflict with schools' rules or policies, as many school systems frown upon such public displays of affection. Educators should help all students understand culturally accepted forms of greeting one another in public. Latinos may have a more relaxed, informal means of communication and treatment of "personal space" than non-Latinos. This relaxed approach can be the source of another conflict in schools: "Hispanics tend to be more informal and flexible about time and punctuality than U.S. natives. For example, Latinos who are invited for an 8 a.m. event may not begin to arrive until 8:30 a.m. or later. Within the Hispanic community, not being on time is a socially acceptable behavior" (Clutter & Zubieta, 2009, p. 3).

Caregiving: Practices and Patterns

Hispanic mothers or female family relatives (e.g., grandmother, aunts, sisters) are the primary caregivers of Hispanic children. Contreras' study (2004) on Puerto Rican adolescent mothers shows that Puerto Rican mothers rely on family members for advice about child care and willingly share the responsibility for their children with other female relatives. In most Hispanic groups, grandmothers have an especially important role to play in child rearing.

Caregiving is a critical issue for Hispanic families, especially given the large percentage of Latina mothers who work outside the home. Many Latino families, especially recently immigrated families, prefer not to use outside child care services for infants and

Boriqua's Reflection: Amanda Maldonado Delgado
Traditional vs. Nontraditional Child-Rearing Practices

I had my first child when I was 22. I found my son to be a colicky baby. The pediatrician suggested stomach drops to ease the pain. Other family members taught me how to make a tea out of star anise (estrella de anis). Both remedies seemed to bring him comfort and by the time he was 6 months, he seemed to outgrow his colic. I do not believe that the anise cured him, but I figured it was worth a try. One of the gifts when he was a baby was an azabache, which is a talisman worn by babies and adults for protections from evil and illnesses, given to him by his great aunt. My son always wore the azabache on a chain around his neck. Elder family members believed that this talisman would watch over him. I agreed but found it hard to believe that a piece of jewelry would protect him from illnesses. When he started on regular foods, I noticed some food allergies. I went straight to an allergist for help. I also relied on my faith and prayed a lot. Some family members saw this as a punishment from God. I tried not to let it bother me and continued to pray that God would help my son and give him the strength to feel better. I had my doubts about the azabache warding off illnesses. I believe that my son's allergies are a result of biological systems, not spiritual interventions.

azabache

Her story in its entirety is available in Appendix A.

toddlers. In some Latin American cultures (Cuban American, Mexican American, Puerto Rican American), mothers-in-law help care for the mother and grandchild during the post-natal period, which is known as *La Cuarentena* or "40 days after delivery" (Meyers, 1994; Whiteside-Mansell, Bradley, & McKelvey, 2009). Other female relatives also help during this period by caring for the new baby's siblings, cooking meals, or cleaning. Cross-culturally, Hispanic fathers less commonly participate in the care of the children. In Bolivia and Peru, however, fathers participate in the care and birthing process (Meyers, 1994).

Breast Feeding, Bottle Feeding, and Weaning

For Latinos, an important aspect of child rearing is a strong emphasis on feeding, especially for infants. Hispanic mothers view feeding in the context of nourishing the infant, but also as a gesture of love. Several Hispanic cultures believe that a chubby baby is a healthy baby. Breast-feeding practices vary among Latino cultural groups, depending upon the level of acculturation. Typically, Hispanic babies are usually breast fed on demand and are weaned off the breast by six months. Pérez-Escamilla (1993) conducted a study on breast-feeding patterns in Latin America and found that babies in Bolivia, Guatemala, and Brazil are usually weaned off the breast by one year.

One study (Bunik et al., 2006) showed that Latina mothers are reluctant to breast feed for several reasons, including a belief that babies benefit from having both breast milk and the nutrients in formula. There is significant pressure from relatives to use feeding to soothe crying babies and promote weight gain. Many of the mothers participating in Bunik et al.'s (2006) study felt that breast feeding is painful, demanding, and embarrassing, and causes changes in their diet and body.

Latino infants are introduced to solid foods early. Cereal may be introduced to babies as young as 2 weeks old. The cereal is mixed into the formula and placed in the baby's bottle at the last feeding to help them sleep through the night. By the age of 2 months, many infants are introduced to cereal mixed with fruit, also placed in the bottle. Bottle nipples are altered with larger holes to facilitate their use with solid foods. By 6 to 12 months, infants are introduced to fresh fruit, fruit-flavored drinks, baby cookies, and such foods as soups, rice and beans, *el potaje* (porridge), and tortillas (Mennella, Ziegler, Briefel, & Novak, 2006).

Bottle feeding may be maintained for prolonged periods of time in Latino families; many bottle feed their babies until they are 3 to 5 years old. Hispanic mothers tend to delay self-feeding until they are sure their children are fully nourished. Consequently, some children beginning school are not yet able to feed themselves. Studies have shown that this prolonged bottle feeding may result in tooth decay and iron deficiencies, especially in Mexican American children, who are typically bottle fed past 15 months of age (Brotanek, Halterman, Auinger, Flores, & Weitzman, 2005). This bottle feeding also may mean that

Mariana Souto-Manning's Reflection

I will never forget the day in which Lucas's preschool teacher told me proudly that he was self-feeding. It was not a skill I valued at a young age. I wanted to feed him (as my mother had done) as I developed a close mother-child bond. To me, the concept of familism, which is so common in Latino cultures, was being crushed in the name of independence. I kept hearing "best practice" for this, "best practice" for that, and started asking myself, "best practice" for whom? It was obvious to me that these "best practices" were not best for Brazilian culture and language.

For Mariana's full reflection, please see Appendix A.

infants receive large quantities of milk and juices (p. 1041), contributing to a greater likelihood of childhood obesity (Kersey, Lipton, Quinn, & Lantos, 2010).

Care providers and teachers especially need to be aware of the feeding practices of Hispanic families and avoid interpreting these customs as babying the children and stifling their independence. In order to maintain a good supportive relationship with Latino parents, care providers and teachers should ask questions about feeding practices and allow time for Hispanic children to acclimate to the school culture. Forcing the issue of independence may cause a conflict with Hispanic child-rearing values. These feeding and other caregiving practices, such as walking the child directly to the teacher and fastening their clothing, etc., are valued as building tight family bonds.

Parent/Child Communication

Of course, the parent/child relationship varies from family to family, in part due to the amount of assimilation or acculturation. Vazquez (2005) explains that parents can maintain good channels of communication with their children by being consistent in what they teach their children and modeling communication with the other adults in the family. Crean (2008) affirms that fathers are highly respected as the authority figure in the family. The mother's role is to mediate any difficulties or problems between fathers and their children. Parents model cultural values, traditions, and practices, including the appreciation of Hispanic folklore (such as *los dichos,* or proverbs); music (different styles of music, such as *salsa, merengue, mariachi,* and *jibaro*); family *cuentos* (stories); as well as traditional recipes and dishes (*mofongo, picadillo, dulce de leche, chile rellenos).* What better way for parents to disseminate the traditions of a culture than by modeling the dancing at celebrations, introducing the traditional music at home, using *los dichos* and/or *los cuentos* when disciplining children, and using *remedies caseros* (home remedies) and medicinal herbs that have been passed down from generation to generation?

Hispanics are proud of their cultural traditions. While previous generations may have felt the need to hide their particular ways of celebrating, dancing, or eating (Rodriquez, 1999), Latino cultural traditions have increasingly become part of the American mainstream. Non-Latinos join us in salsa dancing and celebrating *Cinco de Mayo, Día de los Muertos,* or other holidays.

Hispanic parents place their children first, giving themselves little time to pursue their own personal interests. Parents' lives revolve around the children's activities and needs (Perez, 2006; Vazquez, 2004). Many parents feel it is their duty to overlook their own needs and desires in favor of their children's needs, because the end result will be children who are well-educated and well-mannered. In return, adult children are expected to make sacrifices for their parents. Adult children and grandchildren care for their elderly family

An Ecuadorian Mother's Experience: Myriam Rogers

I spent all of my free time with my family; I gave it all to my three daughters. I sewed for them; I read and read with them. We did almost everything together, but what I did the most was share with them my family stories. I always connected events, books, foods, etc., with them from my culture. I explained to them repeatedly why some things are different for me. I constantly asked for them to just try to understand my point of view. During their teenage years, this proved to be very difficult because my beliefs and principles growing up were not always in line with the ones that their friends shared when they were growing up.

The full reflection is provided in Appendix A.

members, often shunning the use of nursing homes for elderly parents.

Children who have been acculturated to mainstream American society often experience a disconnect between their lifestyle and the more traditional style of Latino parenting. Many find it vexing to live in the parallel worlds of what they know to be accepted by the Hispanic culture and what American culture professes to value: fulfilling one's own needs and interests.

Gender Roles and Distinctions

As mentioned previously, several Hispanic cultural groups still maintain and expect clear distinctions between boys and girls. *Machismo* and *marianismo* are gender-specific constructs in Latino culture. Vazquez (2004, 2005) explains that *machismo* and *marianismo* establish expectations about how individuals should act on the basis of their gender. She argues that placing these constructs on children can be detrimental, because daughters may feel they have to be self-sacrificing to be loved and sons may expect their wives or partners to be subservient and docile. "*Machismo* refers to a constellation of attitudes and behaviors that accompany the leadership or decision-making role that men individually and collectively assume in the home and community" (Guilamo-Ramos et al., 2007, p. 19). In other words, *macho* refers to being virile, aggressive, having physical courage, and being dominant over women. *Machismo* often is considered to include negative characteristics that are not fully understood by the American culture. Arciniega, Anderson, Tovar-Blank, and Tracey (2008) explain that machismo also has positive connotations that date back to the Spanish word "caballero," a gentleman of high station who lives by an ethical code of chivalry (p. 20). Modern-day "machismo" often is reflected in the common stereotype of Latino men as "Latin lovers." Many Hispanic cultures do value machismo and encourage its principles in their male children. They believe that certain values need to be instilled in their male children as potential leaders and heads of family. The root word for macho comes from the pre-Columbian Náhuatl word "mati"—to know—and "macho"—to be known. Aztec men wanted to be known for their courage, bravery, vigor, discipline, and strength (Rodriguez, 1999).

Marianismo is a depiction of the ideal character for Latinas. *Marianismo* derives from the devotion shown to the Virgin Mary, who exemplifies what a Latina should be: spiritual, immaculate, and able to place the wishes of her husband and children before her own desires (Adams, Coltrane, & Parke, 2007; Guilamo-Ramos, 2007). Sometimes, unfortunately, *marianismo* may mean tolerating negative behavior from men, including aggressiveness, sexual infidelity, and egotism. Of course, as Hispanics acculturate to contemporary feminist values, they are raising their daughters with an awareness of women's rights. The following poem, by Judith Cofer-Ortiz (2001), reflects the relationship between a mother and daughter:

Palomita
Wearing a sky-blue skirt
embroidered by an old woman
named Consuelo from a story
she told mami a long time ago
on her island, a cuento
in gold, brown, and silver threads
a shower of sunlight
falling like drops of gold on
a little golden girl
who turns into a silver dove
and flies around and around
a blue sky.

My mami is walking with me in the park.
Palomita, Palomita is the name
she calls me, her little dove,
happy to be going anywhere with her
flying like a bird around and around
my mami in her sky-blue skirt
made from an island story

Child Discipline: Rewards and Punishment

Dating back to the days of Aztec rule, "*la disciplina* has been a major tool in socializing children" (Rodriguez, 1999, p. 236). Hispanics expect absolute obedience from their children. Children need to follow a strict code of behavior (*ley de la casa*) set by their parents. Vazquez (2004) describes the Latin American belief in "open discipline" (p. 113), meaning the responsibility of all adults interacting with children to discipline them. For example, an elderly person in the park can scold a child who is not behaving appropriately. Disobedience, or straying away from the specific code, results in varied means of punishment, which may include corporal punishment. Children who are disrespectful (e.g., talking back or cursing) may be smacked across the mouth or have hot sauce placed on their tongues as a reminder of how unacceptable it is to use bad language. Other acts of unacceptable behavior may prompt a *cocotazo* ("noogie"), or punishments like having to kneel on uncooked rice with bare knees (Fontes, 2002). Fontes (2002) describes how Latino parents who have fewer years of education respond to their children's unacceptable actions

---

Raising My Second-generation Son
Yahaira Caseres

One thing about coming from a large and close family like mine is that everyone knows your business. I feel that this is the same in most large families. Growing up, my aunts had every right to spank or punish me if I even rolled my eyes at them. My cousins and I were raised not by one tough Dominican mother, but by seven. Although my mother was the one that would spank my brother and me, we were never too scared of her. We knew that if we misbehaved, my mother would spank us, but it never really hurt and it would be over in a minute. We would be back playing video games or watching television. Now, my father was very quiet. He never spanked us but we were terrified of him. If he told us to stop jumping, he only had to say it once. My way of raising my child is a bit different from my own upbringing, in that I do not spank my son. I don't believe in hitting my son because it does not solve anything. When I was a child, I used to prefer getting spanked than punished. However, like my parents, I will be involved in my child's education; I will attend the meetings, conferences, take and pick him up from school. I will try to instill in him the importance of family. My husband (who is a Dominican American like me) and I are also choosing to talk to my son in Spanish first. It is important to us that he learns the language of his culture. Overall, my experience has been great. I feel that I am the way I am today because of my strict parents, my close family, my education (the good and the bad), my neighborhood, and my culture.

Read the rest of Yahaira's reflection in Appendix A.

punitively: "The more acculturated the Hispanic family is, the closer their child discipline norms to those of the dominant culture" (Fontes, 2002, p. 5). Many Hispanic families have encountered problems at school or in health care facilities when children are examined for bruises. There is a disconnect with what is considered child abuse and what is considered acceptable discipline for Latinos. Many Latinos believe that government agencies have no right to regulate how they handle discipline in their families.

Fontes (2002) conducted a study on child discipline and abuse and found that Latino parents are apt to shun the advice of any professionals who seem to be criticizing the way their own parents physically punished them. They may feel that the ways in which they were raised (with corporal punishment, for example) did not harm them and, in fact, may believe such practices were beneficial:

Latinos also use other modes for disciplining their children, specifically a folktale monster named *El Cuco*. *El Cuco* or *Coco* is a legendary monster, a Spanish version of the "Boogeyman." The story of *El Cuco* is used by Latino parents to make their children go to sleep or to behave: *"Duérmete niño, duérmete ya, que viene el cuco y te comerá"* (Sleep, my child, or the Cuco will eat you up). Or, you might hear the warning: *Cuidado, ahí viene El Cuco!* (Be careful! The Cuco is coming to get you). Different Hispanic groups have different versions of *El Cuco*. In Mexico, for example, *El Cuco* is *El Cucuy* or *Calaca* (skeleton). In Brazil, *El Cuco* is an alligator-shaped, female monster named *Cuca*. Her mission is the same—to attack children who misbehave or do not go to sleep when told.

Los Dichos (Proverbs) and Consejos (Words of Wisdom)

Every Hispanic family relies on the wisdom passed on by their ancestors. *Los dichos* are short and snappy phrases reflecting Hispanic cultural values that help one make good decisions and offer insight for appropriate action in everyday life situations. They are an important part of Latino oral tradition, passed down from one generation to another, used to guide children's behavior, teach important cultural values of Hispanic heritage, provide advice, and teach valuable lessons.

Perez (2006) clarifies that "*dichos* provide messages of hope, direction and guidance just when we need them. When for some reason or another, a basic truth escapes us, *dichos* put us back on track" (p. 5). In other words, *los dichos* are ingrained reminders that prompt children to be mindful of their actions. They carry a deeper message beyond the face value of the words. When a parent is concerned about their child's choice of associates, they may say, *"Dime con quién andas y te diré quién eres"* (Tell me with whom you hang out, and I will tell you who you are). A few commonly used *dichos* expressed by Hispanic parents are:

Nunca preguntes lo que no te importa.
Mind your own business.

La ropa sucia se lava en casa.
Dirty linen is washed at home. (Family business is family business that is not shared with others outside of the family.)

Embustero conocido, ya nunca es creído.
Known liars are never trustworthy. (Tell the truth at all costs.)

La boca de mentiroso, lo cierto se hace dudoso.
In the mouth of a liar, the truth becomes doubtful. (No one believes a liar.)

Todo lo excesivo es vicioso.
Everything excessive is immoral. (Moderation is key in everyday living.)

Haz bien y no mires a quien.
Always do good and never notice to whom. (Be kind and good to all.)

El que parte y comparte, se queda con la major parte.
He who shares and divides what he has will get the better part.

El que madruga, Dios le ayuda.
Those who rise early receive God's help. (The early bird catches the worm.)

Trabajar para más valer, estudiar para más saber.
Work to have more value, study to have more knowledge.

(Perez, 2006)

Parental use of *los dichos* truly affects the moral development of children. These sayings are embedded in their sub-consciousness, promoting insight and direction in their daily lives.

Summary and Recommendations for Educators and Care Providers

Many factors influence child-rearing practices among Hispanic families. These include ethnicity, socioeconomic growth and development, individual family configurations, and levels of assimilation and acculturation. Care providers and teachers need to be aware of the socio-cultural child-rearing values of Hispanic groups in order to provide more respectful relationships with families. Take into account children's feeding practices, self-help skill development, gender roles, overt and covert discipline practices, and how children relate to their families. The following recommendations are suggested:

- Be sensitive to the boundary between school and home practices, such as those that involve promoting independence in children. Care providers and teachers need to have respect for parents' authority in child rearing and allow children time to acculturate to the school culture. Refrain from deficit model thinking. Be open to the specific practices that will help create authentic relationships with Hispanic children and their families.
- Become aware of and attach importance to Hispanic families' cultural values. This can be done by visiting the children's homes or studying the Latino community.
- Do not be afraid to ask Latino parents about their culture, personal experiences, and child-rearing concerns.
- Reach out to recently arrived Hispanic families in their native language. If an interpreter is necessary, volunteer interpreters may be sought in houses of worship or at community centers. In this way, pertinent information about a child's progress in school can be shared and parents will be more comfortable participating in school programs.

Chapter 4 Questions To Ponder

- Some Hispanic/Latino families with young children in early childhood centers find themselves at odds with American educational practices when it comes to self-feeding routines for toddlers. If confronted by a parent who wishes for their child to be "fed" at lunch or snack time, for fear of their child going hungry, how would you address those concerns?
- Name the four cultural principles (described in this chapter) that guide child rearing for Hispanic/Latino families (Vazquez, 2004). Of the four principles, which do you see most often characterized at your school or center? Provide an example.

- Disciplining a child often can be an issue for Hispanic/Latino families and the schools/ centers, particularly for families who have recently arrived in the United States and who have come from cultures where corporal punishment of a child is expected. How might a teacher address the issue of developmentally/culturally appropriate ways of disciplining a child?

Chapter 4 Web-Based Resources

U.S. Department of Health and Human Services – Hispanic Healthy Marriage Initiative
www.acf.hhs.gov/healthymarriage/about/hispanic_hm_initiative.508.html

Latin Baby Book Club
www.latinbabybookclub.com/

National Latino Children's Institute
www.nlci.org

Salsa, Sabor y Salud (Kraft Foods and NLCI)
www.nlci.org/salsa/indexSSS.htm

National Center for Family Literacy – "Foto Novelas"
www.famlit.org/free-resources/foto-novelas/

Kids Health in Spanish
http://kidshealth.org/parent/en_espanol/index.html#El_crecimiento_y_el_desarrollo

Chapter 5
Education Issues: The Latino/Hispanic Experience

Lilia C. DiBello

"Lo que bien se aprende, nunca se pierde."
(What is well learned is never lost.)

"El que no sabe es como el que no ve."
(One who has no knowledge is like one who does not see.)

Poems by Francisco X. Alarcón

"Primer día de clases"
Parado frente a la "teacher"
Apreté aun más fuerte
La mano de mi abuela
La teacher se sonrió
Dijo algo en inglés, pero yo no entendí
Mi abuela luego me dio su bendición y se fue
Yo me quedé hecho silla en un mundo muy extraño.

"First Day of School"
Standing before the teacher
I squeezed my grandma's hand even harder
The teacher smiled, said something in English, but I did not understand
My grandma then gave me her blessing and left
I felt like a chair left behind in a very strange world.

"Ángel de la guardia"
Cuando más triste y solo me sentía
Queriendo llorar en el salón
La niña sentada al lado mío
De pronto la mano me tomó
Y con los ojos más negros y tristes
Que he visto jamás
Me dijo sin palabras
"No te apures, no estás solo"

"Guardian Angel"
When I felt so sad and all alone
Wanting to cry in the classroom
The girl sitting next to me
Suddenly held my hand
And with the darkest and most tender eyes I've ever seen
Told me without a word
"Don't worry, you are not alone."

Many issues that relate to the education of Hispanics in the United States are worthy of being addressed within this work. The sub-topic of "special education" will be discussed in Chapter 6, as so much is available in the literature that is valuable for care providers and educators. Of primary importance to the ultimate success of any educational program is the need to pay close attention to cultural differences.

Guadalupe Valdes (1996), in her ethnographic study of Mexican American families in the border community of Las Fuentes, found that "without exception, parents expressed very positive views about education. They felt that education was important and that it was their duty as parents to send their children to school" (p. 152). The focus of this chapter is a discussion of key issues affecting Latinos in the United States with respect to educational opportunities.

This chapter addresses attitudes toward education—specifically, how Latino families feel about schooling and the role of the school versus the role of the family. In another section, we explore "Academic Successes and Difficulties" by reviewing literature about the education of Hispanics in the United States, and providing a summary of relevant statistics. The chapter continues with a compilation of laws and policies in the United States affecting Hispanic families, and includes a brief history of bilingual education. A chapter addressing educational issues would not be complete without reviewing models of English language instruction and exploring the learning styles of Latino children. Information regarding Latino teachers is shared prior to a discussion on the education of migrant children. Finally, we explore Hispanics in higher education.

Attitudes Toward Education

For Hispanics who have recently immigrated to the United States, education equals opportunity. It is well documented that one of the major reasons immigrants struggle to make it to the United States is to give their children a chance for a better life than the one they might have had in their homeland (Massey & Redstone Akresh, 2006). Given that the role of the family is so strong in the daily life of Hispanics, one might expect active family input in children's educational lives. Yet, research (Quijada & Alvarez, 2006) has shown that many Latino parents are likely to leave the education of their children to the educators. They respect the teacher as an authority on education. Parents are very supportive of what their children are expected to do in the classroom, and so it is important not to misinterpret a parent's absence at school events. An interview conducted by Gilda Ochoa (2007) with Ana Camacho, a high school teacher, revealed that "Latino parents assume, especially if they are new immigrants, that the teacher and the school know what to do and that they don't have the education to be able to tell the school what to do" (p. 58).

It is difficult to say that the Latino attitude toward education is something we can trace back "to the homeland," because many families are seeking educational opportunities that did not exist in the homeland. Furthermore, one also must consider the myriad variables upon which a decision to move to a new country rests.

> Each migrant has certain goals that have caused him or her to migrate, but whatever the motivations for migration, satisfaction is determined by the objective circumstances encountered after arrival. The circumstances we consider include conditions in the migrant's home country, along with demographic background, education, English-language ability, earnings, prior U.S. experience, and connections to people and institutions in the United States and abroad. (Massey & Redstone Akresh, 2006, p. 956)

Studies show that parents' involvement in their children's schooling is often related to income and education level. These studies defined parental involvement at school through such activities as attending general school meetings, parent-teacher conferences, or a school event; acting as a school volunteer; or serving on a school-related committee (Llagas, 2003).

Academic Successes and Difficulties

It is no secret that Latinos, as a group, have faced academic struggles. When compared with other groups, they are found to have a higher dropout rate, a higher rate of identification for special academic services, lower standardized test scores, and a lower rate of high school completion. In an era when most educators embrace differentiated instruction, it is timely to discuss special needs of populations. In fact, just developing an awareness of successes and difficulties is an important part of the reflective practice required for the establishment of dialogue about education.

In 2004, the Pew Hispanic Center and the Kaiser Family Foundation conducted a national survey about education, asking over 3,000 randomly selected Latinos about attitudes toward public schools and other educational issues. The findings showed that Latinos were very likely to support the public schools and the teachers, and they reported positive feelings about the education being received by their children. Hispanic immigrants rated the schools highest and showed the most confidence in the U.S. education system. Of great interest, however, are the Latino parents' concerns about how their children were being treated in the school system, particularly in terms of equity and standardized testing. Overwhelmingly, the survey respondents were concerned about language issues. Immigrants responded that they perceived a critical need for their children to learn English in schools, while also wanting their children to have the opportunity to retain their home language.

Dropout Rates

Clearly, one of the greatest education issues that needs to be addressed for the Latino population is the alarmingly high dropout rate. The National Center for Education Statistics (2009) reported that the status dropout rate for Hispanic students in 2007 was 21.4%, compared to 5.3% for white students. The "status dropout rate" includes the percentage of youth ages 16 through 24 who are out of school and have not earned a high school diploma or equivalent credential (e.g., a GED). These particular statistics include all Hispanic youth, some who were born and raised in the United States, and others who may be recent immigrants and never attended a U.S. high school. The statistics clearly show a disproportionate number of Latino students not completing the requirements for a high school diploma. This challenge must be overcome in order to address educational issues affecting Latinos. Although the work of such organizations as the Hispanic Scholarship Fund (HSF) and Excelencia in Education has made an impact on the Latino community, the statistics continue to indicate that more must be done to reduce the dropout rates among Hispanic youth in the United States.

Stressors Impacting Educational Experiences

Several researchers have focused their attention on discovering why some Latinos perform well in school and some do not, and whether or not there may be a correlation between variables. A "developmentalist" would argue that the unique nature of each individual learner is of primary significance, and that struggling to summarize individuals as a cultural group is counterproductive. Yet, sociologists and education researchers find value in the opportunity to contemplate the data and discuss the patterns of significance. Ochoa (2007) notes that the vast majority of Latinos in the United States are either immigrants themselves or are children of immigrants, and one's generation greatly influences the way in which one views the schooling experience in the United States.

For example, immigrants to the United States are more likely than their peers born in this country to view schooling as a positive experience, and they tend to rate their teachers as more caring. Recent immigrants have great expectations for their potential to learn a new language and start a new life; as would be expected, the younger the immigrant, the more likely he or she is to complete school and earn a high school diploma. Learning English is critical to the success of most immigrants, and research has shown that those with a strong foundation in their native language are more likely to do better in U.S. schools. Literacy in the home language is an important confounding variable, as is the educational and socioeconomic backgrounds of parents. A student who is literate in his/her home language is more likely to become literate in the English language. Furthermore, if a student has parents with a strong education background (in English or the home language), the student is likely to excel in school and have little problem transitioning to the new language; although this still does not guarantee success in schooling.

An Educational Testing Service (ETS) policy report titled *Fragile Futures: Risk and Vulnerability Among Latino High Achievers* (Gandara, 2005) focused on the challenges that low-income Latino students face in successfully completing high school. The research found that commitments shared by low-income, high-achieving Latino students sometimes create roadblocks to their success.

> These events often relate to the daily dynamic of conducting life without a car, child care, health care, or the money to buy books or pay for bus fare. For Latinos, they are sometimes related to being undocumented and, therefore, to conducting routine business in circuitous ways, and often to issues of language barriers, where the student must be available as a translator or cultural broker for members of the family. And because extended family is considered by Latinos to be the vital network at the core of existence, students may feel a strong responsibility to put the needs of family members ahead of their own immediate commitments. High-achieving students from low-income backgrounds are as likely to be caught up in this web of responsibilities as low-achieving students. (Gandara, 2005, p. 20)

Dotson-Blake et al. (2009) note that Latinos face specific stressors: "Mexican immigrant families with school-aged children manifest systemic concerns directly related to specific stressors experienced by the population, stressors often inseparably related to the individual's or family's immigrant status in their new community" (pp. 232-233). Immigrant families often have difficulty reconciling the differing cultural values between the home environment and the school environment. Children may not be allowed behaviors at home that are tolerated, or even encouraged, at school, and vice versa. Dotson-Blake et al. (2009) also note that intergenerational conflicts may result from differing levels of acculturation. A young adult immigrant student may feel confident about attending a school function after hours because it is something that all the students are doing. However, parents may not permit a young adult to attend a function in the evening without a parent or a chaperone. Yet another stressor involves fear and anxiety over the possibility of a parent's undocumented status, and potential deportation. These are just a few stressors that may impact an immigrant family's relationship with the U.S. education system—all things that must be considered when planning for students who may be learning English as a second language. The ultimate goal would be to establish a good school-home partnership—the success of which lies in the ability of the schools to forge that necessary bond.

A Puerto Rican American Professor's Reflections: Diane Rodriguez

There are many challenges for Latino children and youth who have arrived to the United States without proper documentation for various reasons (e.g., quality of life, education, economics, politics, wars, etc.). For whatever reason these children arrived in the United States, we must ensure that they have an opportunity to succeed and excel in this country. Throughout my work in the Southeast, I have encountered many Latino students who are facing many challenges to move forward in obtaining a university or college degree. I believe that their stories must be heard.

Read more in Appendix A.

Bilingual Education in the United States

Spanish-speaking children arrive in the United States every day, and the influx of new students has had a significant impact on the country's education system and prompted passage of certain laws and policies. We consider here a historical synopsis of bilingual education in the United States. This summary is not meant to be a comprehensive examination of laws and policies affecting Hispanic families. Readers are encouraged to continue their research by considering some of the resources mentioned. And although we address some landmark decisions and policies in key states, the focus for this chapter is mostly on the federal position. It is important to note that this debate is not unique to the United States. In Canada, for example, the French-speaking provinces require that all children be taught in both French and English throughout their time in public education. In Europe, students are often required to learn two and sometimes three languages. China has recently required that their citizens be educated in both English and Chinese.

Following the launch of Sputnik in 1957, the U.S. Congress passed the National Defense Education Act, which provided for funding to increase the number of foreign language programs. The need for foreign language experts had been underscored by the country's experience in World War II. At the same time, however, immigrant children were challenged when entering school by the need to learn English as quickly as possible, and were not always encouraged to continue developing their primary language. A philosophical disconnect was occurring in terms of educational goals for students in the United States—federal support was being given to foreign language programs in high schools, yet native languages were being taken away from young immigrants at the elementary school level. This type of conflicting view with respect to languages continues today across the United States.

In 1964, the Civil Rights Act (www.ourdocuments.gov) outlawed racial segregation in schools, public places, and places of employment. Although not directly written to address the rights of immigrants, the Civil Rights Act brought a focus on equality and prompted citizens to discuss the opportunities afforded to all Americans.

By 1965, Congress passed the Immigration Act, which ended immigration quotas based on national origin (as established by the Naturalization Act of 1906 and subsequent legislation in 1924). Under the Immigration Act, the applicant's occupation became the main factor used in consideration for entry into the country, and preference was to be given to those who had relatives already in the United States. It is important to note that race, religion, color, and national origin would no longer be factors in the selective process for new immigrants (www.historicaldocuments.com/ImmigrationActof1965.htm). "As a result of the 1965 Immigration Act, larger numbers of Asians and Latin Americans started to enter the country. With this demographic shift, more language-minority students from these regions of the world appeared in U.S. classrooms, where bilingual instruction was needed" (Ovando, 2003, p. 7).

The Bilingual Education Act of 1968

The first piece of United States federal legislation to address the needs of minority language speakers was The Bilingual Education Act of 1968 (also known as Title VII of the Elementary and Secondary Education Act, or ESEA). The primary purpose of this Act was to provide federal funds to local school districts in order to meet the education needs of students with limited English proficiency. Interestingly enough, the first draft was originally intended only for Spanish-speaking students, but soon was modified to address the needs of all non-English speaking students. As a direct result of this legislation, multicultural awareness grew within the context of the Civil Rights movement. Individual states began passing laws to bring bilingual education into local school districts, even though the states still maintained a focus on English instruction for immigrants.

In 1970, the Office for Civil Rights (OCR) issued an interpretation of Title VI of the Civil

Rights Act of 1964 regulations that prohibited the denial of access to educational programs because of a student's limited English proficiency. It stated:

> Where the inability to speak and understand the English language excludes national origin minority group children from effective participation in the educational program offered by a school district, the district must take affirmative steps to rectify the language deficiency in order to open its instructional program to these students. (United States Department of Education, 2000)

This ruling opened the door for widespread interpretation of these new documents; it became clear that not all states were in agreement with respect to how these laws and policies were to be implemented. For more details of legislative actions concerning education for English language learners and bilingual education, see Appendix D.

Equal Educational Opportunity Act of 1974

Bilingual education advocates understood that "the failure by an educational agency to take appropriate action to overcome language barriers that impede equal participation by students in an instructional program" (U.S. Department of Education, 2000) meant a violation of Title VI. Despite the federal mandate, however, educators had no specific guidance for implementing programs to meet the needs of these students. There was no specific teaching methodology endorsed by the federal government, and therefore states did not enforce this Act consistently. The Equal Educational Opportunity Act ultimately influenced the implementation of the Bilingual Education Act (1968), because it stated that language barriers must be overcome by instructional programming. The Bilingual Education Act clarified that all programs should prepare students to succeed in an English classroom as soon as possible, while maintaining their native language. Furthermore, the act highlighted the need to establish support centers across the United States for areas with a large concentration of English language learners.

English as a second language (ESL) instruction was to be provided for all students who did not speak English as their primary language, and schools were instructed to educate students in their primary language until they could participate effectively in English-only classrooms. No specifics or standardized approaches were provided. Hence, models differed in school districts across the United States depending on the numbers of children being served.

English Only or Bilingual Education

The conflict between "English Only" advocates and those in favor of bilingual education is not likely to be solved soon. James Crawford posits that the major issue in bilingual accommodation is whether or not bilingual education should be supported by the U.S. government and financed with taxpayer money. In *Hold Your Tongue: Bilingualism and the Politics of English Only* (1993), Crawford states,

> Many fair-minded people, who otherwise cherish individual rights and cultural pluralism, are beginning to wonder whether the national tongue may be an exceptional case. Perhaps "unilingualism" is our best hope of managing diversity, the one bond that might keep us together. If so, it becomes too precious to risk and legislating conformity becomes justifiable. It is my aim to show how mistaken, how shortsighted, and how disastrous that view can be. (Crawford, 1993, p. xii)

Limiting the languages spoken by children and families in the United States seems counter-intuitive. A primary goal for educators and care providers is to meet the needs of the students and their families. As long as this remains a goal of any education system, the debate for "English Only" gets complicated.

Evaluating the call for a "national language" is not a simple matter. It brings up deeply personal issues and questions about whether one language can be of more "worth" than another and about how freedom of speech and expression can be supported. The issue of bilingual accommodation will always be a bone of contention as schools struggle to meet curricular needs and the needs of the communities they serve.

An Ongoing Challenge

Meeting the needs of English language learners will continue to be a challenge in the United States. As of yet, no federally coordinated effort exists to mandate compliance, and so it remains an issue of state implementation. The SERVE Center at the University of North Carolina at Greensboro published *English Language Learners in the Southeast: Research, Policy and Practice* (Mikow-Porto, Humphries, Egelson, O'Connell, & Teague, 2004) in an effort to summarize and share the types of services being offered to ELLs. This report notes that a variety of policies and practices exist regarding the education of ELLs because of the myriad legislative acts, legal decisions, guidelines or "tests," and interpretations that exist at the federal, state, and district levels. As a quick summary of what is happening at the state level, the SERVE document reports that

> States vary considerably in terms of legislation and funding for ELL programs:
> - States that have both legislative provisions and funding for LEP instructional programs include Alaska, Arizona, Arkansas, California, Colorado, Connecticut, Delaware, Florida, Georgia, Idaho, Illinois, Indiana, Iowa, Kansas, Maine, Maryland, Massachusetts, Michigan, Minnesota, Missouri, Nebraska, Nevada, New Hampshire, New Jersey, New Mexico, New York, North Carolina, North Dakota, Oklahoma, Oregon, Rhode Island, Texas, Utah, Vermont, Virginia, Washington, and Wisconsin.
> - Other states, including Kentucky, Montana, Ohio, Pennsylvania, South Dakota, and Wyoming, as well as the District of Columbia, offer legislative guidance but no funding.
> - Meanwhile, states such as Alabama, Hawaii, Louisiana, Mississippi, South Carolina, Tennessee, and West Virginia have neither legislative provisions nor funding for LEP instructional programs in place.
>
> (McKnight & Antunez, as cited in SERVE Report, 2004)

On Language and Culture—Becoming a Bilingual Teacher: Cecilia M. Espinosa

An important aspect of my work as a teacher educator is to help prepare bilingual/biliterate teachers. . . . Each semester I find that they come to my biliteracy class filled with questions about how to best support emergent bilingual children in school. Given the current mandates of the NCLB law, many of them feel the daily pressures of extreme accountability and the narrowing of the curriculum. . . . I strongly believe that given this era of accountability, standardization, and monolingualism, such a stance becomes a much-needed pedagogy of resistance. We begin this process by examining our own life stories about our experiences with different educational settings as speakers of a language other than English. My purpose is to help them reflect individually and collectively on what it was like for them to enter a new culture, a new language, new ways of thinking.

Cecilia Espinosa is an Ecuadorian American bilingual teacher educator.
Her full reflection appears in Appendix A.

The varied implementation will continue to evolve as the needs of English language learners are identified and met. A discussion of instruction models most commonly recognized in school districts is important as educators and care providers consider the best methods for meeting the needs of an increasingly diverse population.

Models of English Language Instruction

As states and local education agencies began designing programs to meet the educational needs of ELL students, a variety of models were conceptualized, and implementation varied depending on the number of students who needed to be served. Border towns, or urban areas with higher concentrations of recent immigrants, typically have disproportionately higher numbers of students to serve, and, consequently, are more likely to try unique models to meet their needs. English as a second language (ESL) services are provided to students in a variety of ways—through pull-out services provided by specially trained teachers or in self-contained classrooms, if large numbers of students require services.

Ovando (2003) describes five popular service models:

- The Structured Immersion Programs: No use of the native language, but students are given specialized ESL instruction tailored to levels of English proficiency.
- The Partial Immersion Programs: Provide ESL instruction, and a small amount of time (e.g., 1 hour each day) may be set aside temporarily for instruction in the native language. The goal is to move to English as quickly as possible.
- The Transitional Bilingual Programs: Extensive instruction provided in the native language as well as in English. However, once a child attains a certain level of English proficiency, he or she is exited into a monolingual English program. The early-exit transitional bilingual programs mainstream students after two years or by the end of the 2nd grade. A late-exit transitional program delays exiting students until the 5th or 6th grade. Programs vary and may not always adhere to these guidelines.
- The Maintenance or Developmental Bilingual Education Programs: Extensive instruction is provided in the native language as well as in English. Unlike students in transitional bilingual education, those in a maintenance or developmental program continue to receive part of their instruction in the native language even after they become proficient in English.
- The Two-Way Immersion Programs (Dual Immersion): Speakers of both languages are placed together in a bilingual classroom to learn each other's language and to work academically in both languages. In a two-way program, the language-majority children become bilingual and biliterate alongside the language-minority children. For example, the English-speaking child learns Spanish, while the Spanish-speaking child learns English within the same classroom.

As the children's needs change, the mode of instructional delivery adapts to those needs

A Dual-Language Teacher: Maren Roedenbeck's Story

I know from my own experience that once you learn to read in a language, you don't forget how to read it, even if you haven't read anything in that language in almost 20 years. Once you decide to start again, you can, and all you have to do to improve is practice.

The full reflection is available in Appendix A.

and to the needs of the system in which they are being delivered. From a stakeholder perspective, schools need to understand which model best meets the needs of their community.

A Shifting Political Landscape

Rachel Moran posits that "despite efforts to frame the bilingual education debate as a scientific argument about the appropriate content of the curriculum for linguistic minority students, the controversy actually reflects a battle over the allocation of discretion to make educational policy" (Moran, 1998, p. 611). Ultimately, at what level are we going to make these types of decisions? Even at the federal level, a consensus has never been reached concerning how to deal with language-minority students in the school systems. After the passing of the Bilingual Education Act and through the late 1980s, it seemed as if the federal government was in full support of meeting the needs of this special population. Yet, individual states, such as California and Arizona, began proposing special legislation to end bilingual education services, with the rationale that the programs seemed to be prohibiting students from moving quickly in and out of the system.

In the 1990s and the first decade of the 21st century, the political landscape had shifted. California passed Proposition 187 in 1994, in an effort to curb unauthorized immigration by suspending social and educational services that were provided to undocumented residents in the state. In 1998, California passed Proposition 227, which essentially approved English as the language of instruction, even for children who did not speak it as their primary language. Bilingual programs were all but shut down in the state of California. A similar debate has ensued in Arizona, Colorado, Massachusetts, and Washington. Proponents of bilingual education—for example, the National Association for Bilingual Education (NABE), which has more than 20,000 members—point to methodologically sound research showing that bilingual education benefits students. NABE's mission is "to advocate for our nation's Bilingual and English Language Learners and families and to cultivate a multilingual multicultural society by supporting and promoting policy, programs, pedagogy, research, and professional development that yield academic success, value native language, lead to English proficiency, and respect cultural and linguistic diversity" (www.nabe.org).

With implementation of the No Child Left Behind Act (2002), the Bilingual Education Act was no longer the federal position on educating ELLs. NCLB Title III, the English Acquisition, Language Enhancement and Academic Achievement Act, required even ELLs to be tested in English in mathematics and language arts, in an effort to account for all learners in the system. Even though immigrant children may not be proficient in English, they are required to be tested after attending school for three consecutive years in the United States. The current focus on accountability and standardized testing is a great challenge for students struggling to learn English as a second language. It remains to be seen what, exactly, the impact of this requirement will be. Educators would not wish to argue for the lowering of standards in order for students to pass examinations—this is not the point. However, the challenge is a significant one. While proponents of NCLB argue that including ELLs will help schools develop an awareness of this population of students, schools with a high concentration of ELLs face the likelihood of lower test scores and lack of funding or direction for them to increase services for students who may be struggling with the assessment. To put the success or failure of a student on a single test, given in a language that the student has yet to learn proficiently, does not seem to be an approach that will allow for students to be successful in the long run.

Information Regarding Latino Teachers

Although Hispanics are the fastest-growing minority group in the United States, Latino teachers are significantly underrepresented. "Today, 40 percent of public school systems are of color, but 90 percent of teachers are white" (Ochoa, 2007, p. 7). The gap is likely to increase, as the rate of students of color is growing faster than the number of teachers of color. The research points to the need for increasing teacher diversity in order to provide students with cultural role models in the classroom (National Collaborative on Diversity in the Teaching Force, 2004).

In July of 2009, Secretary of Education Arne Duncan spoke to the National Council of La Raza in reference to the importance of education in the Hispanic community, stating, "I want to encourage you to develop a new generation of Hispanic teachers. Twenty percent of all public school students in the U.S. are Latino. But only 5 percent of their teachers are Latino." While this disparity does not necessarily indicate a problem in the schools, school systems can consider adopting hiring practices that better reflect the diversity of the student population. An article printed in the *Albuquerque Journal* (Rodriguez, 2009) told the story of Joel Dorado, an immigrant student who had recently moved from Mexico: "In classes with non-Hispanic teachers, [Joel] has felt embarrassed to ask questions or even speak because of the cultural gulf he feels separates him from native students and teachers." One of Joel's teachers, Carlos Ortega, explained that "many Latino students come from cultures where the group is valued more. They may be used to or expect more involvement from teachers or other students when they are having trouble." The highest qualified teacher, regardless of race or ethnicity, should always be the goal; with all qualifications being equal, school systems might consider how a more diverse teacher workforce, reflective of the community at large, could positively influence student learning.

Marilyn Cochran-Smith (2003) has written extensively on the topic of multicultural teacher education. She argues that too many teachers are entering the classroom ill-prepared to teach linguistically and culturally diverse children from urban populations. "They . . . often have difficulty constructing curriculum, instruction, and interactional patterns that are culturally responsive, which means that the students in the greatest academic need are least likely to have access to educational opportunities congruent with their life experiences" (Cochran-Smith, p. 4).

As schools of education work towards reforming their teacher preparation programs, it will be important to consider admissions criteria and marketing strategies that will draw a pool of prospective teachers who will diversify the teaching workforce.

> Latino/a teachers' narratives remind us of the wisdom that comes from our families and how more of this knowledge should be integrated into classrooms and the structure of schools. From their voices, we hear how through resilience, resistance, and family support, they have navigated many exclusionary beliefs and practices. Their stories and perspectives offer hope for the future and concrete strategies for change. (Ochoa, 2007, p. 53)

One teacher can touch the lives of many children, and the benefit of encouraging a more diverse team of educators is the level of awareness that they bring to the context. Angela Lopez Pedrana (2009) notes that

> this awareness is important for all teachers, but for Latino bilingual teachers it is tantamount to being role models to Latino students. Latinos who have learned to navigate through: a null curriculum; competing stories, the hidden curriculum and cognitive dissonance; and have become teachers, are able to help their students address the same issues while in school. (p. 177)

As educators and care providers, a connection with the community is of utmost importance. For schools working with predominantly Hispanic families, every effort should be made to ensure that some members of the educational workforce are representative of the community at large. If this is not possible, the school may be able to work with community leaders to establish a cultural presence in the school that indicates the desire to understand and meet the cultural needs of the families being served.

Migrant Education: A Unique Population

Migrant families represent a unique population, and their educational needs are important to consider. The life of the migrant worker family is often a difficult one, partly as a consequence of the need to travel to where the work is. As they travel with their parents, children in migrant worker households may attend several different schools throughout the academic year. The *Final Report of the President's Advisory Commission on Education Excellence for Hispanic Americans* (U.S. Department of Education, 2003) notes that many Hispanic students are dropping out of school. The report identifies several issues that appear to contribute to the drop-out rate: 1) poor early childhood development and limited emergent literacy rate, due to poverty, limited resources, and high mobility; 2) limited opportunities for early childhood education; and 3) low expectations for Hispanic students. This becomes complicated with "migrant parents having limited educational opportunities, resulting in marginal or no reading skills" (Henderson, 1992, p. 5).

Unfortunately, migrant children and their families face difficult circumstances and an uncertain future (Perry, 1997; St. Pierre, Gamse, Alamprese, Rimdzius, & Tao, 1998). The daily struggle for survival often takes precedence over education. Migrant jobs are affected by unpredictable weather patterns and supply and demand. Furthermore, as Whittaker and Salend (1997) point out, migrant families "receive little assistance from governmental and community agencies. They are often invisible members of the communities in which they work" (p. 483). Migrant workers may need to move thousands of miles to other states in search of work. "Several times a year migrant children may have to adjust to new friends, a second language, different cultural and academic expectations" (Whittaker & Salend, p. 483).

Another challenge that migrant children face is stereotyping by teachers—both conscious and unconscious. Romanowski (2003), in his research on meeting the unique needs of migrant children, explains, "Many teachers were unaware of their own beliefs about migrant students and were influenced by stereotypes that guided their behavior and actions" (p. 29).

Several groups have gathered resources specifically aimed at meeting the needs of migrant families and helping those who work with the migrant population to understand their immediate needs and identify resources for educators. For example, the National Migrant and Seasonal Head Start Association (NMSHSA), a group made up of Migrant and Seasonal Head Start directors, staff, parents, and friends, meets regularly to discuss issues and concerns unique to Migrant and Seasonal Head Start children and their families (www.nmshsaonline.org/). In March 2010, NMSHSA collaborated with the National Education Association to publish and disseminate *Working With Migrant Students: A National Imperative for Head Start Students and Families* (Sanchez-Fuentes & Moreno, 2010). The publication outlines policy priorities necessary to expand and enhance services for the migrant population. It calls for support services, such as medical, dental, mental health, nutrition, housing, and education, to improve the long-term well-being of migrant children and their families.

¡Colorin Colorado! is a bilingual website dedicated to families and educators of English language learners. The resources are extensive, including a recent one called *Resources for Migrant Student Success* (2010). Of great help to educators and care providers is the list of literary resources for children that explore the life of migrant farm workers (www.colorincolorado.org/read/forkids/migrants). Also provided is an extensive list of websites specifically dedicated to providing information and resources for those working with the migrant population.

Vocke (2007) states that "three key factors that impact the children of migrant families are lost school time because of frequent moves, limited ties to the community, and various types of discrimination—economic, social and educational" (p. 6). She offers a guide to meeting the unique education needs of migrant students and a good summary of the limited research available. While it is difficult to ascertain the exact number of children who face these great challenges, data show that approximately 300,000 migrant farmworkers move from place to place as they follow the crops, with as many as 115,000 children accompanying them (Vocke, 2007). Thus, a significant number of youth in the United States are being impacted by this way of life, and the classrooms and teachers are being impacted as well. Therefore, the more information available about this population and their needs, the greater the likelihood that a more effective system of tracking educational progress can be developed.

Higher Education

In March of 2000, then U.S. Secretary of Education Richard W. Riley gave a speech titled "Excelencia Para Todos—Excellence for All: The Progress of Hispanic Education and the Challenges of a New Century." Secretary Riley specifically discussed the need for institutions of higher education to join forces with K-12 systems to create a pathway for student achievement if there was going to be any hope of more Hispanics going to college. He was adamant in noting that institutions of higher education "must be ready to adjust to the growth in the number of Hispanic students and to meet their needs, and they must develop new and creative ways to enlarge the pool of eligible minority applicants to colleges and universities" (p. 12).

What better way to invest in America than to invest in the education of its youth? "Today, 37 percent of the more than 40 million Latinos in this country are under 20 years of age" (Brown, 2009). This is an incredibly large number of young people who deserve the opportunity to seek higher education; the alternative would be to leave an alarmingly large percentage of the U.S. population at risk for not living up to their potential. An analysis of the report "Status and Trends in the Education of Hispanics" (USDOE, 2003) shows that "in 2000, 36 percent of Hispanic high school completers ages 18 to 24 enrolled in colleges and universities, higher than the 27 percent of Hispanic high school completers who enrolled in 1985." This was an encouraging sign, indicating that perhaps Hispanics were becoming increasingly eligible to seek post-secondary education. Yet, further analysis of the data published in this report also showed that the rates of enrollment among

A Mexican American's Reflection: Sylvia Sanchez

At a certain time in the year, large numbers of the children in my classroom disappeared. Their houses were boarded up and they left town. These children entered school after the beginning of the school year and left before the school year ended. The teachers never spoke about them. It was as if they were invisible and had never existed. They were simply gone from one day to the next. We had no idea what happened to them. It was years later, when I was a high school student, that I found out where they went for part of the year. I attended a Presbyterian high school and did volunteer work with children living in migrant labor camps in south Texas. It was through that experience that I finally figured out what happened to all those young children who disappeared every year in elementary school and, eventually, completely disappeared by dropping out before they reached secondary school. They were migrant children who, together with their families, followed the crops up north every year.

To read more of Sylvia's reminiscences, go to Appendix A.

Hispanics remained lower than those of their white peers and that the high school dropout rate for Hispanics remained high (especially among the immigrant groups). In 2000, 10% of Hispanics ages 25 to 29 had completed a bachelor's degree or higher, compared to 34% of whites and 18% of blacks in this young adult age group. Although Hispanics do seem to have more opportunities to earn a degree in higher education, the proportion of Hispanic young adults completing college has not increased since 1990.

The push to support Latino youth in attaining a higher education degree has gained momentum. More than 30 years ago, The Hispanic Scholarship Fund (HSF) was established to provide the Hispanic community with opportunities to earn scholarships for higher education. It has been recognized for providing the Hispanic community with more college scholarships and educational outreach support than any other organization in the United States, awarding more than $280 million in scholarships to more than 90,000 students in need. HSF celebrates the fact that two-thirds of these students were the first in their families to go to college.

In 2000, the HSF Hispanic Education Study (2000), conducted by the Rand Corporation with the help of the Institute of Latino Studies at the University of Notre Dame, examined

Excerpt From an Interview With Ricardo R. Fernández,
President of Lehman College, City University of New York

Q: It is a well-known fact the Latinos in urban areas have a high dropout rate in high school and college as well, especially at the four-year institutions. To what extent do you feel the Latino dropout problem at the college level is institutionalized?

A: Many students in higher education (about 40%) take 6 years to graduate from senior colleges. The average student takes 10-12 credits a semester at Lehman. Most students work part-time and attend school, thus making this the standard as a full load. Many stop attending ("stop out") for various reasons, such as a personal crisis or money issues. . . . There is a crisis in the schools and I am very surprised with the recent Kaiser Family Foundation study, which found that Latino parents neglect to push their kids to work hard (53%). On the contrary, I find that Latino parents always have high aspirations for their children. Keep in mind that in many cases, parents are not high school graduates themselves, and they have had a hard life where the opportunity to go to college was not available to them. The most prominent problem is that Latino parents cannot share with their children what needs to be done on the college level. I would recommend instituting a model outreach program for helping parents in these circumstances. The program should provide students and their parents with a concrete idea and experiences of what college is and entails. Programs could then prepare parents to become mentors for their children throughout their middle and high school years as they prepare for college.

Dr. Fernández also suggests another organization that he is affiliated with that provides support for parents: the Intercultural Development Research Association (IDRA) (www.idra.org). IDRA is a nonprofit organization committed to respecting the knowledge and skills of individuals and building upon the strengths of the students and parents in their schools. So once again, the key dynamic is creating a partnership between parents and the school to ensure success for their children.

The full transcript of Nancy Maldonado's interview with Ricardo R. Fernández is available in Appendix A.

ways to double the number of Latino graduates from institutions of higher education. The projected goals for the class of 2010 with the HSF intervention were:

HSF Study Year 2000 Projections for Class of 2010			
Population Segment in 2010	Projected High School Graduation Rates	Projected College Enrollment Rates	Projected College Completion Rates (BA)
Projected Non-Hispanic White Graduates in 2010	93%	62%	29%
Projected Hispanic Graduates in 2010 (if nothing is done)	70.6%	39.9%	12.5%
Projected Hispanic Graduates in 2010 if HSF is successful	83.3%	57.7%	24.9%

While such a dramatic increase of college scholarship funding for Hispanics would place demands on institutions of higher education, findings from the Rand study indicate an impressive projected return on investment (measured by the projected increase in the number of college graduates): "The Return on Investment from doubling the rate of Hispanic College Graduates is 4:1, or an incredible 400%." Less public funding would be necessary to support families and revenue would increase, as the graduates would be earning taxable income. Most important, once there is a college graduate in the family, the likelihood increases that children born into that family will also pursue a degree. Whether or not the HSF met their goal of doubling the number of Hispanic graduates in 10 years remains to be seen; however, the number of programs and networking for those interested in pursuing a college degree has increased.

> A recent study, conducted by MPR Associates, Inc., one of the nation's leading education consulting firms, found that 80 percent of Hispanic Scholarship Fund (HSF) scholarship recipients graduated within five and a half years—a graduation rate that is almost 30 percent higher than the national average for students of all races and ethnicities during the same period. (www.hsf.net/AboutHSF.aspx?id=32&ekmensel=c580fa7b_8_0_32_2)

Educational Implications for Hispanic/Latino Children and Their Families: A Summary

This chapter has addressed a variety of education-related issues from many different perspectives, including how Latino families feel about schooling and the role of the school versus the family in educating children, and about the successes and difficulties met by Hispanics in attaining education in the United States. Legislation and court cases have impacted the education opportunities for Latino families, specifically in terms of bilingual education. The viewpoint of Latino educators was briefly shared, along with the concerns of migrant families and the struggle for Latino youth to graduate from high school and pursue a higher education degree. The role of the educator and care provider is critical to the Hispanic/Latino population. Perhaps John Dewey put it best in *My Pedagogic Creed* (1987) when he wrote, "I believe that education is the fundamental method of social progress and reform."

Chapter 5 Questions To Ponder

- As an educator, if faced with the challenge of working with a transient migrant farm worker family, what steps might you take to help the student in your classroom feel better connected with his/her peers?
- If given the opportunity to create a bilingual program for your school site, which model of bilingual education do you believe would be most beneficial for the population of students with whom you work? Why?
- In your community, has a federal or state law impacted the work that you do with Latino families and their children? If yes, which one(s)? If no, which law would you like to learn more about as a result of having read this chapter?

Chapter 5 Web-Based Resources

National Association for Bilingual Education
 www.nabe.org
¡Colorin Colorado!
 www.colorincolorado.org/article/36287
Education of Migrant Children in the U.S. by Anneka L. Kindler
 www.neela.gwu.edu/pubs/directions/08.htm
Office of Migrant Education
 www.ed.gov/about/offices/list/oese/ome/index.html
Association of Mexican American Educators
 www.amae.org/
Center for Applied Linguistics (Sheltered Instruction Observation Protocol)
 www.cal.org/siop/
Online Migrant Education Community
 www.migrantstudents.org/
Everything ESL
 www.everythingesl.net/
Excelencia in Education
 www.edexcelencia.org/
Help! They Don't Speak English Starter Kit (Center for Applied Linguistics)
 www.edvantia.org/products/index.cfm?&t=products&c=products&id=515
Hispanic College Fund
 www.hispanicfund.org/
Hispanic Scholarship Fund
 www.hsf.net/
International Reading Association – ELL Resources
 www.reading.org/Resources/ResourcesByTopic/EnglishLearners/Overview.aspx
USDOE Status and Trends in the Education of Hispanics
 http://nces.ed.gov/pubs2003/2003008.pdf
Office for Civil Rights
 www.ed.gov/about/offices/list/ocr/ellresources.html
Questions and Answers on the Rights of Limited-English Proficient Students
 www.ed.gov/about/offices/list/ocr/qa-ell.html
U.S. Department of Education Office of English Language Acquisition's National Clearinghouse for English Language Acquisition & Language Instruction Educational Programs
 www.ncela.gwu.edu/

Chapter 6
Special Needs: Disabilities and Interventions

Nancy S. Maldonado

"No hay mal que por bien no venga."
(There is no bad experience that will not be followed with a good one.)

Several studies have shown that Hispanic American children are under-identified in cognitive disability categories, raising questions about whether the special education needs of these children are being met. This chapter's focus is on issues related to Hispanic American families of children with special needs, giving particular attention to Hispanic families' responses and coping mechanisms when raising a child with disabilities. The chapter sheds light on possible perceptions of disabilities, causation of disabilities, special education services, and recommendations for collaborating with parents, teachers, and service providers. We offer here some information about certain cultural beliefs and practices that may influence families' understanding and handling of disabilities. Remember, however, it is essential that cultural stereotyping be avoided. The individuality of each specific family must be recognized and respected in the context of Latino belief systems.

Culture influences a family's perception of disabilities—how they react to a family member who is disabled. Having a child diagnosed with a disability is a serious, often heart-wrenching, experience. Parents often are stunned by the diagnosis. Some may feel guilt and shame; others may deny that something is wrong with their child. Latino parents of disabled children face a variety of challenges, which may include language barriers, a lack of information, and a need for family and community support as well as financial assistance.

Perceptions of Disabilities

The literature shows that Hispanic families rely on support from their extended families when dealing with a family problem (Gannotti, Handwerker, Groce, & Cruz, 2001). Families who have immigrated often feel isolated in the United States, as they have moved away from that emotional support. Added stress occurs when mothers and their disabled children live in remote areas, or areas where they feel less accepted by the mainstream culture (Bailey et al., 1999). Isolation and lack of English language skills may result in Latino families underutilizing professional and supportive services (Ginsberg, 1992).

For many, religion provides comfort and support, and may help the family "make sense" of a child's disability (Skinner, Correa, Bailey, & Skinner, 2001). Some traditional Hispanic cultural beliefs would view disabilities as a punishment from God. Brice (2002) notes that while many Hispanic parents believe that a child's disability is a punishment, others may consider it a gift from God that will help them become better parents.

Traditional cultural beliefs and attitudes may affect behavioral adjustments toward a child with disabilities. For instance, some Puerto Ricans may look to folk cures and spiritualism, such as when a parent consults an *espiritista* (a medium to the spirit world) to cure a child of his/her affliction (Gannotti et al., 2001). Graf et al.'s (2007) study found that Mexicans, unlike acculturated Mexican Americans, also believe that disabilities, illness, and death are punishment for transgressions, unacceptable behaviors, or sin.

It is possible that a Hispanic family may attribute a child's disability to the "evil eye" (*el mal de ojo*). Many cultures around the globe believe in the "evil eye." While beliefs surrounding *el mal de ojo* vary, it often is considered to be a "curse" given out of jealousy. The perceived result of *el mal de ojo* usually is illness or some kind of disfiguration of the victim (Maldonado-Duran, Munguia-Wellamn, Lubin, & Lartigue, 2002). It is believed that this curse (or *maldición*) can cause a child to be disabled or disfigured.

Other possible cultural beliefs about the cause for a child's disability include a belief that the disability is the result of not satisfying a pregnant woman's cravings or the result of a pregnant woman suffering a *susto* (shock) to the system during pregnancy as a result of an earthquake, accident, or fall. Some Hispanic cultures believe that "women who do not wear a safety pin under their clothing for protection against a full moon or an eclipse may give birth to a child with a cleft palate" (Brice, 2002, p. 79). One common Latino superstition states that a pregnant woman who touches her belly during a lunar eclipse may bear a child with a prominent birthmark or disfigurement. Some believe that if pregnant women sleep on their stomachs or see an "abnormal" (disfigured) person, they will give birth to a disabled child (Lamorey, 2002).

In several Hispanic cultures, certain practices are followed to protect a child after birth, such as dressing the infant in red or fastening a red ribbon on the child's cradle to ward off evil. Mexican markets sell a black and red seed called *el ojo de venado* (deer's eye), which can be worn around the baby's neck or wrist as a protective measure (Maldonado-Duran et al., 2002). An *azebache*, a small black stone on a gold pin, bracelet, or chain, may be worn by the baby to ward off *el mal de ojo*. Chains with charms including crucifixes or hunchbacks are also used to ward off evil intentions. Wearing a talisman or charm as a form of protection is also a common practice in the Middle East, Western Africa, and the Mediterranean.

El ojo de venado

Causation of Disabilities: Heredity, Genetics, and Medical Factors

The Latino Journal (2009) reports that Hispanic women have a higher risk of birth defects, possibly because only 21% take folic acid to prevent birth defects, as compared to 40% of white women. A study by Canfield et al. (1996) found an increase of anencephaly (impartial brain and skull matter, leading to death) and spina bifida in parts of Texas bordering Mexico. The Ninth International Congress of Human Genetics (1999) researched births with congenital malformations and disabilities in Latin America. Chile reported 2.97% of their live births were children with congenital malformations, and Colombia reported 2.8%. Cuba reported 3.36 per 1,000 births had spina bifida, 1.73 had cleft palate, and 8.0 had Down syndrome. Ecuador reported 3% of newborns had congenital disabilities and 9% had Down syndrome, while Mexico reported that one out of 50 births have one or more congenital malformations. Puerto Rico reported that they have the world's highest rate of albinism, 5 in every 10,000 births (pp. 410-414). These statistics reflect some of the disabilities that immigrant Hispanic children could have when they come to U.S. schools.

Historical View of Latino Children and Special Education Services

In the past, many of the children designated to receive special education services were identified as needing these services based on inappropriate and inaccurate IQ testing in English. Figueroa (2005) conducted research on learning-disabled children who came from homes where Spanish was the only spoken language. He specifically looked at assessment, curriculum and instructive services, and prevalence rates. His findings depict a series of discrepancies between language and math aptitude/achievement scores, nonverbal IQ and academic achievement, and verbal and nonverbal measures of intelligence.

Other findings show that Latino children are overrepresented in learning disability diagnoses throughout the United States. For example, "In California, Latino children make up approximately 50% of the learning disabled population" (p. 165). Several studies show similar findings of overrepresentation of Hispanic children in special education (Agbenyega & Jiggetts, 1999; Artiles, Rueda, Salazar, & Higareda, 2005; Brice, 2002; Figueroa, 2005; Zhao & Modarresi, 2010). California, which has one of the highest numbers of second language learners in the United States, has shown an overrepresentation of Latino children in special education since the 1970s. Spanish-speaking children who were tested in English scored low, and thus were labeled as learning disabled or mentally retarded.

Such practices led to legislation and court cases. For example, *Diana vs. California State Board of Education* (1970) contested the use of IQ testing as a means of placing Latino children in special education. The ruling stressed that children should be tested in their native language. Despite such rulings and subsequent related legislation, Latino children, particularly those who are second language learners (ELLs), are still overrepresented in special education (Artiles et al., 2005). Another interesting finding from the Artiles study shows that second language learners in English immersion programs were more likely to be placed in special education programs than those in other support language programs. This finding warrants further investigation, since language immersion programs stress the second language and disregard the native language.

Latino children are also overrepresented in special education programs in New York City. Agbenyega and Jiggetts (1999) found a strong correlation between schools in poverty areas and children placed in special education, specifically children of Hispanic heritage. They recommend more advocacy to educate Latino and minority parents about the types of services and interventions that are available to them, as well as resources for school communities in poor economic areas. As important as it is, knowledge of the multi-faceted Hispanic culture, including country of origin, family traditions, religious practices, acculturation, and socioeconomic background, is not enough to provide valid support to families. The point here is to steer clear of assumptions that may lead to negative stereotyping.

Special Education Services

As a result of inappropriate placements in special education programs, many Hispanic parents are wary of intervention, special education, and therapeutic services that are available for children with disabilities. The cultural and language barriers that Latinos experience in health care systems also lead to mistrust of diagnoses and prescribed services. The best results for Latino children with disabilities occur when the school community builds a link between the school culture and the parents' acceptance of the disability, its cause, its therapies, and accessible support systems (Lamorey, 2002).

School and health care systems need to understand the cultural and folkloric values of Latino families as they relate to disabilities. Understanding cultural interpretations of a disability is crucial for building trust, creating supportive partnerships, and fostering communication. Partnerships between families, school systems, and intervention service providers are crucial to developing appropriate intervention services.

Joseph-DiCaprio, Garwick, Kohrman, and Blum (1999) interviewed 52 physicians regarding the role of family culture on pediatric care of children with chronic and disabling conditions. The physicians stressed the importance of communication with families and children to gain the families' trust. They also stated that each individual case is different and should be treated as such, and that care providers from the family's cultural group should be consulted (p. 1034). A study by Hardin, Mereoiu, Hung, and Scott (2009) found several disproportionally contributing factors affecting special education services for young English language learners, such as insufficient number of bilingual professionals and skilled interpreters, communication obstacles, and conflicting measures that challenge important partnerships with parents of ELLs. Attention also should be given to the nonverbal communication patterns among Latinos in the form of body language and speech intonation, to make certain that messages are clearly communicated and understood (Langdon, 2009).

Special education professionals need to consider several factors when referring Latino children for special education services. Testing Spanish-speaking children or bilingual children requires taking several assessment measures to differentiate a language disorder from a language difference (Brice, 2002). The point is to minimize bias in testing procedures by using varied forms of non-standardized assessments. Brice (2002) recommends taking the following steps when testing Hispanic children:

- Test children in both languages
- Create supportive relationships between children and parents
- Report standardized scores with caution if the assessment was not standardized in respect to specific cultural groups and language
- Confer with and involve parents
- Confer with other professionals from a similar background (Mexican, Puerto Rican, Cuban, etc.).

Another option to consider when planning instructional interventions is "sheltered instruction." The premise of this intervention is to facilitate higher levels of academic achievement for students with limited English by providing them with meaningful instruction in the content areas as the students slowly improve in English proficiency. This helps avoid a watered-down curriculum, as students are able to work on certain content at a higher level even though their language skills are in a state of transition.

Recommendations for Collaborating With Parents, Teachers, and Service Providers

Parental "ways of thinking" are important factors at any level of children's education, but are crucial to providing valid services for children with special needs. Hispanic parents whose sole language is Spanish may struggle to fully participate in the education of their children. Puerto Rican and Mexican mothers from Florida and Arizona, who were interviewed via the phone about their experiences with special education, voiced their frustration and disappointment as to how services were chosen. "They claimed that professionals (teachers and therapeutic providers) did not listen to their concerns and opinions, but placated them" (Alvarez-McHattan & Correa, 2005, p. 137). River-Bermudez's (1998) study notes that Puerto Rican parents asked for more social support from their spouses, families, friends, community, and church, especially during critical periods (when accepting and understanding diagnoses). Support from close and extended family, in terms of helping with household chores, babysitting, and meeting financial needs, was also valued and requested. The key is for teachers and service providers to take an introspective look at their own cultural background's views on disabilities and its implications on how they interact with Latino children and their families.

It is quite clear that all parents need to be reassured and supported when a child is recommended for special education (Hardin, Mereoiu, Hung, & Scott, 2009). Keeping all of these multi-faceted factors in mind will help to engage Latino parents in supporting the interventions and treatments prescribed for their child. All parents want their children to be successful in school, have productive lives, and contribute to society. Hispanic parents desire the same for their children with disabilities, and express concerns as to whether their children will be independent and able to care for themselves as adults. They want information about their children's disability, prescribed services, and how to teach them at home. Engaging Latino parents in this dialogue will develop true partnerships and successful interventions for their children.

Teachers and service providers can develop supportive relationships with Latino families of children with disabilities by emphasizing warm, individualized styles of communication, an unperturbed sense of time, and knowledge about the children's needs. Moreover, teachers and providers should be aware of a parent's possible mindset about disabilities based on their mystical, religious, and supernatural aspects. Teachers and service providers must do their homework and research the particular cultural values, belief systems, and practices of the Latino families in their programs and communities. In doing so, they can establish sincere partnerships with parents, built on a foundation of mutual trust, respect, and support for the betterment of Latino children with disabilities. Treat each family and child as unique, however, and do not make assumptions about cultural values and beliefs systems simply because a family speaks Spanish.

The following suggestions are recommended for successful engagement of Hispanic parents of children with disabilities in order to develop the best viable interventions:

- Refrain from stereotyping all Hispanic families as having the same belief system
- Understand the specific Latino cultural group's interpretations of disabilities
- Treat every family as uniquely individual, chatting with them about their belief systems, language, and country of origin
- Understand religious and spiritual practices in relation to children with disabilities
- Be knowledgeable of communication styles (e.g., eye contact, touching), and about uses of titles (e.g., Mr., Mrs., Señor, Señora) that project a tone of respect
- Be aware that language as well as cultural issues impact the quality of care and understanding of specific disabilities
- Use assessment instruments that are suitable for programs serving Spanish-speaking children and their families
- Provide flyers or articles on specific disabilities written in Spanish
- Conduct initial meetings about referring children for special education during home visits to develop sound engagement and trust with families
- Provide interpreters (especially from the particular Hispanic group—Mexican, Puerto Rican, Cuban, Dominican, etc.) during meetings with parents about referrals, interventions, and special education.

Maria's Reflection: Dominican Naturalized Citizen (translated)

As an immigrant in this country, it was very hard to advocate for my daughter. I could express my concerns over her language development. I did have an interpreter, but I felt that she was not saying what I was saying concerning my daughter's language development and her lack of attention. You know, as an immigrant you don't trust anyone, but I had to trust the interpreter to say my words and get help for my daughter. After a few months of meetings and translated sessions, my daughter did get services. They started first in Spanish and then changed to English. She's in the 4th grade now and receives her therapy in the classroom. I think she is okay, but the therapist and the school personnel feel that she needs more help.

Chapter 6 Questions To Ponder:

- Educators are often faced with the difficult task of referring a child who may be struggling in class to receive special services. If a child in your school/center speaks English as a second language, what steps are in place at your site to ensure that language is not the issue?
- Miami-Dade and Monroe counties, in Florida, established the Parent to Parent of Miami network to support parents of children with special needs. Visit the Parent to Parent website (www.ptopmiami.org/). What did you learn about establishing a community of support for children with special needs?
- Read the Federal Policy on Disproportionality regarding IDEA: (http://idea.ed.gov/explore/view/p/%2Croot%2Cdynamic%2CQaCorner%2C9%2C). How do these recommendations directly affect your center/school? How might they specifically affect Hispanic children?

Chapter 6 Web-Based Resources

Council for Exceptional Children (Hispanic Caucus)
  www.cec.sped.org
The Latino Institute, Inc.
  www.latinoinstitute.us/
Division for Culturally and Linguistically Diverse Exceptional Learners (DDEL)
  www.ddelcec.org
National Education Association—"Focus on Hispanics: Special Education and ELLs"
  www.nea.org/assets/docs/hispanicfocus07.pdf
ASPIRA
  www.aspira.org
National Center for Latinos With Disabilities
  http://clas.uiuc.edu/special/progdesc/cl00480il/cl00480.html
Parent to Parent of Miami
  www.ptopmiami.org/ The Mid-Atlantic Equity Consortium http://www.maec.org

Chapter 7
Images of Hispanic Families: Film, Television, and Children's Literature

Nancy S. Maldonado

"El que es ciego de nación, nunca sabe a dónde anda."
(He who is blind to his own nation will never know where he is traveling.)

The increase in the Hispanic population in the United States has led to a parallel increase of Hispanics and Hispanic culture appearing in the media. Popular culture today celebrates the appointment of Supreme Court Justice Sonia Sotomayor, the number of home runs hit by Latino major leaguers, and the addition of George Lopez to the cadre of late-night television hosts. We track the lives of Latino celebrities like Jennifer Lopez and Marc Anthony; we welcome the addition of MTV Latino awards and the evolution of People *magazine "en espanol." And as we read* People *or watch television, we might be eating nachos and cheese or other Hispanic-origin foods that have become more mainstream choices.*

The media has a major influence on our understanding of cultural contexts outside of school and family. For example, exaggerated representations of Latinos on television and in movies often feed into stereotypes. We can understand and celebrate the commonalities of Latino traditions, accepting specific traits often associated with our cultures. Yet, it should be made clear that not every Mexican wears a sombrero, not every Cuban plays dominos, and not every Puerto Rican owns a set of maracas.

A Look at Hispanic/Latino Stereotypes

Research on Hispanic stereotypes (Jackson, 1995; Marin, 1984; Peterson & Ramirez, 1971) dating back to the 1970s indicate that Hispanics have been viewed as lazy, cruel, ignorant, and pugnacious (Jackson, 1995). Most recently, Hispanics often are perceived as not valuing education, since they have the highest high school dropout rate in the United States and consequently low numbers in higher education. The basis for these stereotypes often lies in the harsh realities of everyday life (i.e., language and cultural barriers and poverty) that many Latinos face, which require them to choose between using their money to finish school or to help their families (Shear, 2007).

Aronson (2004) states that we are all exposed to stereotypes that influence our perceptions of particular groups and create biases and myths about a particular group's character and value systems. Young (2009) examines common myths about Latinos, such as "Latinas work as housekeepers," "Latinas are sexy sirens," "Hispanics come to America illegally," "Hispanics do not want to speak English," and "Latinos are not hard workers." She dispels each of the aforementioned stereotypes, providing research and data on Hispanics in the United States. For example, while some hard-working Latinas are indeed housekeepers, others are lawyers, teachers, doctors, nurses, journalists, real estate brokers, etc. Yet, damaging stereotypes still permeate society's perceptions of Hispanics.

Hispanics are proud of their particular ethnicities. Their physical appearance can reflect a wide range of skin and eye color, hair color and texture, and height. Yet, certain stereotypes and generalizations exist. Hernandez (2009) studied the stereotype of Cuban "chonga girls" in South Florida, a term sometimes used to refer to young women who wear large hoop earrings, identification necklaces, a lot of hair gel, suggestive clothing, and speak "Spanglish" (English and Spanish mixed into a dialect). She examines the "emergence of this stereotype on the Internet, print media, and contemporary visual art in order to understand how chonga bodies produce and reflect discourses about Latinas' sexuality, ethnicity and class" (p. 64). Young Hispanic girls receive mixed messages about whether the chonga image is a correct depiction of who they are or who they should be. A Rodriguez et al. study (2000) on "labeling" (stereotyping) discusses the most damaging stereotype bestowed on Mexican American women—that they are "submissive, docile and with no ambitions other than producing children" (p. 516).

Many stereotypes develop about Latinos when English is not their first language. Yet, studies have shown that second- and third-generation Latinos in the United States have lost Spanish as their first language (Mora, Villa, & Davila, 2006; Suro & Passel, 2003) as they acculturate to American culture. Second-generation Latinos tend to be bilingual, whereas third-generation Latinos are primarily English speakers (Suro & Passel, 2003).

Language does reflect culture. When speaking to many Hispanics, one may notice a

Juan's Story

The population at Penn State University was at that time (in the 1980s) overwhelmingly European American. . . . I was . . . a young male working in a child development center, and, in terms of my appearance, although I have light skin, I used to wear my hair in a big curly afro, and had a beard and mustache. Add to that a heavy Spanish accent, and you get the picture. . . . There is a particular experience that I will never be able to forget. Each head-teacher at the child care center was assigned to be the primary caregiver for one of the infants. As a head-teacher, I was assigned to take care of a healthy, beautiful, 6-month-old blond/blue-eyed boy who physically resembled his parents. . . . Part of my responsibilities was to greet the mother in the morning, when she brought her baby, her only child, to the center and to ease the transition. At the beginning of that morning routine, and for some time after, that I remember as being a bit too long, the boy would cry every morning as he was being given to me by his mother. As a result, the mother's eyes would get watery . . . with tears eventually rolling down her cheeks. Although I knew that this was (and continues to be) a common scene at day care centers and elementary schools all over the world, I could not help but think how this mother must have been feeling. She was leaving her only child with a young Hispanic male, with some of the physical characteristics of what has been associated, in this country, with being a rebel, a bohemian, or at times even a terrorist.

To read all of Juan's reflection, go to Appendix A.

A Puerto Rican American's Reflection: Grace Ibanez-Freidman

I was about 15, and was with my father walking toward the boardwalk of Rockaway Beach in New York City, where we were spending a few days of vacation time. The sun was very hot, and I was looking forward to joining my sisters and mother on the beach for the afternoon. For reasons I don't recall, my father and I paused and sat on one of the benches near the boardwalk. Out of the corner of my eye I saw a mother with a toddler. The mother had let go, and the child went tottering toward my direction. As she reached my bench, she began to trip forward. I immediately reached out to grab the child before she fell on the hard concrete. The mother came running and shouted out to me, "Don't touch her, I don't want her touched by a Puerto Rican." My father said nothing: my humiliation was complete.

"flavor" to their language. For example, switching languages (code switching) within a conversation is very common: "*Vamos a la tienda a comprar dulce de coco* (let's go to the store to buy coconut candy) because I have a yen for it today." Even those third- or fourth-generation Hispanics who have limited ability in speaking Spanish still understand their culture, and embrace their "Hispanicness" while they are emerged in the "American experience." Yet, this celebration of Latino culture may be perceived as anti-American. Jackson (1995) studied overall attitudes of Anglos toward Latinos, finding several negative perceptions. Hispanics were perceived to place more value on "salvation and religious or mystical experiences rather than on pursuing knowledge, good health, economic prosperity and financial independence" (p. 7). Recent immigrants were perceived to be refusing to learn English (Young, 2009).

The influx of Latino cultures into American neighborhoods has not been a simple process, due to the misinterpretation of who Latinos are and what they can contribute to communities. The current political situation surrounding issues of immigration further complicates matters. Some proposed legislation has sought to classify undocumented immigrants as

Carlos Lopez Leiva: Realizations of My Own Skin

In the early 2000s, I came to the United States. As I arrived, I immediately started noticing all the different adjectives or "social identities" bestowed upon me. I officially became not only an "alien" or immigrant, but also a Hispanic (this term for me has a European connotation) and not a Latino. By looking as I do, some people have considered me and made me feel "different"—though we all are—and, at times, through glances, reactions, and/or avoidances, have also marked me as a "dangerous" person, such as a mugger or a thief. This picture becomes even more complicated, as I speak my second language, English, with an accent. The reactions have ranged from simply not being able to understand what I say, to questioning the validity of or simply ignoring my claims, based on how they sound in my voice.

It has been through these negative experiences, through my own skin, that I have come to better understand the pain and the fear of exclusion. Being on both sides forced me to stand against approaches that I considered unjust, as well as to live and face unjust actions, not only against me but also to those like me.

For the complete essay, see Appendix A.

felons and a threat to national security. Such portrayals fuel negative perceptions of who Latinos are and what they bring to the American experience.

Some people in historically Anglo communities feel their way of life is being threatened when they see Hispanic culture and language taking a more prominent place. Thus, they create walls of separation among people living in American communities. Residents may worry about their neighborhood's cultural shift as they witness the growth of Latino businesses, churches, and catering halls for Hispanic celebrations. Discrimination by Anglo residents, fueled by stereotypes and misleading information about Latinos, continues (Woodrick & Grey, 2002).

One recent study (Dovidio, Gluszek, John, Ditlmann, & Lagunes, 2010) showed differential treatment given to "white" and Latino shoppers. Stores in the study that offered gift certificates quoted a minimum dollar amount higher than $10 more frequently for Latino shoppers than for white shoppers. Sales clerks also asked for the shopper's identity more frequently when the shopper was Latino than when the shopper was white. The researchers conclude, "To the extent that Latinos are centrally implicated in the controversy about illegal immigration, the more frequent requests for identification from Latinos than from Anglos could be motivated, at least in part, by suspicions of legal status" (p. 74).

Where Do Latino Stereotypes Come From?

Aside from the political controversies associated with immigration, what are other sources of negative attitudes toward Latinos? How do individuals who have little or no direct contact with Hispanics develop and believe stereotypes about Hispanics being lazy, non-educated, violent, and criminally minded? Many outside the Latino experience are introduced to Latino culture through the media.

Mainstream Television

While some television shows (e.g., *The George Lopez Show*, *Ugly Betty*, *Freddie,* and the classic *I Love Lucy*) can be positive, portraying Hispanic families dealing with everyday issues of work, family relationships, and culture, other prime time television programs help perpetuate stereotypes. Hispanics are often portrayed as gardeners, housekeepers, car mechanics, and criminals. A study conducted by Children Now and the National Hispanic

When I Was a Native American:
A Second-generation Puerto Rican, Terry Louise Sebastian

My title reflects an experience I had back in 1994 when I came to terms with my ethnicity. I am a second-generation Puerto Rican, born in New York City and raised for the early part of my childhood in Spanish Harlem. After teaching in New York City for 16 years, I decided to teach in Little Wound High School on a Lakota reservation in South Dakota. Living on an Indian reservation is like living in another country, literally. Different issues, problems, and lifestyles. Once a month, I drove 88 miles off the reservation to Rapid City to do my shopping. I encountered a serious issue when shopping at a local merchant. I noticed that I was being watched closely and followed. It made me feel quite uncomfortable, being stalked in that way. Once back on the reservation, I shared my experience with a colleague. She informed me that since I looked like a Native American, I was treated as one. In all my years being raised in Spanish Harlem and in the Bronx, I never had encountered an experience as I did in South Dakota. I learned what it was like to be in another person's shoes. This experience truly sensitized me to the racism, insensitivity, and humiliation of being a Native American.

Foundation for the Arts (2002) analyzed 3,172 television characters appearing on the six major networks during the fall 2001-02 prime time segments, finding:

- Latino characters made up 4% of the prime time population, an improvement from the 2% of the previous year. However, Latinos at that time represented 12.5% of the U.S. population.
- Latinos accounted for 2% of all primary recurring characters, the same as the previous year.
- Four out of five Latino characters appeared in secondary and tertiary roles.
- Two-thirds of Latino characters were male.
- Latino male characters most often appeared in law-enforcing occupations or as criminals.
- Latina characters most often appeared in the roles of nurse, clerical worker, or domestic worker.
- Latina characters were younger, on average, than those of the overall female prime time population. (p. 5)

Mastro and Behm-Morawitz (2005) analyzed the regularity and quality of Latino portrayals during the 2002 prime time television season. Their findings also showed that Hispanics were typically cast in secondary and/or non-recurring roles, that depictions of Latinos have "historically been confined to a narrow set of stereotypical characters (the criminal, the law enforcer, the Latin lover, the Harlot, and the comic/buffoon)," and that most of the comic roles were characterized by "heavy accents, laziness, secondary status and lack of intelligence" (p. 111). Subervi, Torres, and Montalvo (2005) studied the portrayal of Latinos on news broadcasts, finding that "immigration and crime have been the dominant topics for Latino stories over the past 10 years. Out of 1,201 stories, these two topics have accounted for 36% of coverage" (p. 5). They found that the various issues or news features related to Latinos were often presented via a "problem lens" and hardly ever depicted Latinos' positive contributions. Intentional or not, stereotypes, particularly negative ones on television, influence viewers' ways of thinking about Hispanics and their culture.

Spanish Television

Univision and Telemundo have been at the forefront of Spanish language television for many years; although they are in direct competition for a very specific market (Spanish speakers), they have managed to secure their audiences and the U.S. market has welcomed and easily sustained both stations. Writing about these two leaders in the industry, Guillermo Gibens (2008) cited that although Univision is the larger of the two stations, claiming to reach 99% of the U.S. Spanish-speakers, Telemundo also reaches a significant portion of the market (claiming to reach 93% of U.S. Spanish speakers). Both stations are headquartered in the South Florida area, with affiliate television stations, radio stations, online Internet portals, and record companies located all over the world.

Historically, there has been a need to establish Spanish language television stations in the United States because the Hispanic community expressed a desire for a station that could positively portray their identity and also communicate news and programming in Spanish. Furthermore, as would be expected, these news stations could carry programming and news from Spanish-speaking countries, allowing immigrants from those countries to keep up with events and culture from their home communities.

Growing as rapidly as the Hispanic population in the United States, Spanish language television is increasingly becoming a significant force in American television. Univision is the fifth largest network in the United States, after ABC, CBS, NBC, and Fox (Market, 2009, p. 45). Spanish language programming includes variety shows, talk shows, news, sports, and current events. A considerable proportion of the viewership follow the popular telenovelas (soap operas). The telenovela genre has a significant impact on Latino popular culture. These popular shows have adapted to address their Hispanic viewership in the United States of all generations, from the most recent immigrant to third-generation Hispanics.

Initially, the Spanish telenovela was overloaded with stereotypes of powerful men and submissive women involved in dramas based on religion, culture, language, nationalism, and personal values (Alvarez-Gonzalez, 2010). Common characters from past telenovelas often were searching for the perfect husband, looking for a lost love, escaping from bad situations, or dealing with issues of love, betrayal, and death. Telenovelas today address social issues, including drug trafficking, infidelity and marital problems, alternative sexualities, the political climate, and economic problems (Adams, 2005). Romance is the underlying concept in these episodic telenovelas, which are produced in several Latin American countries, namely Mexico, Brazil (in Portuguese), Venezuela, Colombia, Peru, and Argentina. The telenovelas from different countries are slightly different in content; for example, Mexican telenovelas are melodramatic, Colombian shows are comedic, and Brazilian melodramas portray realism of society instead of the individual (Barrera & Bielby, 2001). For example, the Brazilian telenovela "El Clon" (2002) is the story of a cloned young man and the love he has for a Muslim woman. Because of its popularity, it was translated from Portuguese to Spanish. *El Clon* presented everyday problems such as drug abuse and divorce, as well as such current "hot topics" as cloning and the Islamic culture (Alvarez-Gonzalez, 2010).

Angeleri (2011) notes that telenovellas are no more stereotypic than their American soap opera counterparts, and the stereotypes allow viewers to easily understand characters' motivations and make connections with certain personality traits they may share with the people onscreen. There *are* differences between the telenovela and the American soap opera. Namely, the American soap opera is geared mainly for female audiences during the day, while telenovelas are shown at night to a wider range of audiences that include both males and females. One critical concern is the highly sexualized content in telenovelas. Rios (2011) finds that telenovelas do not address risky behaviors or serious social problems, thus leaving younger viewers to form opinions based on incomplete or faulty information. Intentional or not, stereotypes, particularly negative ones on television, may consciously or unconsciously influence viewers' ways of thinking about Hispanics and their culture.

Film

The film media's take on Hispanic culture and life has stirred plenty of controversy regarding who has portrayed Latinos in movies and what characters they represent. In *The Perez Family* (1995), for example, Italian American actress Marisa Tomei played an immigrant Cuban prostitute who recruits other Cubans at an immigrants' detention center to act as a nuclear family in order to attain quicker access to the American mainland. Anjelica Huston, another non-Hispanic actress, also played a Latina in the movie. Tomei was asked to "gain 18 pounds and wear a bronzing lotion because the film's producer felt she was not dark or plump enough to play a Cuban prostitute" (Isais, 1997). Furthermore, the film fed into stereotypes of immigrants being deceiving, manipulating, and scheming individuals who do whatever it takes to immigrate to the United States.

Fortunately, more recent films address some of the realities of certain Latino experiences from a more positive perspective. For example, *La Misma Luna* (Under the Same Moon) (2008), with a cast of mostly Hispanic television and film actors, is a sentimental story of Carlitos, a young boy being raised by his elderly grandmother in Mexico, while his mother works in the United States without required documentation. The death of his grandmother forces Carlitos to cross the border without authorization to find his mother in Los Angeles. The film follows Carlitos' dangerous and painful quest through Texas, Arizona, and, finally, Los Angeles. His mother's struggles working as a housekeeper and nanny and the struggles of migrant workers on a tomato farm being raided by the INS are portrayed vividly in this powerful film. Another film that portrays the struggles of Latino immigrants is *El Norte* (The North) (1983), which depicts two Guatemalan Indians, Enrique and Rosa, who suffer through various experiences that require extreme levels of courage and fortitude in their quest to find work, learn English, and make a life in the United States.

Contemporary Latino life is portrayed in other worthwhile films. In *Real Women Have Curves* (2002), Ana, a Mexican American teenager about to graduate from high school, shares her story as a girl from a working-class family. Ana's conflict typifies the cross-cultural barrier that many first-generation Hispanic Americans encounter. Ana's English teacher and mentor (also Latino) believes Ana is an intelligent student capable of going to a university. But Ana's mother insists that Ana stay at home and join her sister in making dresses in a sweatshop. Ana works at the factory, but applies to Columbia University and challenges her mother's expectations. When her mother pressures Ana to lose weight so she can fit into the small dress sizes they make in the factory, Ana strips and claims that "real" women of Hispanic backgrounds have curves. Ana's character continues to grow as she witnesses her father's struggle as a gardener and listens to her grandfather's advice on being American and pursuing her dreams.

The aforementioned films depict the strengths and closeness of Hispanic families and the struggles associated with coming to grips with the American experience. Nevertheless, many films still reflect the traditional stereotypes of Hispanics as drug dealers, subservient women, sexy sirens, and male convicts (e.g., *Stand and Deliver* (1988), *El Mariachi* (1993), *Carlito's Way* (1993), *Mi Vida Loca* (1994), *La Lengua de las Mariposas* (1999), *The Girl on the Stone (La Niña en la Piedra)* (2005), and *Illegal Tenders* (2007)). This list is by no means exhaustive, and readers are encouraged to visit such websites as that of the National Hispanic Media Coalition (www.nhmc.org) for further information.

Rodriguez (1997) provides a series of questions to consider when viewing portrayals of Hispanics in films. The same criteria can be used for analyzing Latino characters in novels, books, and other media. The following questions are a sampling:

- What is the character's function with regard to the plot? Is the character positive or negative? If positive, are they heroic, charitable, competent? If negative, are they malevolent, greedy, foolish, incompetent?
- Does the character commit crimes?
- Does the character use controlled substances? What is used and how often?
- What are the character's goals? How are they attained? Through legal or illegal means?

Children's Literature

Although several studies have shown an increase in the representation of Latino cultures in children's books over the last 40 years, gender and racial stereotyping remain in the portrayal of Hispanics in children's books (Mendoza & Reese, 2001; Nilsson, 2005; Perez-Stable, 1997). We know that books aid in the development of greater awareness and understanding of diverse cultures and languages through character portrayals. A number of genres (picture books, poetry, folktales, fiction, etc.) provide distinguishing insights into Latino cultures, ways of thinking, and social mores. For many Latinos, children's books are the first introduction to their own culture as well as other cultures.

Children's literature can play a significant role in home settings and classrooms by providing strong images of Latinos presented in a positive light. This medium is an excellent way for teachers, parents, and care providers to provide children with opportunities to see themselves and to learn about and come to understand others from diverse cultures. A selection of children's literature on Hispanic cultures should share accurate and authentic images of Latinos (Mendoza & Reese, 2001). Consider the ethnicity of the authors. Children's books written by Latino authors about their own particular cultures provide a more authentic sense of Hispanics.

Mexican American writer Arthur Dorros, in *Abuela* (1991), writes about the warm relationship of Rosalba and her *abuela* (grandmother). He based the story on his own experiences as a child listening to his grandmother's stories. Alma Flor Ada, a Cuban American, has written several children's books based on stories she heard as a child from her parents and grandparents. In *I Love Saturdays and Domingos* (2002), Ada provides a positive perspective about living in a bi-cultural world. In this picture book, the main character shares her experiences listening to her Latino grandparents and her Anglo grandparents tell stories about their own particular cultural heritages. This book provides a positive look at cultural diversity, focusing on the warm relationships between the main character and her multicultural parents.

Appendix B provides a list of children's books on Hispanic culture that avoid gender and racial stereotypes. We also include a selected list of books for adult readers, teachers, parents, and care providers that will help them become more sensitized to Latino culture. Some key points for parents, teachers, and care providers to keep mind are:

- Use picture books to introduce children to the various Latino cultures.
- Avoid books that limit the portrayal of Hispanics to farm workers, laborers, and homemakers, and select those that show Hispanic characters, particularly women, in contemporary roles.
- Select books written by Hispanic authors that convey authentic experiences from their own lives. Care should be taken when recommending books written by non-Hispanic authors, in order to ensure that they provide a non-biased view.
- Elementary school-age children should read autobiographies and biographies of Latinos to raise their awareness of the numerous contributions made to society by Latinos.
- Look for stories that use Spanish words and phrases in the vernacular of the particular Hispanic group (i.e., Mexican, Cuban, Dominican, etc.). Ensure that some of the vocabulary among specific Latino groups is derived from different contexts.
- Select books that show respect for the cultures represented in classrooms, programs, and homes. For example, book selections for classrooms populated by Puerto Ricans and Dominican children should reflect their cultures.
- Learn to enunciate Spanish words properly; many children's books include glossaries for definitions and pronunciation guides.
- Educators and care providers should read novels, autobiographies, and biographies to learn more about the history and culture of the Latino groups in classrooms, schools, or programs.

Summary and Recommendations for Educators and Care Providers

A research study by Gaztambide-Fernández and Guerrero (2010) showed that the

> Negative stereotypes associated with the ethnolinguistic background as well as the intellectual and linguistic capabilities of Latino/as can have a deleterious effect on the interactions between students and educators. These interactions then lead some Latino/a students to negatively perceive their schooling experiences. (p. 63)

Gaztambide-Fernández and Guerrero are specifically referring to stereotypes that may be ingrained in many school cultures. In this chapter, we explained how stereotypes are disseminated through media outlets, such as television, film, and children's literature.

Stereotypes also may be derived from personal experiences in workplaces and schools with members of a cultural group that become unjustly generalized to the entire culture and also transferred to other, similar cultures.

We cannot emphasize enough how important it is for teachers and care providers to become aware of the various Latino cultures represented in their classrooms and centers. The following suggestions can help sensitize individuals to the cultures of specific Hispanic groups in the community:

- Conduct neighborhood studies about cultural events, holiday celebrations (religious/non-religious, folkloric)
- Attend a religious service other than one from your own religious practice
- Be present at community events for family gatherings
- Eat in community restaurants
- Shop at local businesses
- Read local newspapers
- Immerse yourself in the community ambiance.

Teachers and care providers who pursue such firsthand experiences will be able to keep abreast of cultural, ethnic, economic, and linguistic changes in the communities they serve, and thus will be able to provide better service to children and their families.

Chapter 7 Questions To Ponder:

- Consider a favorite movie/television show with a Hispanic/Latino character. In what ways did this character's use of language affect your perception of his/her ethnicity? (e.g., How did Ricky Ricardo's use of language on the "I Love Lucy" television show help to establish his character?)
- The role a character plays in a children's book influences how children perceive cultural groups. How are books selected for your school/center? How many books are available for students that provide a positive, non-stereotypical view of Hispanics/Latinos?

Chapter 7 Web-Based Resources

National Hispanic Media Coalition
www.nhmc.org
Latinos for Internet Freedom
www.latinonetlibre.com/
Al Otro Lado (Documentary)
www.pbs.org/pov/alotrolado/
Beyond the Border—*Mas Alla de la Frontera*
www.pbs.org/itvs/beyondtheborder/
Border Film Project: Photos of Migrants & Minutemen on the U.S.-Mexico Border
www.borderfilmproject.com/en/index.php
Hispanics and the Media
www.pbs.org/newshour/bb/media/jan-june01/hispanic_3-13.html
ESPN *Deportes*
http://espndeportes.espn.go.com/
Univision
www.univision.com
Telemundo
http://msnlatino.telemundo.com/

People Magazine en Espanol
www.peopleenespanol.com/pespanol/
Colorín Colorado
www.colorinolorado.org
Alma Flor Ada
http://almaflorada.com/
Barahona Center for the Study of Books in Spanish for Children and Adolescents
http://csbs.csusm.edu/csbs/www.book_eng.book_home?lang=SP
Cody's Cuentos – Classic Children's Fairytales in Spanish
www.codyscuentos.com/
Cultivating Readers – Family Literacy
www.famlit.org/pdf/cultivating-readers.pdf
Pat Mora
www.patmora.com/dia.htm
Iguana Magazine (for ages 7 to 12 in Spanish)
www.nicagal.com/iguana/eng/
Lee y Seras
www.leeyseras.net/
Maya and Miguel – PBS Kids
http://pbskids.org/mayaandmiguel/flash.html
Multicultural Education Internet Resource Guide
http://jan.ucc.nau.edu/~jar/Multi.html
Parents' Choice—Children's Media and Toy Reviews (Chicano and Chicana Books)
www.parents-choice.org/article.cfm?art_id=338&the_page=reading_list
American Library Association—Pura Belpre Award
www.ala.org/ala/mgrps/divs/alsc/awardsgrants/bookmedia/belpremedal/index.cfm
Reading is Fundamental—*Semillitas de Aprendizaje*
www.rif.org/kids/leadingtoreading/es/leadingtoreading.htm

Chapter 8
Celebrations, Traditions, and Fiestas: "Salsa y Sabor"

Lilia C. DiBello and Nancy S. Maldonado

"Salud, amor, pesetas y tiempo para disfrutarlo!"
(Good health, love, money, and time to enjoy them!)

Celebrations in Hispanic homes reflect religious beliefs and cultural practices from the home country as well as adaptations of holidays assimilated from the new culture. Latinos are diverse in their celebratory practices, and the manner in which they choose to celebrate has much to do with where they are currently living and their particular cultural identity. Traditions are handed down, yet it is recognized that subtle changes occur with each generation as families try to hold onto cultural practices while incorporating new customs. For example, South American celebrations of Christmas do not include the "Santa Claus" tradition. However, South Americans who now live in the United States continue their traditional practice of celebrating the visit from Los Reyes Magos (Three Kings), while also incorporating a visit from St. Nick.

In this chapter, we discuss holidays that may be celebrated by Hispanic families, including political and historical holidays, folkloric holidays, and traditional religious celebrations. This exploration is not intended to be exhaustive, but rather representative of the myriad customs that keep specific characteristics of Latino heritage alive. Also important to note is the fact that many of the celebrations discussed in this chapter may have a religious grounding, given the strong connection many Hispanics/Latinos have with the Roman Catholic faith. Although recent research indicates a shift in the religions being practiced by Latinos in the United States, many of the celebrations grounded in the Catholic faith do remain paramount for many families.

Salsa y Sabor: Eating Habits and Traditions

Salsa y Sabor: The heart and soul of the culture.
Salsa (music and dance, the rhythm of the culture) and Sabor (soul, the flavor, as in the flavor of the culture, or why we do what we do).

In Hispanic cultures, as in many cultures, families come together during mealtimes to share their experiences during the day, uphold cultural values, and maintain family traditions. In Hispanic countries, a light meal is served for breakfast. *El almuerzo*, commonly known as lunch in the United States, consists of several courses and is usually the main meal of the day. It is served promptly from 12 noon and lasts until 2 p.m. It is expected that all family members will come home from school or work to dine together, and then take a nap—*la siesta*. This practice can be traced back to the traditions of Spain. Newly arrived immigrants find it difficult to continue this practice in the United States, however. For starters, they cannot find all of their country's foods and products, and American work and school schedules conflict with the practice of *la siesta* (Clutter & Zubieta, 2009).

Margarita's Reflection: I Was Always Hungry

When I arrived to the United States in 1982, I had no idea of the amount of hunger I would feel when I started working. I will never forget the pain I experienced on the first day at work in the Lorel factory. I usually had a breakfast of crackers, cheese, and two cups of coffee. My day began at 6 a.m. By my first break at 10:45, I was hungry. I had another cup of coffee and then went back to work. We had a 12 noon break for lunch. I was told to be back in 45 minutes. I panicked. How could I go home to have my almuerzo? My cousin said, "You will get used to it. The almuerzo here is at 6 p.m." It took me six months to get used to having a snack for my lunch period.

Cuban/Chilean American Reflection:
Annette Macari
Growing Up Organic

Something my mother said during the interview struck me as funny but so true. When Cristina (my daughter) asked her to describe what the food in Cuba was like compared to the United States, Abuelita remarked, "We only ate organic food in Cuba." She then went on to explain that the food consisted of local products that went from the farm directly to the table. Coffee beans were roasted in the oven that morning, and the smell of the roasting was better than anything you could find at the grocery store now. . . .

My husband's company wanted us to relocate to the Midwest. . . . Suddenly, I was at a loss. For some of the meals I was used to preparing, I had trouble finding ingredients. . . . I was on a quest to find these foods near where I lived. I found a store that had select items from the Goya brand that were placed in the "international" aisle. I laughed at that. . . . Never had I missed Cuban food so much. It was in my soul and I didn't know it. The only thing left to do was to learn to make it myself. I started going through my Cuban cookbook that I bought before leaving Miami and making those familiar foods myself. I learned to make black beans from scratch. I make my own sofrito now. There is still much to learn, but I am enjoying it so much. I am also teaching my children about these wonderful Cuban foods and helping them to grow to love the culture—the organic way.

For the complete text of Annette's reflection, see Appendix A.

At the onset of dusk, *la merienda*, a light snack of coffee and bread or sandwiches is traditionally provided. This informal meal is more of a snack and it precedes *la cena*, a small supper served as the last meal of the day. When guests come for dinner in Hispanic households, a customary post-meal practice is *la sobremesa*—socializing over coffee or perhaps an after-dinner drink. Most Hispanics adopt the American three-meal system very quickly, due to school and work time schedules. The NPD Group market research company claims that while Latinos are "more likely to cook from scratch than non-Hispanics, . . . the importance of homemade cooking declines as Hispanics acculturate" (www.npd.com/press/ releases/press_051216a.html).

Celebrations: Political and Historical Days of Celebration

While traditions vary for Latinos in the United States, we have noted that many still celebrate the independence days of their home countries. For some, they do not carry as much significance in the United States as they may have had at home, given that they are not paid holidays. Most Hispanics ultimately identify with July 4th, although they will make note of the independence days for their home countries. In Table 1 (p. 94) we provide a chart of independence days for various countries. It is important for teachers and care providers to become aware of these holidays; families may choose to give their children a holiday from school on their home countries' patriotic holidays. Or children may come to school dressed up in their best or in folkloric clothing to commemorate the holiday.

As the numbers of Latinos in the United States increase, their traditions and celebrations will become more and more a part of American culture. In recognition of these various independence day holidays, the U.S. Congress passed a proclamation of National Hispanic Heritage week in 1968. Twenty years later, they designated the period from September 15 to October 15 as National Heritage Month. As Table 1 shows, many Hispanic countries celebrate their independence during this highlighted period.

Columbus Day: Two Views

In the United States, Columbus Day is celebrated to mark Christopher Columbus' arrival in America. Celebrating the Europeans' discovery of the Americas and the consequent meaning for European descendents is one perspective. But what was the reaction of the indigenous cultures already living in the western continent?

Some Hispanics change the focus on October 12 (the accepted date of Columbus' arrival) to *El Día de la Raza* (Day of the Race). "When Latin Americans refer to 'race,' they are speaking of their Spanish and indigenous roots, and October 12th becomes a day to celebrate that mixed heritage" (Menard, 2004, p. 132). As educators and care providers, it is important for us to tell the whole story. When we celebrate Columbus Day/*El Día de la Raza,* we have an opportunity to go beyond the rhetoric and represent both perspectives.

Michelle's Experience

I have worked at a Head Start program in the Bronx for the past 12 years. In the last five years, a significant number of Mexican families have moved into a predominantly African American neighborhood. A couple of years ago, our center's picture day was on September 16th. Our staff was shocked when eight of the Mexican children came dressed up in velvet suits and mini ball gowns. Their parents said they were celebrating Mexican Independence Day and they were so happy that the children would be photographed in the ethnic garb.

I learned that Mexico's independence from Spain is September 16th, not May 5th! Cinco de Mayo celebrates the Mexican army's victory over the French in 1682.

Table 1. Dates Celebrating Independence Day of Hispanic Countries
Qué Viva La Patria!

Country	Months											
	Jan	*Feb*	*Mar*	*Apr*	*May*	*June*	*July*	*Aug*	*Sept*	*Oct*	*Nov*	*Dec*
Bolivia								5th				
Chile									18th			
Colombia							20th					
Costa Rica									15th			
Cuba	1st											
Dominican Republic		27th										
Ecuador								10th				
El Salvador									15th			
Guatemala									15th			
Nicaragua									15th			
Honduras									15th			
Argentina					25th							
Mexico									16th			
Panama											3rd	
Paraguay					14th & 15th							
Peru							28th					
Uruguay								25th				
Venezuela							5th					

Celebrations: Holidays and Folkloric Practices

Holidays

Año Nuevo. As in most cultures, the celebration of the New Year is a time for reflection and renewal. Aside from the familiar rituals of counting down to midnight, using noisemakers, and drinking champagne, Hispanics may practice the custom of eating 12 grapes at the start of the New Year. The grapes symbolize the 12 months of the year. This practice stems from a period in Spanish history when a surplus of grapes was harvested. Many Hispanics carry on the tradition, which has been passed on from generation to generation.

In another tradition, Hispanics may wear special colors on New Year's Eve. Each color carries a message of significance. For example, in the Mexican tradition, one is encouraged to wear red underwear if seeking love in the New Year and yellow underwear to bring prosperity and good fortune. White represents the cleansing and renewal that is the underlying theme as Venezuelans symbolically sweep out the old with a broom (others may take a bucket of water and throw it out the front door).

***El Día de las Madres* (Mother's Day).** Mothers are very significant in the lives of Latinos. "The Latino family dynamic is matriarchal" (Menard, 2004, p. 47), and so it is no surprise that the holiday carries special significance in the Hispanic community. Many Hispanic countries have adopted the American tradition of honoring mothers on the second Sunday in May. Mexicans celebrate Mother's Day on May 10th and Dominicans celebrate it on the last Sunday of May.

For Mexican Americans, *el Día de las Madres* may begin with a serenade from a mariachi band and/or a special service at church. Gifts are showered on mothers—food, flowers, chocolates, and sometimes bigger gifts. Some Latinos practice the tradition of wearing carnation corsages on Mother's Day—red for those whose mothers are still alive, pink for those whose mothers are far away, and white for those honoring deceased mothers.

***El Día de los Muertos* (Day of the Dead).** *El Día de los Muertos,* celebrated from October 31st to November 2nd, is a Mexican holiday to honor the dead. November 2nd is the Roman Catholic holiday of "All Souls Day," which is spent mourning and praying for

American versus Mexican Practices in Honoring the Dead: Linda K. Parkyn

American Ritual
It is 1963, and I am ten years old. We are in the car on the way to the cemetery and I am surrounded in the backseat by geraniums. It is Memorial Day, and we are going to plant geraniums on the graves of my grandparents. I remember this day every year of my childhood. My Mom does the planting. My Dad does not have a planting job; he is there only to carry the geraniums and fetch the water. My mother is silent. She digs deep into the Pennsylvania soil, and she remembers those who have come before her. When finished, the three of us stand respectfully for a few minutes and then we leave.

Mexican Ritual
I am on the bus in Aguascalientes, Mexico, and I am surrounded by the Mexican flower that most resembles marigolds. The flowers are bigger and brighter than marigolds, but they are still orange and smelly. It is November 1, Day of the Dead in Mexico, and everyone is jostling each other on the bus ride to the town cemetery. In this cemetery, everybody has a job. It is bustling with activity! . . . All the people are singing and telling stories about those who have come before them to live and die on this earth. Long into the Aguascalientes evening, families sit on warm blankets, eat the favorite foods of their ancestors, and, yes, even talk to those who have come and gone before them. November 2 is the festival of the dead, a time to remember, to bring the favorite food and drink of those you love and see no more. It is especially a time to tell the stories of their loved ones to the next generation. It is a time to assure themselves that those whom they love have gone to a better place.

The Blending of Traditions
My mother died recently, and I thought once more, on the anniversary of Day of the Dead, November 1 and 2, about those geraniums in the hard Pennsylvania soil. I built an altar in our home in memory of my Mom. I placed her knitting needles and her cookie cutters next to her picture, along with a nameplate from the back door of our old house. In true Mexican spirit, as I played with her memory, I felt a peace about her death that I had not experienced before.

For the complete text of her reflection, see Appendix A.

deceased family and friends. In many Mexican homes, *El Día de los Muertos* is a time to honor the dead and share stories about them with children in families. This Aztec tradition, said to be over 3,000 years old, is celebrated with incense, candles, skull decorations, food, and dancing. Death is not feared, but rather is celebrated; it is believed that the dead come back to their families on these days to celebrate with them.

Cultural Traditions and Folkloric Practices

Quinceañeras (15th Birthday). The "Quinces," the 15th-year birthday celebration, is the recognition of a young lady coming of age in the Latino culture. Most Latino groups share this celebration. The closest American equivalent to this celebration would be a Sweet Sixteen party, a debutante cotillion, or perhaps the Bat Mitzvah for 13-year-old girls in the Jewish tradition. Parents begin planning for the *quinceañera* the moment a daughter is born. The privileges that emerge after this rite of passage are many. After their *quinceañera*, daughters can engage in beauty routines that signify adulthood and the end of childhood. Some *quinceañera* celebrations rival wedding ceremonies, with up to 14 *damas y caballeros* serving as attendants in the honoree's "court."

Modern-day quince celebrations have become part of mainstream American culture, and are even portrayed in a popular MTV series "Quiero Mis Quinces" (www.mtv.org). Depending on their own family traditions, some Latinos incorporate a church service as part of the quinces in order to have a blessing bestowed upon the young lady. It is not uncommon to have the mother crown the daughter with a tiara and the father replace the girl's flat shoes with high heels. Many factors determine whether or not a young woman has a quinces celebration. Given the extravagance that some of the celebrations entail, financial constraints may prevent a family from hosting such an event. Some feel that the women's liberation movement has lessened the desire to promote a coming-of-age milestone in this way (Lopez-Rayo, 2007). Family tradition is also key. Some families may consider adopting a more Americanized version of the celebration (i.e., Quinceañera Cruises or Destination Quinceañera Celebrations-Disney), which would combine a family vacation with the birthday celebration.

The following poem by Judith Ortiz Cofer sheds light on the significance of the coming of age for a young girl celebrating her quiñce.

Quinceañera, by Judith Ortiz Cofer (1987)
My dolls have been put away like dead
children in a chest I will carry
with me when I marry.
I reach under my skirt to feel
a satin slip bought for this day. It is soft
as the inside of my thighs. My hair
has been nailed back with my mother's
black hairpins to my skull. Her hands
stretched my eyes open as she twisted
braids into a tight circle at the nape
of my neck. I am to wash my own clothes
and sheets from this day on, as if
the fluids of my body were poison, as if
the little trickle of blood I believe
travels from my heart to the world were
shameful. Is not the blood of saints and
men in battle beautiful? Do Christ's hands
not bleed into your eyes from His cross?

At night I hear myself growing and wake
to find my hands drifting of their own will
to soothe skin stretched tight
over my bones,
I am wound like the guts of a clock,
Waiting for each hour to release me.

Cumpleaños (Birthdays) – Piñatas. Although the 15th year holds special recognition for girls, other birthdays may be celebrated with parties as well. Children are showered with gifts, cake, and ice cream; typically, parties have a theme. Family members from every generation gather alongside neighbors and friends to celebrate and sing "Happy Birthday" in English and Spanish.

The piñata is a unique aspect of many Hispanic birthday celebrations. Piñatas come in a variety of shapes and are filled with candy, confetti, and prizes. Children eagerly wait to fill their party bags with loot from the piñata. Some piñatas are made with ribbons hanging from the underside; when the signal is given, pulling on the ribbons will release the treats. Other piñatas are completely sealed. Blindfolded children are spun several times to keep them off balance and someone uses a pulley to keep the piñata moving; the children use a bat or stick to try to hit the piñata and break it open. The youngest of the children is given the first chance to break it.

A distinctive way to acknowledge Hispanic children and adults on their birthdays is singing the traditional song *Las Mañanitas*. This song is sung on the morning of the birthday to wake up the loved one. The lyrics are as follows:

Las Mañanitas
Estas son las mañanitas, que cantaba el Rey David,
Hoy por ser día de tu santo, te las cantamos a ti,
Despierta, mi bien, despierta, mira que ya amaneció,
Ya los pajarillos cantan, la luna ya se metió.

Que linda está la mañana en que vengo a saludarte,
Venimos todos con gusto y placer a felicitarte,
Ya viene amaneciendo, ya la luz del día nos dio,
Levántate de mañana, mira que ya amaneció.

El día en que tu naciste nacieron todas las flores
En la pila del bautismo, cantaron los ruiseñores
Quisiera ser solecito para entrar por tu ventana
y darte los buenos días acostadita en tu cama

English translation:
This is the morning song that King David sang
Because today is your saint's day, we're singing it for you

Wake up, my dear, wake up, look, it is already dawn
The birds are already singing and the moon has set

How lovely is the morning in which I come to greet you
We all came with joy and pleasure to congratulate you

The morning is coming now, the sun is giving us its light
Get up in the morning, look, it is already dawn

The day you were born all the flowers were born
On the baptismal font the nightingales sang

I would like to be the sunshine to enter through your window
to wish you good morning while you're lying in your bed

http://www.lyricsmania.com

Bodas (Weddings). Weddings are important celebrations in most cultures and societies. In the Catholic tradition, it is one of the seven sacraments. From the Catholic Latino perspective, marriage is a sacred lifetime commitment. Yet separation and divorce rates for Latinos are increasing (Padilla & Borrero, 2006). In the last century, families would struggle to stay together for the sake of the children. As Latinos assimilate more into modern U.S. society, however, they are more likely to find separation and divorce to be acceptable options.

Nevertheless, the wedding ceremony and the merger of two families are still very significant events in the lives of Latinos. Preparations for a wedding ceremony can be extensive. For many Latinos, the actual ceremony still incorporates many rituals and traditions dating back to the Moors of Spain. In this way, the *bodas* (weddings) link older generations to the happy couple.

The bride may enter the ceremony wearing a white gown and a veil covered with orange blossoms, representing her purity. During the ceremony, the placing of a figure eight-shaped *lazo* (yoke) on the bride and the groom symbolizes unity. The *lazo* is a rosary, a satin cord, or a string of flowers that can be placed over the shoulders or around the couple's waists. Instead of the *lazo*, other Hispanics use a *mantilla* (veil) to represent the unity of the couple. In some traditions, it is the *madrina* (godmother) who pins the *mantilla* around the shoulders of the bride and groom before they receive the priest's blessing of their union.

The lengthy ceremony typically includes the wedding ceremony nested within the traditional Catholic mass. No Hispanic wedding would be complete without hearing the "Ave Maria" hymn at some point during the mass. Parents bestow a customary *bendición* (blessing) that solidifies the union of the couple.

Another common ritual found in Hispanic wedding ceremonies is the offering of the *arras* (coins). Typically, 13 coins are used as part of the ceremony, which symbolically represent the dowry offered to the groom and his family. This practice, handed down from generation to generation, is said to be a pledge of commitment. Some say the number 13 represents Jesus and the 12 apostles. Depending on the community custom, the *arras* may be presented in a small cask or on a tray. The arras may have been precursors to the traditional wedding rings, but Latinos now use both the arras and wedding rings for the exchange of vows.

After the ceremony, a traditional wedding reception involves food, drink, and music. A father might dance with his daughter to the popular song "*De Nina a Mujer*." Another common practice is the "dollar dance," in which the bride or the groom is festooned with money in exchange for a dance. Present-day couples make choices as to which of these marital rituals they select for their own special day.

Bautizmos (Baptism). Baptism is another one of the seven sacraments of the Catholic faith, a rite to expunge "original sin" from the baby. In the Hispanic culture, *bautizo* (baptism) is the first introduction of the infant to the church community. *Bautizos* also provide a means for welcoming children into the family while officially announcing the child's Christian name.

Latino parents choose family members or good friends to be *padrinos* (godparents). This is a serious role; *la madrina* (godmother) and *el padrino* (godfather) have a say over the development of a child's spirituality. They provide spiritual guidance and so should be of the most excellent character. "Being a padrino requires two-way communication, which means being in close contact with your compadres so that they can get to know and love your children and support them in their spiritual and moral development" (Rodriguez, 1999, p. 63).

Primera Comunion (First Communion). First communion is another sacrament in the Roman Catholic church. After several months (sometimes years) of preparation and after receiving the sacrament of reconciliation (forgiveness of sins), First Communion is the first time a child receives the Eucharist (a wafer blessed by the priest). Traditionally, a child's First Communion occurs anywhere between the ages of 7 and 9.

In the United States, First Communion takes place during the Lenten season (the 40 days prior to Easter Sunday). However, in Mexico, First Communion is commonly celebrated on December 8th, the Day of the Immaculate Conception (Rodriguez, 1999, p. 64). By tradition, children wear white for the ceremony. In some communities, both boys and girls wear all white; however, contemporary trends no longer require boys to do so. First Communion is a very solemn rite of passage that is typically celebrated by the whole family and documented by a traditional photograph showing the child kneeling with a Bible and rosary in hand.

Funerales (Funerals). Just as one celebrates the arrival of a new family member at birth, it is customary to participate in a ceremony when a loved one passes away. Several Hispanic cultural rituals and traditions can be followed to mark the passing. Some similarities should be noted. Generally speaking, Hispanics consider death to be a natural part of the life cycle. Within the Catholic tradition, Hispanics participate in a ceremony or special event to celebrate the life of a loved one or friend who has passed. Even if their ties to the Catholic Church are no longer strong, most Hispanic families will gather to participate in a ritual that is presided over by a clergy member.

It is understood that the final moments are to be shared with family members, particularly if a person has been ill. These are opportunities to say "goodbye," and for the dying to receive love, care, and protection from their loved ones. It is not uncommon for someone to choose to stay at home when it becomes clear that his or her time is near. In Latino tradition, it is typically preferred to be surrounded by loved ones, rather than face death alone. After a death, Hispanic families traditionally hold a *velorio* (wake), where friends and family gather to pay their last respects.

Wakes traditionally include time for prayer through a *novena*—a commitment to engage in nine days of prayer seeking special graces. Often, this may include saying the rosary. Personal items are placed in the casket for the loved one as a final token to be shared before saying goodbye. As part of the Latino tradition, family members stay with the body until the burial. Many funeral homes accommodate a family's desire to have a *velorio* that lasts well into the night or perhaps even until the day of the burial or cremation ceremony.

The funeral ceremony follows the wake. For some, a mass may be said at church in honor of the departed prior to the burial. For others, a procession of cars follows the hearse directly from the funeral home to the cemetery, where a small service is held on the grounds. It is still a common custom to send flowers to the funeral home for the wake, and these flowers follow the hearse in a special car and are placed on top of the casket in a mound after the burial.

Many Latinos with close ties to a home country will have two funeral ceremonies—the first in the new country (the United States) and a second funeral in the homeland. The body is transported to the home country to be buried with other family members. Educators and care providers need to be sensitive to rituals that might extend over longer periods of time than expected. Traditions have evolved as Hispanics in America have adapted to their communities and the need to accommodate school and employment schedules.

Following the burial, another social gathering may take place with a meal or reception.

The family gathers to eat and to comfort one another as well as to share memories of their loved one. Hispanics typically believe that death is a phase that one must pass through in order to reach the afterlife. It is often comforting for mourners to think that the spirit of the loved one who passed away will continue to bring strength, comfort, and guidance to those who remain in this world.

Please keep in mind that these traditions associated with death and burial have been generalized and do not reflect the variety of rituals particular to certain religions that many Latinos are now embracing.

Summary and Recommendations for Educators and Care Providers

Latinos are diverse in their celebrations of political, religious, or family holidays. The manner in which they choose to celebrate has much to do with where they are currently living and specific cultural practices and rituals from their heritage. Hispanic traditions are handed down from one generation to the next, but it is recognized that subtle changes occur with each passing of a generation. As can be seen in the reflections shared in this chapter, many Latinos experience a disconnect between how they were raised and their association with new cultural values and practices.

Latino family celebrations project a strong sense of solidarity, whether it is for a child's christening, a wedding, a funeral, or a political holiday. Their traditions are enduring and become part of the American landscape as they blend with new traditions.

It is imperative for teachers and care providers to become aware of the various family holiday traditions and customs being practiced by the children in their classrooms, multi-service centers, and community organizations. With that knowledge, they will understand why children may be absent from school for family observances. The following suggestions can help build understanding of traditions followed by your community's families:

- Visit churches of the different denominations represented in their schools and community, as well as recreation centers, bodegas, beauty salons, notions stores, bakeries, and other businesses that cater to Hispanic families.
- Reach out to families and be accepting of their cultural practices without judgment. For example, understand that a child could be absent from school for over two weeks while the family returns to the Dominican Republic for a burial, prayers, and family grieving.
- Reassure families that their cultural practices are strengths they can share with other children and their families in classrooms.
- Support Latino culture and family by making it part of your curriculum. For example, include authentic materials in the classroom that represent the culture, such as a Puerto Rican, Cuban, or Mexican pilón (a mortar and pestle used to grind and/or mash garlic, herbs, and seasonings). Also include children's books about Hispanic celebrations, birthdays, piñatas, and cooking.

Chapter 8 Questions To Ponder

- What is your favorite celebration discussed in this chapter? How does this celebration compare/contrast to a festivity in your community? Which Hispanic/Latino celebration do you wish to learn more about?
- When celebrating different cultures at schools/centers, it is common to dedicate a day, a week, or a month to the topic. How do you celebrate cultures in your community? Do you agree/disagree with specifically dedicating a period of time to the celebration of Hispanic heritage?

Chapter 8 Web-Based Resources

Hispanic Heritage Month
http://hispanicheritagemonth.gov/
The Strachwitz Frontera Collection of Mexican and Mexican American Recordings
http://frontera.library.ucla.edu//
Smithsonian Education – Hispanic Heritage Resources
http://smithsonianeducation.org/heritage_month/hhm/index.html
Hispanic Culture Online
www.hispanic-culture-online.com/hispanic-holidays.html
Mis Quince Magazine
www.misquincemag.com/
El Boricua
www.elboricua.com/
Puerto Rican Folkloric Dance
www.prfdance.org/
Calle Ocho Festival Miami
www.carnavalmiami.com/calle8/
Goya Recipes
www.goya.com/english/recipes/categories/favorites-by-region
Lyrics Mania
www.lyricsmania.com

Concluding Thoughts

As we come to the end of this journey writing *Hispanic/Latino American Families in the United States*, we have learned about the diversity that characterizes Latino cultural identities. Moreover, we solidified our own Hispanic/Latino cultural identities by researching our heritage, traditions, and cultural values. During this process, we created a new lens for discussing and analyzing what we already knew about our culture. Along the way, we encountered surprises that really opened our eyes to historical facts, issues, customs, and traditions that we had accepted as our own, but now had the opportunity to truly comprehend.

We offer this labor of love as a gift to all educators and care providers, with the hope that it provides insight into who Hispanic/Latino children and their families really are. As early childhood teacher educators, we take pride in encouraging our students to look at the children in their classrooms and realize that it is their responsibility, as educators and caregivers, to foster a sense of self-identity in children. Ingrained in our philosophy of education is the belief that all children have a right to a child-centered experience. As a result of our research for this work, our framework has shifted to include a belief that a child-centered cultural awareness should be celebrated in all children's educational experiences.

We have increased our appreciation of the need for strong, respectful relationships between home and school, in order to have the most effective approaches for teaching and learning about all cultures. Our own challenges, as parents trying to pass on our Latina cultural experiences and values, have made us conscious of how much can be lost with each passing generation, beginning with our language. The struggles that we face trying to maintain the native language in our own households has led us to reflect about the different world our children live in. With the increase of Latino awareness in the American experience, we are hopeful that our children and grandchildren and subsequent generations will truly embrace and be proud of their Latino/Hispanic culture. As a wise Latina once told her daughter, "Don't worry, in time you will come to appreciate who you are."

In closing, we share a letter to a *recién nacido* (newborn) written by his grandmother. This letter is a reflection of who many young Americans are today.

Dear Vincent and Alicia,

I am writing to you today because I have realized we have not spoken about language and language identity. I am your abuelita, grandma, nonna, baka . . . and there are lots of things I will tell you throughout your life. Today, I will tell you about your language background and your language identity.

Yes, I know this seems like a strange thing to talk to you about, especially since I have already chosen a language in which to communicate with you. I am writing in English because right now you live in the United States, where the dominant language is English. Even though you live in a bilingual household and have a bi-

lingual family, your first language will probably be English. When I was a young person, I never expected to be bilingual, nor multilingual as I am today. So, one never knows what this life will bring us.

Furthermore, there has been a lot of research into the relationship between language and identity. Theories point to the idea that the language a person speaks is related to that person's identity. That identity is formed by living in that person's culture.

I will talk about your family—your ancestors and the language they spoke. I will also talk a little about the specialized language they needed, depending on their occupations and interests.

Your Dad's Family

Your Paternal Great-Great-Grandparents—Michael and Marie Catherine

These great-great-grandparents are my paternal grandparents. They were my father's parents. They were born in Croatia, when it was called Austria-Hungary. Your great-grandpa and grandma came to the United States separately; they met and married in Chicago. They spoke Croatian when they arrived in the United States; they learned English as adults. I still remember that they did not speak perfect English; they sometimes struggled to make themselves understood to me. They did not come from the same city in Croatia. By the time I was old enough to understand, their country was no longer called Austria-Hungary, it was the nation-state of Yugoslavia. The political pendulum has now shifted back; today, their homeland is called Croatia.

They spoke the same language and had the same understanding of how the world worked, the roles of men and women, and they KNEW that they needed English to get ahead and earn money. That was the immigrant experience in the first decade of the 1900s when they arrived in the United States. Both of your great-grandparents settled on the south side of Chicago. There were lots of Croatian immigrants there, and they lived in a bilingual community where people spoke Croatian first and English as a second language. My grandpa, Michael, worked in the steel mills in the northeast corner of Illinois—where Illinois meets Indiana at the bottom corner of Lake Michigan. It was the kind of work that new immigrants to this country do—long hard hours, trying to make good money to support their families. My paternal grandparents were city people; they spoke of the bureaucracy of the big city, hot city nights in summer, and cold drafty houses of Chicago in winter.

Your Paternal Great-Great-Grandparents—Thomas and Mary Ann

These great-great-grandparents are my maternal grandparents. They are my mother's parents. They were from England—a city named Sheffield. They had two children who were born in England, and then they immigrated to the United States, where they settled in Iowa. In Iowa, they had three more children, including my mother. My grandma died in the great influenza epidemic of 1918, only six months after my mom was born. As a result, my grandpa put my mom up for adoption; he felt he could not take care of 4 children and a new little baby.

My grandpa worked in the coal mines, the strip mines that were very bad for his health and the environment. They all spoke English, first English from England and then Midwestern English. Their talk was the language of people who live in rural areas, have gardens in the hot Midwestern summers, and know about tractors, land, vegetables, and mining.

Your Paternal Great-Grandparents—Paul Matthew and Susan Amy

These great-grandparents come from my side of the family. My mom, Susan Amy, was born in rural Iowa in 1918, the year WWI ended and the year of the great influenza epidemic that took my grandma. She grew up in a small city—Des Moines, Iowa. It is in the middle of the Midwest, where at that time EVERYONE spoke English. People there know about rural life, but also know about city life. But their city life is not that of a place like Chicago where my dad's people lived. My mom and her family had always spoken English—that was their only language. It made their immigration process easy; they shared a language with the people in the new land. But even so, they were immigrants and you could tell by their traditions, customs, beliefs, and languages.

My dad, Paul Matthew, was born in 1912, in Chicago. His was a totally different language story. When he was in primary school, he studied in a Catholic school where the language of instruction was German. Then, even in primary school, the students were taught Spanish. He spoke Croatian at home with his parents and English with his friends. At that time, he was living in four languages. However, as I became a young person and young adult I never heard him speak any language other than English. He did the majority of his education in English. As a young person he learned the value of education; he always wanted to go to college, but that dream was never fulfilled. He was only able to do some courses in night school after he finished his high school degree. He worked for the U.S. government all of his life—the U.S. Postal Service, to be exact. He worked his way up the ladder and eventually worked with the team that developed the zip code system. He had little formal education, but he was a believer in education. He always read and studied the dictionary.

Your Paternal Great-Grandparents—Victor Hugo and Rosa Alicia

These are your grandpa Hugo's parents. Your grandpa was born in Mexico, to a Guatemalan man and a Mexican woman. Your grandpa's father claims to be Guatemalan to this day, but he has lived in Mexico for around 65 years. He speaks Mexican Spanish and anyone who would meet him would be sure he is Mexican. Still, he defines himself as a Guatemalan. Funny, isn't it? How his identity is still formed by his nationality even after all of these years.

Your grandpa's mother, Rosa Alicia, was born in the rural State of Mexico, in a small town. Not many generations ago, the people in this small town spoke Nahuatl, an indigenous language of Mexico. Some of the people who live in that area today still speak this indigenous language. But none of your great-grandma's family report speaking Nahuatl. The reason why they no longer speak this language is that it is not encouraged in Mexico to speak indigenous languages at this time; speaking an indigenous language in Mexico is not prestigious. Actually, indigenous languages are not called languages by most people; they are referred to as "dialects." This implies they are less important. If someone speaks an indigenous language and Spanish in Mexico it is only recently in that their bilingualism has been noticed. In Mexico, just as in the United States, there is a prestigious majority language—Spanish—that everyone is expected to speak.

Your grandparents—Victor Hugo, Jr. and Ruth.

When I (Ruth) was a young person, I began studying French in the 7th grade when I was about 11 years old. I continued studying French until I graduated high school. That was about six years of study. When I graduated, my oral comprehension was pretty good, and I was able to read literature (with the help of a dictionary). When I met your grandpa, I began to come in contact with written Spanish; he would buy the newspaper, or leave his books around. I soon discovered that I was able to understand written Spanish from the French I had learned in high school. As an adult, I began to take Spanish classes at a local university. I had the advantage of my French knowledge and was able to quickly read in Spanish. In the early 1980s, your grandpa and I moved from Chicago to Mexico City. It was then that I learned how much Spanish I did <u>not</u> know. I had a very hard time understanding when people talked to me. I have always worked as a teacher, and for a long time I was an English teacher. I began to learn about language learning and how important it is. Also, it was here that I began to learn all that I know about the relationship between *language learning and language identity.*

I first met your grandpa, Victor Hugo, Jr., in Chicago. Chicago is a big city that is home to people from many different parts of the world. Your paternal grandpa, Victor Hugo, Jr., is your dad's father; he came to the United States to work as a young man. He and his brother, your great-uncle Pepe, lived around the corner from the social service center where I worked. One of the things we did was to offer free English classes. When we met, I did not speak Spanish and your grandpa did not speak English. Seems impossible, right? Yes, we did not share any language. Soon, your grandpa began to learn English. He was diligent in his studies. He studied at his work place and after work he went to an ESL program for adults. He was quickly able to function in English both in his workplace and at school. Pretty soon we were able to understand each other. So, he became bilingual before I did.

Your Mom's Family

Your Great-Grandparents—Martha and Gilbert and Marie Catherine and Victor

Your mom's grandparents on both sides were descendants of Italian speakers and understood and spoke Italian. They lived in the big cities of New York State—New York, Syracuse, and Utica. They were born in the United States and were part of the American culture, although they shared their Italian customs and food with many people in the area who came from Italy. Their language was the language of cities also.

Your Maternal Grandparents—Vicki and Carl

Your maternal grandparents, or your mom's parents, were born of Italian stock, to speakers of Italian. Your grandparents are both business people. Your grandma, Vicki, has a business in her home. She works with young children and has a big influence in their language learning. Your grandpa, Carl, uses his language skills as a sales person. They are both speakers of English. They never spoke Italian unless it was necessary to communicate with their relatives who spoke that language. However, Italian is still part of their life and traditions through food today. They speak the language of Italian food; pasta, sauces, and cheeses.

Your Parents—Victor and Kimberly

Now it is time to talk to you about your parents. Your mom, Kimberly, was born in the United States to English-speaking parents. She always studied in English. She attended elementary and high school in New York, but as a young adult moved to Tampa, Florida. Living in Florida in today's globalized, diverse environment, she has firsthand, day-to-day contact with people who speak languages other than English. She is not surprised when people address her in a language other than English and she can even respond minimally to Spanish speakers. She is a monolingual speaker of English who understands that other people speak other languages.

Your dad, my son Victor Matthew, was born in Mexico, and his first language was Spanish. But he always lived in a bilingual environment. His maternal grandparents—his mom's parents—spoke only English; his paternal grandparents—his dad's parents—spoke only Spanish. His cousins, the ones from his father's family, could never understand how he could read/write/speak in English. He was in contact with a lot of people who spoke English, even in Mexico. In my work, I had a lot of contact with people from the United States and the United Kingdom. They rarely spoke Spanish. Also, I had friends who only spoke English. He was able to go back and forth in this bilingual world. As an adolescent, he would serve as a tour guide in our Mexican city for my international English-speaking colleagues. There is another fact that is interesting about your father. In spite of his strong language abilities, he did not like school, nor was he successful at school. He is a smart man linguistically, but he did not learn to apply his abilities in an institutionalized school setting. Later in his life, he learned to value formal education and got his college degree.

So, what does all of this mean for you as young people? It means you come from linguistically and culturally very diverse stock. Also, it means that although you perhaps do not understand today, your ancestors spoke many languages and had different understandings of what it means to be bilingual. They also came from different occupations and skills; therefore, they spoke many different languages in their jobs and workplaces. As you get to know us better, you will learn things about language from all of us, but the thing I would like you to learn is that your language identity is and can be as diverse as you allow it to be. Learning more than one language allows you to build cognitive skills and understand the people who live around you. I hope that by the time you can read this, you have already learned this in your daily life while growing up. It is one of the many things I hope to teach you.

Con mucho amor,
Tu abuelita,
Ruth

amazon.com

Returns Are Easy!
Most items can be refunded, exchanged, or replaced when returned in original and unopened condition. Visit http://www.amazon.com/returns to start your return, or http://www.amazon.com/help for more information on return policies.

Your order of May 5, 2012 (Order ID 103-9332896-9269836)

Qty.	Item	Item Price	Total
1	**Hispanic/Latino American Families in the United States: An Introduction for Educators and Care Providers** Paperback **(** P-2-C102D263 **) 0871731797**	$22.00	$22.0

This shipment completes your order.

Have feedback on how we packaged your order? Tell us at www.amazon.com/packaging.

Subtotal	$22.0
Shipping & Handling	$1.5
Promotional Certificate	$-1.5
Tax Collected	$1.7
Order Total	$23.7
Paid via credit/debit	$23.7
Balance due	$0.0

508/DysFYjmsR/-1 of 1-//1L/sss-us/6283397/0517-08:00/0517-06:14

V4

Appendix A
Latino Reflections

We extend our thanks to the contributors who shared their experiences with candor, articulacy, and love of their Latino heritage.

Ruth Ban - Assistant Professor, Barry University, Florida, and Profesor Universidad Autonoma de Aguas Calientes, AGS, Mexico
Michelle Rose Banks - Head Start Director, New York
Ingrid Brioso - Student, North Carolina
Maria Elena Buria - Early Childhood Teacher Educator, Florida
Yahaira Caseres - Preschool Teacher, New York
Amanda Maldonado Delgado - Head Start Head Teacher, New York
Margarita Dominguez-Figueroa (pseudonym) - New York
Elena Echevarria-Martinez - Adult Services, Special Education, New York
Dr. Cecilia Espinosa - Associate Professor, Lehman College, Bronx, New York
Dr. Ricardo R. Fernández - President, Lehman College of the City University of New York
Dr. Grace Ibanez-Friedman - Retired Associate Professor, St. John's University, New York
Carlos Lopez Leiva - Center for the Math Education of Latinos/as, Illinois
Maria Lopez (pseudonym) - Esthetician, Dominican Republic
Annette Fajardo Macari - Banker and mother of three, Florida
Dr. Juan Morales-Flores - Assistant Professor, Kingsborough Community College, New York
Dr. Linda K. Parkyn - North Park University, Professor of Spanish, Illinois
Raul Pimental (pseudonym) - Mechanic, Connecticut
Raquel Quesada - Assistant Principal, PS 71, New York
Dr. Diane Rodriguez-Luterbach - Associate Professor, East Carolina University, North Carolina
Maren Roedenbeck - Dual Language Teacher, Miami-Dade County Public Schools, Florida
Myriam Rogers - Spanish Immersion Teacher, Montgomery County Public Schools, Maryland
Dr. Lilliam Rosado - Professor, New Jersey City University
Dr. Sylvia Sánchez - Associate Professor, George Mason University, Virginia
Terry Louise Sebastian - Physical Education Teacher, New York
Dr. Mariana Souto-Manning - Associate Professor, Teachers College, Columbia University, New York
Jennifer Vallejo - ESOL Teacher, Missouri

My Family Has a Proud History: Grace Ibanez Friedman

My family has a proud history, as well as its share of ne'er-do-wells: my maternal great grandfather was involved in the Grito de Lares revolution against Spain; his female cousin went to jail for sewing the first Puerto Rican flag. On the paternal side, both my great grandfather and grandfather fought against Teddy Roosevelt. One became known for establishing the first newspaper in Arecibo, Puerto Rico, and he was among the first charter members of the Society of Puerto Rican Photographers.

It was nearly impossible to feel good in the United States when I grew up. The view of Puerto Ricans in the 1950s where I lived in New York City was very negative. We were called Marine Tigers, named after a ship that brought over many Puerto Ricans to the shores of New York and the east coast. Television, which was new at the time, had negative stereotypes of Latinos. My parents were upset, of course, and to protect us, forbade us from speaking Spanish outside the home, although we were encouraged to speak it in the home—especially by my mother. This developed a bifurcation in me, proud on the inside and uncomfortable on the outside. It wasn't until my late 20s that I integrated the two personas into one.

I worked for four years at the Puerto Rican Congress of New Jersey, a statewide, multipurpose, social activist organization. There I was reprogrammed, surrounded by so many qualified and diverse Puerto Ricans and other Latinos, that the fear of being stereotyped disappeared. Replacing it was a proud and integrated self, knowing not just my personal history, but the overall histories of all Latinos in the United States. One of my first acts of my new self was to write a resource guide for persons interested in developing a bilingual/bicultural child care center. This became my master's thesis, which, to my great pride, was stolen shortly after it was placed on the shelves of Bank Street College, and it was later entered into ERIC—the national resource base for educational reports and writings. It filled a hole in me, and helped many organizations, including the 12 child care centers that I personally helped to develop over 30 years ago—which are still functioning.

As I look back, I am grateful that I never lost my basic connection to my past, despite the years of living almost in an underground space, much like the main character in Ralph Ellison's *Invisible Man*. It is good to be one whole self all the time, visible and viable.

A Puerto Rican Daughter Reflects: Raquel Quesada

If one's life is molded by the experiences of our formative early years, then I am proof that what I have accomplished professionally, what I have emulated as a mother and as a friend, and what has driven my spiritual beliefs were profoundly shaped by my early experiences as a young Puerto Rican immigrant girl to the United States. From all the many remembrances that bombard my memories and spark around in my mind, the one that seems to stand out most is that of separating from my father when he came to New York to work and earn enough money to send to our family.

Every night I prayed that I would soon see him. I learned, early on, that a prayer does not have be structured and prescribed. My prayers were a quiet and private conversation that rocked me to sleep as I silently cried out for a loved one. Seeing my father at the airport after one year, gaunt and frail from working the midnight shift as a factory worker, instilled in me the resolution to work hard.

My love of books started when my dad saved for several weeks to be able to buy me my very first book, *The Three Billy Goats Gruff*. I begged him to buy me the book, not realizing that he could not afford to buy me the book right away. I learned to be strong and to have patience, and I learned about the sacrifices a parent makes for their children. I learned to walk tall and ignore the looks and comments that hurt, and instead seized the opportunities that gave us hope. School became the place where I was "rich" in good grades and where I was helped by many caring teachers. Later on, going to college was never really discussed, it was just understood that it would be. No negotiations.

The day that my dad died, I cried and then I reflected. A surge of energy came over me and I knew that everything would work out. The strength, courage, and love with which I was raised, and which were such a part of our Puerto Rican immigrant experience, were still with me. This quiet and humble man was probably the greatest teacher I ever had.

A Cuban Refugee's Story: Maria Elena Buria

I was 8 years old when the plane landed at Miami International Airport. Almost 50 years have elapsed since that eventful day, yet I can still feel and visualize the whole experience as if it had occurred just yesterday. It is hard to comprehend how a 30-minute flight, covering a distance of only 90 miles, could have such a profound and life-changing impact—but it did. Life would never again be the same for me or my family. It was on that day when we said goodbye to the land where we had first met life—the island paradise that would forever texture and color our life's canvas—and placed all our hopes, dreams, and uncertainties on the promise of a new land—a land that we would, from that day forth, call "home." Our departure from Cuba brought with it new opportunities and challenges, as well as a new adjective: "refugee"—the umbrella term for our sadness, alienation, unity, hope and, most of all, gratitude.

About a month after our arrival here in the States, Father found employment. He had been a real estate developer back in Cuba; he would now be working at a clothing factory, making $45 per week. We had spent our first month in the United States living with relatives; now employed, Father was able to rent a place of our own. The $95 a month, two-bedroom, white duplex was located in a quiet and somewhat friendly low-income neighborhood. It was not exactly the two-story home Father had built back in Cuba when marrying Mother—there were definitely no chandeliers, granite floors, or a housekeeper to take care of the cooking and cleaning. It was a small apartment, but clean—no one complained—it was our new home. There was no complaining either about having cornmeal and "arne del refugio"—the canned meat we received from the government—on the daily menu. My parents and grandmother were just grateful for the food and the $100 we were given monthly for the first six months. Until his last days, Father would constantly speak of the generosity of America.

We had left Castro's Cuba in 1960. When my sisters and I enrolled in the nearby elementary school, we were the first Cuban children in the school. We were a novelty, and were treated as such in the early days. We were fair skinned, had straight fine hair—with my oldest sister, Maria Victoria, being blond. Thus, we didn't look much different than the other children in terms of physical characteristics. But our expensive gabardine dresses, cashmere sweaters, and Mary Jane shoes were not exactly fashion staples for the other children. Between the way we dressed, and the fact that we didn't speak English, it was obvious to all—especially the other children—that we weren't from the neighborhood. Whether for good or bad, we stood out—receiving constant attention from everyone.

We had attended an all-girls' Catholic school back in Cuba. It was a very structured, strict, and academically demanding school. Our new school in the United States seemed less rigid and less academically demanding than our school in Cuba—a welcome relief—but given that we did not speak very much English, and had never shared classroom space with boys, it was all new and quite stressful. I had always been somewhat shy, but this new environment pushed me deeper into shyness—a shyness that would haunt me throughout childhood and heightened my profound feelings of alienation. There was always this tugging feeling of not belonging—not "here" or "there."

I recall the day my 1st-grade teacher, Mrs. Rock—a somewhat elderly and kind-mannered lady—called me to the front of the room and asked me to name the items pictured on a large chart that she had been using to teach me English. Although I was somewhat afraid of her, I liked Mrs. Rock: I could tell that she genuinely wanted to help me and would go out of her way to spend one-on-one time with me to teach me English. And so as I pointed to each item on the chart, I called out the corresponding word. The children laughed every time I made a mistake—laughing even louder the time I used the word "chicken" when it should have been "kitchen." The embarrassment was overwhelming—I had to fight back the tears. I did not want to go to school the following day, but of course, Mother made me. I was always afraid that the children would again laugh, and although I knew that what Mrs. Rock was doing was good for me, I resented it with a passion—it made me suffer so that I would stay up into the wee hours just worrying and stressing. Having to go to school had become torture for me.

I spent 4th grade in a bilingual classroom. Mrs. Stack was my new teacher—she, too, was very kind and nice. By then, a large number of Cuban children had immigrated to the States and had enrolled in our school. Fourth grade was less stressful than the previous year, or the years that would follow—I felt more at home now that my classmates were all like me. But this less stressful time would not last long, as the following year I was placed back in a regular classroom.

English as a second language had been part of our curriculum since I had started in kindergarten back in Cuba, so by 5th grade—two years after our arrival—I had a pretty good command of the language. The academic part, especially math and science, came easily to me. The education I had received back in Cuba had helped me to be ahead of my classmates in these two areas. It wasn't long before I was doing well in all the other subject areas as well, except, of course, in music and P.E.—these require socialization, something that had been very hard for me since day one in our new school.

Soon after starting 5th grade, I made friends with a girl name Patty. Patty had been nice to me since day one. She could tell that I was shy and went out of her way to befriend me and make me feel part of her little group. Patty was the first friend that I had made in school since arriving there. One afternoon during recess, I overheard Patty inviting all the other girls to her birthday party. She had invited every girl in the class. I was all excited, waiting for my turn. Patty's birthday would be the first party I would be attending since arriving in the United States. I couldn't wait. "I wish I could invite you to my birthday party, but my father doesn't allow Cubans in our house." She said more, but those are the only words spoken by Patty that I heard—and never forgot. I was speechless and too stunned and hurt to even cry. I completely distanced myself from all the other children—even Patty—from that day on. I would be 20 years old and a junior at the University of Florida before I was to again make a friend. It had been that painful.

I was now in the 6th grade: the day, November 22, 1963—another horrendous day I would never forget. The sequence of events is a bit blurry, but this is what I do remember. We had received word that President Kennedy had been shot. We were standing in line out on the yard waiting to go back to our classroom—we had just finished with recess. "They said that a Cuban went into the President's office and shot him!" The words were coming from George, one of my classmates. I have no idea where he had heard such a thing or why he was saying it; all I know is that pure fright came over me. Somehow, the fear we had experienced prior to our leaving Cuba all came back to me—I was trembling. A horrible slide show began to play in my mind: a man being shot by a firing squad on television; militia men all dressed in olive green uniforms and carrying rifles getting off a jeep across from our home; my mother sitting on the bed and crying while my sisters and I huddled around her. It all came back to me like a terrible nightmare. We returned to our classroom and took our seats. I continued to tremble while the slide show continued to play in my mind. At some point word came that President Kennedy was dead. Our teacher began to cry uncontrollably while sitting at her desk and holding her face between her hands. The principal ran in and was holding her as she continued her loud crying. Other adults came into the classroom, and they, too, were crying. My fear grew—all I could think of was that everyone was going to be angry at me because a Cuban had killed the President and that they would hurt me. I raised the top of my desk and stuck my head inside—as to hide so no one could see me or get me. The President was dead—there would be chaos and violence. I just stayed hiding my head in the desk and crying, just wanting to go home to my mother. That day seemed like an eternity.

Halfway through that torturous year, I was transferred back to a bilingual classroom. I couldn't understand why. Yes, I rarely opened my mouth to speak, but by now I had become fluent in English and along with Michelle B., had the highest grades in the class. I again cried uncontrollably. Even though I was miserable in that class, at least it was a familiar place. I would now be placed in a totally new environment where I didn't know anyone. I felt as if a great injustice had been done to me. I hated school. I did not want to go back. It was a daily battle to get me to go to school from that day on. I would sit on my grandmother's rocking chair until way into the morning hours and just rock my anger and anxiety away. By morning I would always be exhausted from no sleep, but no matter the excuse, I was not allowed to stay home. To my parents, education was not negotiable—only illness would keep us home. I could not understand why my parents seemed blind to what I was going through. It was many years later—when I was no longer a child—that I was able to understand that part of the reason my parents could not fully comprehend or see what I was going through was the fact that they, too, were trying to adjust to their new home while mourning the loss of their country and the life and loved ones they had left behind—not to mention having to deal with the realities of everyday survival.

We had moved several times during those first few years. As more of our relatives immigrated, we had to make room for them by renting a bigger house. Since Father was still working at a factory and making little money, the house needed to be bigger, but the rent cost would have to remain the same—this meant moving into an older and more rundown home! Now I had two reasons for not getting any sleep—my anxiety over school and having to fry in the Florida heat because there was no air conditioning and we had to cover ourselves—head and all—at night to protect ourselves from the rats that shared the house with us! Life was rough, but at least we had a large yard in which my sisters and I could play. We welcomed this change. While at play, we forgot our troubles.

Time passed and somehow I made it through elementary school and began middle school. I was now bused to a school that was quite far from home. The school was in a very rough neighborhood—nothing like I had experienced before. We had lived in poor neighborhoods since our arrival in the States, but they had been relatively quiet and peaceful neighborhoods, not prone to any violence. Now, for the first time in my life, I witnessed two girls fighting. I was shocked! I could not imagine the nuns back in my school in Cuba allowing such a thing to occur—it just wouldn't. It would not be ladylike. My culture shock, as well as my awareness, was now expanding into new realms. As I stated earlier, Father had been a very successful real estate developer back in Cuba. His financial success had allowed us to live a life shielded from many people's harsh realities. We now were living in those realities and the adjustment was not easy—not for me or anyone else. But, this was our new life—there was no other choice but to adjust and keep moving forward.

It was now winter—I was in the 8th grade and a teenager. I had long before outgrown my beautiful gabardine dresses and cashmere sweaters. My homeroom teacher was taking roll. "It's cold. How can your parents send you to school without a coat?" she asked in a judgmental kind of voice while pointing her finger at me and shaking her head. "I don't have a coat," I replied in such a low voice that no one heard me—probably not even the teacher. And so she continued to belittle my parents and make negative comments about

Cuban immigrants. I just kept my head down and did not say anything else—I was embarrassed enough. Now everyone knew that I didn't have a coat. What my classmates or teacher didn't know is that my mother and father were not irresponsible or negligent parents; it's just that they didn't have the money to buy us coats. But we didn't need a coat; my mother always made sure that we were dressed warmly by layering several pullovers and sweaters. Unfortunately, my homeroom teacher had not taken the time to notice that Mother had "bundled" me up.

In time, 8th grade ended like all the other years that had come before it and those that were to follow. There would be more painful moments for me to experience, more alienation and isolation to overcome, more adjusting. But as the years went by, my new life began to feel as if it was my real life—the life that I had been meant to live—a good life—a happy life. I no longer felt like a stranger in someone else's home—but instead, I felt as if I was home—this new land called "America" was home. Yet, somewhere in the deep caves of my soul, there will always be this small, empty space filled with a longing that will never be met. I suppose it's like the longing felt by an adopted child once he/she grows up—that little, almost silent, voice that asks: What would it have been like?

Cuban Immigrant's Reflection: Ingrid Brioso (Spanish)

Lourdes querida,

Hace tiempo que no sé de ti.

Ayer fui a un mall, desde el mediodía, a buscar un trabajo. Visité muchas tiendas y me fui con sólo una respuesta. Una respuesta entre los treinta lugares que visité. El día anterior había entrado a una tienda y había llenado una aplicación después de hablar con la empleada de ese turno. Fue la misma mujer que me recibió hoy, me recordaba y me dijo que había apartado mi aplicación, que le había comentado al gerente que alguien con buena presencia había pedido empleo esa tarde, que debería esperar su llamada. Noté que su inglés era pobre así que no me preocupó el mío. Ese fue el resultado de mis inadagaciones en el Mall. Luego crucé la avenida en el carro, que es inmensa, y entré a un lugar llamado Barnes and Nobles, es una cadena de librerías que se pueden encontrar e todo el país. El lugar es hermoso, gigante, lleno de libros, con música instrumental baja o el tema Bésame mucho. . . . Pregunté por alguna plaza pero no había ninguna libre, una pena porque me fascinaría trabajar ahí; sin embargo me quedé en el lugar, lo recorrí un poco. Los libros puedes cogerlos y sentarte a leer. Así estuve leyendo a Jack London en inglés por una hora, decidí darme ese regalo; y ya cuando eran las cinco decidí salir para ir al otro mall, que queda del otro lado del vecindario. El primero era cerrado, hermético, gigante pero el segundo es una calle alargada con tiendas a los lados, con un Barnes and Nobles también. Fui directamente a él pero no hubo nada disponible y entonces decidí caminar un poco por las tiendas. Llegué a una llamada "Havana nine" recordé los cuentos de Alberto de "tonite" el juego de palabras y todo, entré y vi muchas guayaberas, todas importadas desde China, lo que me provocó mucha risa y luego me fui a unos estantes con fotos de La Habana. Eran llas seis y estaba buscando trabajo desde las doce, en ese mall no había nada disponible salí a la calle y de alguna forma me sentí un poco sola, viendo a todo el mundo reunido, paseando, pero eso son sólo algunos momentos, sólo eso, una comparación triste y hermosa entre los días y las noches. Y gracias a ese estado de nostalgia, a la tarde hermosa, a estar en un lugar que no es el mismo me entró un sentimiento una necesidad de hablar con alguien y vi a una muchacha que acababa de salir de una tienda para sentarse en un banco en la acera y fumar un cigarro, una empleda vestida de negro, me acerqué a ella como si le dijera algo más trascendente, más revelador y sincero y le pregunté: Do you know if there is any openings for employment right there? Y me dijo que sí, que estaban contratando. Me puse muy feliz y entré y todo cambió. . . . Era un lugar pequeño con luz tenue y música clásica, como si siempre fuera de noche ahí, las paredes llenas de estantes con vinos, una especie de cava con un bar, su nombre es The great merchant (wine boutique and bar). . . . Había un muchacho sentado en el frente y le pregunté. Me dijo que sí que estaban en el proceso de seleccionar y emplear, fue muy amable y hasta me extendió una tarjeta por si yo tenía alguna duda. Le dije que venía de Cuba y que me preocupaba no haber trabajado nunca aquí, que me preocupaba que eso me pusiera en desventaja. Y empecé a llenar la aplicación. Estaba feliz y tranquila y disfruté el inglés. Me acerqué a preguntarle algo y por alguna razón que no recuerdo deduje lo que sucedía y quise saber si él sería el entrevistador, me dijo que sí, ni siquiera quiso que continuara llenando la aplicación, sólo mi manera de contactarme, y me aseguró que sabría de ellos a principio de esta semana. Cuando salí miré la tarjeta y descubrí que era el administrador de la tienda y yo afortunadamente nunca lo supe, lo que me permitió desenvolverme con naturalidad, fluidez en el lenguaje y seriedad. Yo sola dije de mí sin hablar mucho, y creo que él supo notarlo. Ese fue el final de mi día. Necesité tantas negativas para que pasara algo realmente bueno.

Me he vuelto una mujer, o algo distinto de lo que era ya. Las experiencia se me han acumulado en los huesos, en la mente, en la forma de hablar y la de andar. Antes andaba encojida, ahora no es que el andar sea más erquido sino que los huesos son más pesados, más fuertes. He tenido que recorrer todo lo que no viví en tres meses. Hoy se cumplen tres meses desde que estoy aquí . . . hoy sería ese 30 de frebrero a tres distancias de montarme en el avión. Cuánta ilusión en ingenuidad cargaban esas alas. Ya estoy durmiendo más tranquila. Me levanto a las siete para llegar a las clases de inglés a las nueve. Debo manejar una hora a setenta millas. Nunca había pobado tanta velocidad yo sola, tanta velocidad distinta en momentos tan adversos. Y tan buenos por lo que enseñan a sentir. Manejo cada mañana y miro a la derecha, al asiento vacío a mi lado y trato de verme desde afuera, como en una película, pero son mis manos las que sostienen el timón, por primera vez. Por primera vez, en tres meses, sostengo el timón que me llevará a dónde yo quiera. Por ahora estudio inglés y busco trabajo. Manejo y lo veo todo, duermo, pienso. A veces me pregunto el por qué de este cambio, de esta nueva visión de todo. Agradezco el crecimiento que me provoca tanta adversidad y sí, tengo mucho que decir. . . .

Espero que estés bien. Nunca voy a olvidar el recibimiento que me diste, tu cariño y tu sinceridad, sin conocerme.

Cualquier cosa, aquí me tienes.

Ingrid.

Ingrid's Reflection: English Translation

Dear Lourdes:

It has been awhile since I last heard from you.

Yesterday I went to a mall around noon, to look for a job. I visited many stores and left only with one answer . . . a possibility . . . one after visiting 30 places. The day before, I had been to a store and filled out an application after speaking to an employee. . . . That same lady received me today and she remembered me and told me that she had set my application aside and had given it to the manager, explaining that someone with a good presence had applied and that I should wait for his call. I noticed that her English was poor so I did not worry about mine. That was the end result of my inquiries at the mall.

Later, I went across this huge avenue in the car and went into a place called Barnes and Noble, one of a chain of bookstores throughout the nation. It is a giant, beautiful place full of books, with instrumental music softly playing in the background. "Besame mucho" was heard as I walked the stalls. . . . I asked if there was a job opening, but they did not have one. Too bad, because I would have been fascinated working there. I wandered around and realized that you can take a book and sit down to read it and I decided to give myself a treat and read Jack London—in English—for about an hour before I went to the other end of our neighborhood to another mall.

The first was a huge enclosed mall, but the second was a long street with stores on both sides of the street and with another Barnes and Noble and I went directly to it, but there was nothing available there, either, so I decided to walk around the stores. I arrived at a store called Havana Nine that reminded me of the stories of Alberto de "tonite," the play on words and all. I saw so many *guayaberas* imported from China, which made me laugh, and then went to an area that had photos of La Habana.

It was then six o'clock and I had started looking for a job since noon and there were no available jobs in this mall, either, so I went back to the street and somehow I felt a little alone watching everyone strolling together and having a good time . . . but it was only a few moments, just that, a sad but beautiful comparison between nights and days. And thanks to that nostalgic feeling, the beauty of the afternoon and being in a place that is not the same, I had this sudden need to speak to someone, and I saw a young lady who had come out of store to sit on a bench to smoke a cigarette. She was an employee all dressed in black and I approached her as if I was going to tell her something important, revealing, transcendental, sincere . . . and I asked her: "Do you know if there are any openings for employment right there?" and she said yes, that they were hiring. I became very happy and went in and all changed. It was a small place with soft lights and classical music, as if it was nighttime inside there. The walls were covered with wine cellars. The place is called The Great Merchant (a wine boutique and bar). There was a young man sitting at the entrance and I asked him. He told me that they were in the process of selecting and hiring. He was very nice and even extended a business card, just in case I had any doubts.

I explained that I had come from Cuba and was worried because I had never worked here before and was concerned that it would put me at a disadvantage, but nevertheless I began to fill out the application. I felt happy and at peace and enjoyed the English. I went toward him to ask him something, and for whatever reason I realized what was happening and asked him if he would be the interviewer. He answered yes and told me not to even continue with the application except for the contact information, and he assured me that they would contact me by at the beginning of the week. When I left and looked at his business card I discovered that he was the manager of the store, and fortunately I never knew it, which helped me to proceed with ease, to maintain a fluid and serene use of the English language. I was able to describe myself without much talk and he noticed it. That was the end of my day. I needed so many negative moments in order for something really good to happen.

I have become a woman, or something different than what I had been. The experiences are gathering in my bones, in my mind, in the way I speak and the way I walk. Before, I was a little shy; now, it's not that I stand taller, but that my bones seem heavier, stronger. I have had to live in three months all that I was not able to live before. I have been here for three months today. Sometimes, I ask myself why I have to live all of these changes. I appreciate the growth that has provoked so much adversity. Yes . . . I have so much more to say.

Chapter 2: Health Care Stories

Elena's Reflection

I grew up in a multi-generational household. My grandparents and my great grandmother lived with us in a 5-room apartment in Alphabet City in the lower East Side of Manhattan. We lived in a neighborhood with many Latinos—Cuban and Puerto Rican, mostly. The elders always assembled together after Mass to walk to the bakery to get fresh bread (*pan de agua*). I would tag along with my grandmothers and listen to their conversations about religion, regular gossip, and home remedies. They made special teas for different ailments, but there was one product that, without fail, was in every medicine cabinet or night table; Vicks Vapor Rub! As a young child, I recall the extensive use of Vick's Vapor Rub in our household. My *abuela* (grandmother) used Vick's for headaches by placing a layer of Vick's on her forehead, covered by a bandana, until her headache disappeared. My mother also applied Vick's on her abdomen for bad menstrual cramps and my father inserted globs of Vick's into his nostrils to clear his congestion.

Lilliam's Reflection: "Que Dios quiera"

My parents watched over my colds carefully in the winter as they often turned into congestion, wheezing, and then asthma. Difficult nights would bring my grandmother from her house to my bed. She would intervene with rubbing alcohol, oregano herb tea, and prayers. Getting well was only possible with the help of God. All her prayers ended in "Que Dios quiera"—only through God's will.

Chapter 3: Religious Reflections

God's Ways Are Unpredictable: Jennifer Vallejo

I want to share my story with you. I want to tell you a real story, a story that has joy and pain, as well as some victories and some failures. I hope it brings you hope and courage in your journey as an immigrant. This is the story of the time I have been in the United States since I came from my country.

I was born in La Paz, Bolivia, the capital with the highest elevation in the world (located at 12,000 feet above sea level). I grew up in La Paz, a beautiful city, surrounded by snowy mountains, valleys, and amazing geographic places. I graduated from high school and after that, from college with a bachelor's degree in social communication arts. I thought I would never leave Bolivia. I love my country, its geography, multiculturalism, and uniqueness in many ways. However, God had different plans for my life.

As a child, it was very painful to see my dad leaving my home and my country to go to the United States to get a better life, to give my sister and me better opportunities in life. As an 11-year-old, nothing was better than having my dad by my side, holding my hand and telling me that everything would be fine. I believe that is why I did not really consider coming to the United States. In fact, I even refused to study English because I thought I would never need it (something I deeply regretted later in my life). After many years, my dad got his American citizenship. Soon after that, he claimed my sister and me. At that time, I was about to graduate from college. I had other plans for the future. I wanted to go to Spain. I wanted to explore the Old World. However, there was something different written in my divine destiny.

In February 2000, I arrived to Miami, Florida. This time I was coming with a big, sealed yellow envelope that said I was an American resident. I barely spoke any English. I did not drive a car. Honestly, I did not know what I was getting into. Six months later, I was deeply homesick. Everything was different, and my family, friends, food, and favorite places were thousands of miles away. I wanted to go back. It was then I had a real encounter with Jesus. It changed my entire life and the way I see people, life, spend money and time. I began looking at things from a different point of view. I knew God had a plan for my life. My attitude changed and I started looking at the opportunities I had around me.

I decided that I had to learn English if I wanted to get somewhere in this country. First, I started studying by myself with a basic English grammar book. I used to wake up very early every morning and go over grammar rules. A few months later, I enrolled on a program at college called VESOL (Vocational English as a Second Language). At that time, every day was a challenge, from taking the bus to stopping myself from feeling homesick. The first two years, I used public transportation to move around Miami to commute to college and to work. If you know something about public transportation, you know you need lots of patience and time. Going by bus every day gave me another perspective about the United States. Not everything that I have seen in the movies was true, but also I could see how many people were fighting to get a place in this society. I saw frustration, hopelessness, kindness, simplicity, and hope. I realized I was not the only one feeling homesick. I stopped complaining once I actually realized I was in a better place than many other immigrants who were going on the bus with me, day in and day out.

It took me a big effort to learn English. Actually, learning English is a lifelong learning experience for me. I spent countless hours at the English lab at college trying to figure out the verb "to be" and other tenses. After a year of studying English, I could understand some, but talking was so painful and embarrassing that it took my whole being to say a simple phrase. However, I was determined to learn English. It was a crazy language for me. Almost all the grammatical rules had exceptions, and the same letter had too many different sounds for me to remember the pronunciation. However, my perseverance was not enough; I had great English teachers who helped me to believe that I could actually speak English someday. To this day, I am thankful to them.

I also decided to become independent as soon as possible. Shortly after I learned the basic skills to survive I started looking for a job. My first job was as a waitress. It only lasted for a month. Then, I worked as a cashier, and as a sales person. Afterwards, I worked as a page in a bookmobile public library. My job at the library helped me to improve my English skills. Many people believe that living in Miami makes it hard to learn English; however, I think it takes two things to learn a new language: desire and faith. It took me at least three years to feel a little bit comfortable with the language. I had a good job, I finally started liking the place I was living in, and I was feeling less homesick. However, something was missing.

I began to pray about what God wanted me to do. I really had in my heart to work with children. It was then that I received a letter from Barry University. It was an invitation to apply for a master's degree in early childhood education. It did not require having a background in education. The process to apply for me was long because I was not a native English speaker. I needed to take different tests, translate transcripts, and validate my foreign degree.

Getting the master's degree was a journey. When I started, I looked at the credits and all the classes I had to take, and I saw a huge mountain that I was not sure I could climb. I remember the first year; it took me hours to write a paper. Along the way, I found good people who helped me to proofread my schoolwork, encouraged me, and supported me all the way. I will always be thankful to those who helped me. Making presentations in front of my class was hard. I used to memorize everything to make sure I was saying the right thing and everybody could understand me. The second year of the master's was easier. But I got more confidence in my command of English. Finally, the day came and I graduated with a master's degree in May 2005 from Barry University.

Then, I began to work in a dual-language school as a Spanish and math 2nd-grade teacher. It was a great experience. I taught Spanish to non-native Spanish speakers. I could totally relate to them as they learned. As a teacher, it was amazing for me to see the process in my students from not knowing a word in Spanish to making sentences, reading, and writing in another language. I taught for two years in that dual-language school. I believe that working as a teacher is one of the most rewarding professions. I realized how much I enjoyed working with children and seeing the learning process in their lives.

Although I was really happy working as a teacher, I wanted to serve God with all my heart. An opportunity rose up, and I decided to change directions. I quit my job as a teacher and moved to Kansas City, Missouri, and joined the mission base of the International House of Prayer as an intercessory missionary. I worked as a missionary for a year and a half. I learned to live a very simple life. When I first moved to Kansas City, somehow I had to start all over again. I was in a different culture again. I was excited to get to know more about the American culture as well as other cultures.

I wanted to serve God and He wanted to surprise me, and He sure did. In January of 2007, I met my husband in a divine way. God united us in the same place. Six months after we met, we said "I do" and promised to one another before God that we would be together for the rest of our lives. Miguel, my husband, is from Spain. Although we speak the same language, we had to get to know each other's cultures. He had an advantage since he served in Bolivia for two years as a missionary. It has been the most wonderful time in my life.

After I got married, I got a job in a public school as an ESOL teacher. When I look back, it amazes me what God has done in my life. It is a wonder for me to be teaching English now. Most of my students are immigrants or immigrants' children from Mexico, El Salvador, and Guatemala. I am so thankful to be a bridge between both languages and cultures. I often tell them that they need to share their hearts between Spanish and English. I teach them to be proud of their culture and to love learning, so they can become lifelong learners, and to be confident of themselves.

God's ways are unpredictable. I believe everybody has a divine destiny. Being an immigrant here in the United States (or any other country) is not easy. Leaving home, family, friends, and places that you love is painful. Being in a new place and having to overcome challenges produces an inner battle in your soul that can kill you or make you stronger. It is not easy to succeed in a place that you do not really know. However, if you have faith, boldness, and endurance, you can overcome more than you would ever imagine. It has been almost nine years since I came from my country to the United States. During those years, many times, I felt like quitting. I know it was God's grace that carried me through all the way. I still believe someday I will go back to Bolivia. I would like to help the street children in my country. I have not accomplished all my dreams, but I am sure I am where I supposed to be, and I am doing what I am supposed to be doing. I pray you will find your path and you will have the strength and wisdom to overcome your problems and succeed in this country, which is a nation for many nations.

Raul Pimental's Reflection: A Dominican Living in Two Spiritual Worlds

I grew up in the South Bronx in the 1970s, a first-born son to parents from the Dominican Republic. I began my education in a very small private Catholic school. I was brought up Roman Catholic and attended El Colegio de San Marcos in Santo Domingo, the capital. I was taught by nuns, attended church every morning with my classmates, and did all of my sacraments in that church. I thought myself to be an extremely religious child. I did the "altar boy thing" also and had already decided at age 10 to become a priest.

Unfortunately for me, my mother left me in my aunt's care when she left for the United States to make a better life for my sister and me. We moved to a new *barrio* (neighborhood) and lived with my mother's sister, who was the *barrio*'s *espiritísta*. That is, she practiced Santeria and was the chief priestess in our town. My world was turned upside down. Not only did I miss my mother, but now I was still attending San Marcos, a good Catholic boy, and exposed to Santeria. I was so confused with the lives of the saints as I knew them and their dual personalities in the Santeria religion. I felt awkward in the Catholic church and soon stopped being an altar boy. I began to help my aunt create her altars to Changó and San Lazaro, and also began to understand her role as a Santeria *espiritísta* and advice counselor to all who came to her house for advice of a spiritual nature.

Two years later, my mother was able to bring me and my sister to America! I went to public school because Catholic schools were so expensive and my mother could not afford them. I worked at my uncle's *bodega*, where I found many of the religious artifacts used for Santeria. I felt comfortable and uncomfortable at the same time. Needless to say, after being exposed to both spiritual worlds, I still felt like I was lacking something. I went to college for two years, [where I] took a course in Far Eastern Religions with a professor who really opened my eyes to true spiritualism. Today, I am 54 years old, a Buddhist, and very content in my third spiritual world!

Chapter 4: Child-Rearing Stories

Boriqua's Reflection: Amanda Maldonado Delgado
Traditional vs. Nontraditional Child-rearing Practices

When I think about my own child-rearing practices, I must reflect on my own childhood. I guess because, after all, growing up in a nontraditional Puerto Rican household is the basis of my own child-rearing practices. I call my Hispanic upbringing nontraditional, since I am third-generation Puerto Rican. Things changed quite a bit in my family after the second and third generations were born. For example, my grandmother always wanted me to become a professional and not act subservient as she was to my grandfather. She liked the American ways but missed the "island." She was happy to raise her family in New York, speak English, and work in the "city." My great grandmother, the first to immigrate to the United States, was a working mother, which was not common in the 1920s for newly arrived Latinos.

I was raised in the Bronx, where my parents stressed the importance of being strong and educated in the American way, but also to respect the culture. When I was sick, they relied on the expertise of my pediatrician. But my grandparents believed in natural remedies from Puerto Rico, of course. They recommended these first because they were proven for generations. Growing up, I remember my house was always trying to balance traditional Puerto Rican practices with American practices.

I had my first child when I was 22. I found my son to be a colicky baby. The pediatrician suggested stomach drops to ease the pain. Other family members taught me how to make a tea out of star anise (*estrella de anis*). Both remedies seemed to bring him comfort and by the time he was 6 months, he seemed to outgrow his colic. I do not believe that the anise cured him, but I figured it was worth a try. One of the gifts when he was a baby was an *azabache*, which is a talisman worn by babies and adults for protections from evil and illnesses, given to him by his great aunt. My son always wore the *azabache* on a chain around his neck. Elder family members believed that this talisman would watch over him. I agreed but found it hard to believe that a piece of jewelry would protect him from illnesses. When he started on regular foods, I noticed some food allergies. I went straight to an allergist for help. I also relied on my faith and prayed a lot. Some family members saw this as a punishment from God. I tried not to let it bother me and continued to pray that God would help my son and give him the strength to feel better. I had my doubts about the *azabache* warding off illnesses. I believe that my son's allergies are a result of biological systems, not spiritual interventions.

When my son was 4, I gave birth to another beautiful baby, a girl. Because of some minor issues, she was admitted into the neonatal intensive care unit. I sent my prayers to God and asked him to help the doctors care for her. After two weeks, she was finally sent home. Unfortunately, her dad, my father, and I had to take her back to the hospital, this time with a fever and diarrhea. They had to admit her until the tests from the newborn screening were in to rule out anything more serious. We all shared many prayers and tears. Again, some family elders members believed we were being punished by God for something. Other families believed that due to my son's allergies, I must have been doing something wrong during my pregnancies. I had faith in the doctors and believed she would be okay. She left the hospital strong and fighting. Family members suggested taping a quarter to her belly to "fix" her "outie" belly button. Once again, I sided with the doctors, who believed that this would cause more discomfort than good. Learning from my prior experience of feeding my son table food at an early age (Puerto Rican traditional practice), I introduced her to foods at 8 months. Once again, my husband and I noticed food allergies. I could not believe it after all the nursing I had done. Family members told me an old saying that translates to "whatever does not kill you won't hurt you." I watched them say this as children put dirty toys and dirty food into their mouths. This saying was one that I knew I would never apply to my children. Once again, I agreed with my doctors, who told me to sanitize everything. I always felt I was right and wrong with whatever practices or remedies I chose as I tried to balance the traditional Puerto Rican versus non-traditional American practices.

My children are growing up in a similar way to my own upbringing. My husband and I must read ingredients on every food, soap, and lotion etc. to avoid allergies. We see an allergist at least once a year. I have a deep celebrated faith and take my children to church as much as I can.

My faith in God, I believe, is what gets me through the tough times. My husband does not celebrate his faith as much as I do. I believe he comes from the traditional side that thinks we are somehow being punished. I choose to dwell on the positive and thank God for blessing us with two intelligent, healthy, and strong children who have overcome many obstacles in their young lives. I thank my family for instilling in me a love of my culture but allowing me to "be me" and develop my own beliefs. My children both enjoy Spanish food and hearing about crazy stories passed down from their great-grandparents.

guayabera

Another conflict in balancing dual-cultural child-rearing practices is having family members requiring me to dress my son with a *guayabera*. I have to say, that look never appealed to me. I prefer him with jeans and sneakers and some kind of punky tee-shirt. Family members would also like me to see my daughter with braids and poofy dresses. I think her wild hair and mini-skirts suit her personality better. I do, however, value our cultural value about education. Education was always a topic of conversation when all of the generations were together. Nothing was lost in translation. I will stress the value of education to both of my children. I also expect them to value our extended family with lots of "tios" (uncles) and "titis" (aunties) just as much as I did. I expect my son to defend his sister and vice versa. In the Latino tradition, we hope our children are always happy and feel loved forever. We want them to know about their heritage and pass it on to the next generation, but also have faith in God and know that He will never punish us. Home remedies are okay, but I much rather they respect the opinions of doctors. But I would love for them to keep their Puerto Rican values and traditions, such as food, education, and speaking up for themselves.

Mariana Souto-Manning: A Brazilian Reflection
A Young Latino-American Child and His Family Negotiate Home and School Borderlands

Before I ever became a mother, I decided that my child(ren) would be bilingual. I immigrated to the United States as an adult, yet most of my family remains in Brazil. In addition to knowing the advantages of being bilingual in a larger way (e.g., in terms of developing cognitive flexibility), I was committed to teaching my children about their roots and fostering relationships between them and my Brazilian relatives. To do so, they would have to experience Brazilian culture and language—to be able to communicate and develop relationships with family in Brazil. When I made this commitment, I never imagined how hard it would be, at least initially.

I had become accustomed to hearing about how children should speak English only or they would be disadvantaged one way or another (Souto-Manning, 2006). The hardest part of this journey was to negotiate my bilingual commitment against so-called "best practices," which rapidly became ingrained in my own child's beliefs, narratives, and practices as he began to attend preschool. Without crossing the physical borderlands that delineate a country's territory, my own child had to learn how to negotiate crossing borders day in and day out, in terms of both culture and language, as he ventured between school and home contexts.

When my oldest child (who is now 6) first entered preschool, he quickly noticed that he was different. Most of the other children in his class were white and monolingual. He was bilingual and had olive-colored skin, heritage from his mother's Brazilianess. At age 2, without explicit prompting from his teacher, he protested against speaking Portuguese. He protested when his mother took him to school. He wanted his white, American father to do so. He wanted to fit in, and so he reacted to daily border crossings with cries and screams upon hearing any Portuguese being spoken.

At such a young age, Lucas had to navigate a complex journey of crossing the borderlands that separated home and school cultural and linguistic practices. These cultural practices often appeared conflicting. As he did not hear Portuguese spoken in his classroom nor see Brazilian cultural values being lived there, he decided these were wrong and undesirable (as he often expressed). He fought to eliminate them. He would yell, cry, and scream at the first sound of Portuguese. He would inform his Brazilian mother that he should feed himself and put his clothes on without her assistance. In Brazil, however, young children learn these skills somewhat later. He forcefully and repeatedly sought to refute Brazilian language and culture.

But Lucas was not the only one voicing this message. As a Brazilian immigrant and Lucas's mother, I heard from many people how my child (who did not utter a combination of two words until 22 months) was delayed because of Portuguese. I was, again and again, given the message that what I was doing was wrong and inappropriate, that Portuguese was a malady that would weaken his ability to speak English and grow academically. I heard from a special education teacher that if I were to speak Portuguese to him, he would end up in special education (Souto-Manning, 2006).

In school, Lucas was deemed developmentally delayed because he could not feed himself and perform other behaviors deemed age-appropriate according to (mono)culturally situated assessments, such as the Denver Developmental Screening Test and the Ages and Stages Questionnaire. I was told, over and over, that he needed to feed himself independently, to dress himself independently, and to perform other behaviors independently. I was never asked how this fit within my cultural background. It didn't. I was raised to believe that interdependence is better than independence—that helping each other is better than being better than someone, and that young children should be dependent on their mothers.

Throughout Lucas's early preschool years (birth through 3), I was told that I needed to work on certain skills with him so that he would not fall behind. Nowhere was it recognized that some of these very skills went against Brazilian cultural practices (e.g., independence vs. interdependence). The developmentally appropriate practice (DAP) (Bredekamp & Copple, 1997) guide was honored over my background, my upbringing, my cultural practices (Souto-Manning, 2009a). In no way was the DAP guide acknowledged as a culturally situated set of practices (Genishi & Goodwin, 2008). If we are to foster children's development in early education, teachers need to recognize the cultural nature of development (Rogoff, 2003). They need to know that in Brazil, children learn cursive writing in kindergarten and not in 3rd grade, for example. In India, for example, children learn the abstract concepts of left and right much earlier than in the United States (Rogoff, 2003). Culture determines the way that children develop. Obviously, each family is unique and culture manifests itself in particular ways. So, learning from families in order to educate young ones is essential.

I will never forget the day in which Lucas's preschool teacher told me proudly that he was self-feeding. It was not a skill I valued at a young age. I wanted (as my mother had done) to feed him as I developed a close mother-child bond. To me, the concept of familism, which is so common in Latino cultures, was being crushed in the name of independence. I kept hearing "best practice" for this, "best practice" for that, and started asking myself, "best practice" for whom? It was obvious to me that these "best practices" were not best for Brazilian culture and language.

Nevertheless, the message I was being given was so strong that I started wavering and doubting my own judgment. Was I doing the best thing by putting my child through such an ordeal? I was being told from so many sides that he needed to assimilate, that to succeed, he needed to embody American ways of knowing, that even as a professional educator I started doubting my own beliefs. This is reflected in many of my journal entries in which I questioned my own beliefs and practices.

Despite some insecurity regarding those "best" practices, I knew that it was best for Lucas to speak Portuguese. I had been speaking Portuguese and English with him for all of his life and he was able to speak both. For a period of six months to a year, Lucas refused to speak Portuguese, and responded by ignoring me, yelling at me, or even, at times, throwing things at me. While this was painful—and I wondered if this resolve would affect my relationship with my child, long-term—I decided to continue speaking Portuguese with him as well as English. Giving up Portuguese would be akin to severing relationships with half of his family, not being able to speak with his grandmother, uncles, and many others who loved him dearly. I stuck with my decision. It was not easy. I was met with much protest, with much anger.

After what now seems to have been a short period (yet which seemed to last forever when I was immersed in it), Lucas slowly stopped protesting. Initially, my bids in Portuguese were met with English responses and acknowledgments. Then, as time went by, Lucas started speaking Portuguese with me and with my Brazilian family members. Obviously, he sees more of an authentic need to speak Portuguese with people like his grandmother, who does not speak English.

Lucas started understanding that even though school and home might seem like different worlds, he did not need to choose one or the other (Souto-Manning, 2009b). He could and would continue to cross borders each day as he went from home to school and school to home. Together, we negotiated ways to engage in a second border crossing. This border crossing was much longer and more recursive than the first one—when I came into the United States. It happens every day, and many days, several times each day, as Lucas negotiates his home and school contexts.

Lucas is now 6 years old and is in kindergarten in a public school. In his class, multiple languages are valued. He now understands speaking another language in terms of strengths. He knows that everyone is unique and that speaking many languages is special. He is proud of his bilingualism and is striving to become trilingual as he plays with Spanish-speaking peers. Furthermore, Lucas has developed in terms of his "measurable" language and cognitive development, as measured by standardized test scores. We recently received notice that Lucas scored very high on these standardized tests and qualified to receive gifted services in five areas—including oral and written language. At the same time that Lucas's academic and verbal development is valued in school, he continues honoring concepts that are dear to my home culture (Souto-Manning, 2009a), such as familism and interdependence. In terms of language, he engages in long virtual visits in Portuguese at least once a week, in addition to now initiating talk in Portuguese with me, with his father, and with his younger brother.

Reflecting back on this second border crossing, which was much rougher in the beginning, I realize that we finally found routes that would not lead us to strain ourselves. I must challenge the idea of "best practices" and "developmentally appropriate practices," as they are (mono)culturally situated and promote processes of subtraction and erasure (Valenzuela, 1999) in children from immigrant families, in children from families like my own.

References

Bredekamp, S., & Copple, C. (Eds.). (1997). *Developmentally appropriate practice in early childhood programs* (Rev. ed.). Washington, DC: National Association for the Education of Young Children.

Genishi, C., & Goodwin, A. L. (Eds.). (2008). *Diversities in early childhood education: Rethinking and doing.* New York, NY: Routledge.

Rogoff, B. (2003). *The cultural nature of human development.* New York, NY: Oxford University Press.

Souto-Manning, M. (2006). A critical look at bilingualism discourse in public schools: Auto/ethnographic reflections of a vulnerable observer. *Bilingual Research Journal, 29*(2), 439-458.

Souto-Manning, M. (2009a). Educating Latino children: International perspectives and values in early education. *Childhood Education, 85*, 182-186.

Souto-Manning, M. (2009b). Syncretic home literacies: Learning to read in two languages and three worlds. In G. Li (Ed.), *Multicultural families, home literacies, and mainstream schooling.* Charlotte, NC: Information Age Publishing.

Valenzuela, A. (1999). *Subtractive schooling: U.S.-Mexican youth and the politics of caring.* Albany, NY: State University of New York Press.

An Ecuadorian Mother's Experience: Myriam Rogers

What you are about to read is something that I've been wanting to put together for a while now. It's a story of struggle, joy, love, and luck. This is the story of my life.

I begin my story at the age of 25. That was when I found out that I would be leaving my country for the first time in my life. After 25 years in Ecuador, living in a very close-knit family as the youngest of 10 children, this was my first opportunity to branch out on my own. I was fortunate enough to get a scholarship to study in New York and Chicago, two of America's greatest cities! You could imagine my elation over this amazing opportunity to study in the States for a year! This was eventually replaced with feelings of disappointment and discouragement when it ended up being a bad experience for me. My living experiences with people that I didn't understand or have anything in common with, coupled with the coldest weather I've ever been subjected to in my entire life, didn't allow for many good memories of my stay in America. When the year was over, I could hardly wait to go back to my country. I guess it's fair to say that I definitely went back with a sour taste in my mouth. I knew that I would never return. As far as I was concerned, there was nothing in the States that called for my attention and I didn't have the slightest desire to return.

How wrong I was. Destiny definitely had a different plan for me. When I was back in Ecuador, and was working with the Peace Corps in Quito teaching Spanish to American volunteers, I met someone. His name was Dick and he was a Texan who was very easy to talk with and even easier to get along with. As much as I tried to deny it or ignore it, I couldn't help recognizing that we connected in a certain way. My feelings of denial all stemmed from the fact that he was American, which doesn't seem fair, but if you were in my shoes the year that I studied in the States, you'd understand. We met in October. He asked me out in December, and we dated over the course of four or five weekends. It was hard to see each other because he was living 8 hours from Quito, where I lived and worked. In the end, feelings got the better of me and we got married on February 14th.

Our plan was to move in together after our civil ceremony and have the real wedding that summer so that his family could be a part of it. My family, especially my mom, disagreed completely with moving in together and postponing the real wedding and said, "Everything or nothing." Dick's response was "everything," so we made all the arrangements in 10 days and got married in February.

We lived in Quito while he completed his two years with the Peace Corps and during that time, we had our first daughter. We moved to Texas with our 7-month-old daughter and soon after our return, we found out that we were pregnant again! Only this time we were expecting not one child, but two! We were having twins! I learned the word "twins" that day during my visit to the doctor. I was happy, sad, worried, and happy again; we went home crying with a mixture of feelings, happy and sad, content and concern. Dick still was looking for a job and since my condition was pre-existing, we knew that our babies and I would not be covered by the insurance.

When we were making plans to move back to the United States, I was excited about all of the opportunities that were waiting for me. I was told that my Spanish would open doors for me and that I'd be so overwhelmed with job offers, that I'd have a hard time choosing one. Well, reality was a little different! I came to the States pregnant with twins and a 7-month-old baby, living in a completely new and foreign place to me. I quickly realized that finding a job was going to be a job in and of itself.

I always knew what I wanted to do with my life professionally. My career goals were never a question for me. I wanted to teach, plain and simple, and nothing was going to change my mind. Not even when I found out that it was going to take about 8 or 9 years for me to complete the classwork that would validate my degree and allow me to teach. I would like to add that I was already coming to the States with two teaching degrees from my country, so all of the coursework for the years to come were in addition to the two degrees I'd already earned.

Yes, it took me eight long years of taking night classes at several universities! This was a trying time for me because I was also working full time at a school in Houston, Texas, and at a magnet school in Maryland after we moved north. As you can imagine, my time was very limited. My lack of English was also a detriment as I studied and did every assigned project with my three daughters on the weekends. Some projects were more challenging than others, but each one was a new experience and required a different way of completing it.

Another requirement to validate my degree was to pass the entire NTE (National Teacher Examination), which was obviously only given in English. To prepare for the Listening and Comprehension part of the exam, I was going to have to be able to understand and repeat different conversations. Panic was what I felt, but I soon came up with the solution to my problem. Every morning on my long drive to work I would listen to different talk shows instead of music. After listening for a while, I would lower the volume and try to repeat what I'd just heard. Days, weeks, and even months went by filled with frustration because I understood almost everything, but I couldn't repeat it. The frustration I felt every morning became my motivation. One day I came home and as I was telling my husband some news I heard on the radio, I started to cry. My husband was surprised because the news was good so I shouldn't be crying. I explained to him that I was not crying because of the news, but because I was finally able to repeat what I'd heard on the radio. "Here comes victory!" I said as I moved one step closer to my dream of teaching.

Later on, I found out that my daughters used to hide the NTE envelopes because without understanding completely what was in the envelopes, they were cognizant enough to realize that each time I received one in the mail, I got sad. At times, my scores were less than one point below what was required to pass. It took a few tries, but I did it! I passed the tests and I became a teacher in the States!! The job was all mine. That same day, I received the most beautiful bouquet of roses and I felt on top of the world.

I could almost repeat the saying "It takes a village to teach a child." It took a whole family to make my dream a reality. For each project, I had a different idea. For each homework assignment, I needed help in different ways. My mother-in-law was also a teacher and she was a godsend. She would advise me and recommend books that she knew would be easier to read because, remember, my first language was Spanish and I had not yet learned English. That wasn't my top priority at the time! I had a house to run; I had babies to feed, read to, bathe, love; and I had a husband to take care of. My daughters were my students and my audience. My husband was my secretary and, remarkably, he did it without ever complaining! Dick gathered all my papers and made them look neat and professional. I don't know what I would've done without his help!

I look back on those days and I realize now how hard they were; at that time, however, it never occurred to me that I couldn't do it or that it would be close to impossible. Teaching was always my dream and I made it my reality every single day. This dedication and hard work has paid off through the years with professional accomplishments of winning grant awards, being nominated for teacher of the year in Montgomery County, being observed and videotaped by other professionals as an exemplary teacher in an immersion program, traveling to Spain to observe and offer guidance for an immersion program in Majorca, and running my own summer camp to teach 5- and 6-year-olds about the food and traditions of countries in South America.

I spent all of my free time with my family; I gave it all to my three daughters. I sewed for them; I read and read with them. We did almost everything together, but what I did the most was share with them my family stories. I always connected events, books, foods, etc., with them from my culture. I explained to them repeatedly why some things are different for me. I constantly asked for them to just try to understand my point of view. During their teenager years, this proved to be very difficult, because my beliefs and principles growing up were not always in line with the ones that their friends shared when they were growing up.

In 1992, I won a grant from the *Washington Post,* making a family trip back to Ecuador possible. I was able to immerse my children in my culture and was blessed with the opportunity to show them firsthand where I came from. They had the chance to see my family and my background and thankfully, little by little, they began to understand ME.

The sweetest part of this entire story of my life is that now, my three daughters are grown women and in each of them, they show a little bit of me. They like my food, they cook my food, they ask to hear my stories, and they want me in their lives. They celebrate who they are and I see that they are very proud of what they are and where they come from. They have embraced both cultures. A huge contributing factor is my husband, a very calm and patient man with good ears that are always ready to listen. He always gave his full support to all of my dreams, visions, and adventures. I always feel at ease knowing that, in his words, I am his partner for life and his favorite person to go anywhere and everywhere with.

That is the story of struggle, joy, love, and luck. Most of the struggles are behind me. Joy and love for my family and career are still my driving forces. I am lucky to have learned the cultures of two countries and, with a little more luck, my grandchildren will also get to hear my stories and taste the food of Ecuador.

Yahaira Caseres' Reflection: Raising my Second-generation Son in a Dominican American Household

My name is Yahaira Caseres. I am 27 years old. I am married and have a 2-year-old son. I was born in New York City, but raised in the South Bronx. My parents are both Dominican, so I consider myself a Dominican American or, as some say in the Dominican Republic, a Dominican York. I have a younger brother and an older half sister, who moved seven years ago to the United States. My family and I are very close. I come from two large families. From my mother's side, I have 11 aunts and uncles and 34 cousins. From my father's side, I have eight aunts and uncles and many more cousins. I am not sure how many cousins I have from my father's side of the family because they all live in the Dominican Republic, so I do not really know them. As for my mother's side of the family, most of us live near each other. We spend every holiday, birthday, and almost every weekend together. We are really close. My family reminds me of the family in the movie *My Big Fat Greek Wedding*. We are loud, we love to eat, we fight, we gossip; but most important, we love each other.

We use any excuse to have a party and dance. However, holidays are the best. My mother, aunts, and uncles cook a bunch of delicious food. For instance, on Thanksgiving, we have a roasted turkey, turkey stew (*pavo guisado*), chicken, and roasted pork shoulders (*pernil*). These are just the meats. There is so much food that most of us take some home for the next day. The older generation has spoiled my generation rotten. We never cook. One of us might do a salad, but that is it. Last Thanksgiving, I decided to surprise them and made a delicious pumpkin cornbread. The funny thing is that they did not believe I made it from scratch because I hate to cook and it was the first time I had ever brought anything. The ones that arrange every holiday, picnic, and so forth are my mother and my two aunts. They have become the head of the family since my grandmother passed away 11 years ago.

My grandfather is 93 years old. At parties, he dances all night and hits on women, which is kind of gross. However, he does keeps us laughing all of the time, even when he does not mean to. He is very old school, so he does not understand many of the things that are happening in the family. For example, he does not understand why my cousin is a lesbian, or another cousin is gay, or why a couple of us have tattoos and or piercings. Since he was born in 1914, we do not let his comments bother us.

One thing about coming from a large and close family like mine is that everyone knows your business. I feel that this is the same in most large families. Growing up, my aunts had every right to spank or punish me if I even rolled my eyes at them. My cousins and I were raised, not by one tough Dominican mother, but by seven. Although my mother was the one that would spank my brother and me, we were never too scared of her. We knew that if we misbehaved, my mother would spank us, but it never really hurt and it would be over in a minute. We would be back playing video games or watching television. Now, my father was very quiet. He never spanked us but we were terrified of him. If he told us to stop jumping, he only had to say it once.

I learned to speak English by watching *The Simpsons*. I learned to read and write in English when I was transferred from a bilingual class to a monolingual class in the 3rd grade. The teacher who taught me how to read and write was Ms. Thompson. She was a petite African American lady with thick glasses. She always wore pants and floral blouses. Ms. Thompson was a sweet lady with a soft, gentle, yet firm voice. I remember that she worked with me a lot, one-on-one, because I really needed it. The bilingual classes that I was in rarely gave English work. Thus, I do not understand why they called them bilingual. After I was transferred, I had a hard time with schoolwork at home. My parents did not know any English, so if my neighbor wasn't home to help me, I had to try to figure it out myself. My parents tried to stay as involved as they could. They helped me with math homework, never missed a parent-teacher conference, and assisted at a few school meetings. Eventually, they stopped going to the school meetings because they were always held in English. At the parent-teacher conferences, I often had to be a translator. The toughest thing was telling my mother any complaints that my teachers had about me. I remember thinking, maybe I should not tell her this part; but I was always too scared to lie.

By the time I reached the 4th grade, I knew how to read and write at grade level. However, since I still had a thick accent, my reading did not sound as good as other children's did. When I read aloud, the teacher would correct me frequently, which, ultimately, led me to hate reading aloud in front of the class. As I mispronounced words, other children would laugh at me. One time, even my 4th-grade teacher laughed at the way I pronounced "New York." I still remember feeling embarrassed and wanting to cry. I even asked my mother to change me back to a Spanish class. That experience made me not want to participate in class. Even when I knew the answer, I would never raise my hand. I did love to speak, read, and write in English, because it was still so new to me. I loved writing book reports. I could read to myself, write my report, and get a good grade, which, I felt, proved that I was smart.

Now, as an adult, I prefer to work on my own. I believe the reason why is because growing up, I worked at home by myself often. My brother had it a little easier than me. He had me at home to help him with any homework and to speak English to. Still unlike me, my brother was in bilingual class until the end of 8th grade. He can read, write, and speak Spanish perfectly. However, he does not read or write in English at the level of a high school graduate. So when he did go to college, he never went back after the first semester. His bilingual experience was like mine, with minimal work in English.

My way of raising my child is a bit different from my own upbringing, in that I do not spank my son. I don't believe in hitting my son because it does not solve anything. When I was a child, I used to prefer getting spanked than punished. However, like my parents, I will be involved in my child's education; I will attend the meetings, conferences, take and pick him up from school. I will try to instill in him the importance of family. My husband (who is a Dominican American like me) and I are also choosing to talk to my son in Spanish first. It is important to us that he learns the language of his culture. Overall, my experience has been great. I feel that I am the way I am today because of my strict parents, my close family, my education (the good and the bad), my neighborhood, and my culture.

Chapter 5: Reflections About Education

A Puerto Rican American Professor's Reflections: Diane Rodriguez

There are many challenges for Latino children and youth who have arrived to the United States without proper documentation for various reasons (e.g., quality of life, education, economics, politics, wars, etc.). For whatever reason these children arrived in the United States, we must ensure that they have an opportunity to succeed and excel in this country. Throughout my work in the Southeast, I have encountered many Latino students who are facing many challenges to move forward in obtaining a university or college degree. I believe that their stories must be heard. The following are a few selected stories:

Silent Voice

My name is José. I arrived to this country five years ago, full of hopes and dreams: hopes that were turning into dreams; dreams that were limited. Some of them are still reachable and some are almost untouchable. When I arrived to this country, everything was really hard, especially the learning of a new language. When I entered the United States, I also entered a new world. Everything was different and I felt like a stranger. Most of the time, I have had somebody that supported me. I have received a lot of support from my teachers. They support everyone in every moment, but especially if you are in the process of learning English. Most of them understand that this learning process is difficult enough for a grown person, let alone a young student who is being placed in a classroom where everything is new and in a different language. After a few years, I started to adapt to this country. Now I know more people and I am still learning the language as I go. I understand that learning a second language is a lifetime process, but I am patient. I am more confident now about how the language is used and how I can use it and benefit from knowing it, at school, at work, and in social situations. One of my biggest dreams is to be a registered nurse. I want to be a nurse because I really love to help other people. Helping others gives me a special sensation and feeling that is hard to describe. It is a sensation that is hard to forget. My plan to make this dream a reality is by going to a university and getting my degree, but there are some walls that are impeding my dream. These walls are difficult to climb, but I know that with the help of people who care about our dreams and hopes, we will be able to overcome this impediment. Again, we are receiving all the help we can get from our teachers now, but we need somebody in the government that could represent us and our dreams to become better citizens in order to help a growing community that will, in turn, help this country.

Reflection of Tim Cintron, Schoolteacher

In May 2008, the North Carolina Community College System (NCCCS) stopped admitting undocumented immigrants into degree-seeking programs. The NCCCS will still allow high school students to take community college classes and adults to take non-college level courses, such as GED, English as a second language, and continuing education classes. Prior to this decision, all 58 community colleges in the system admitted undocumented aliens, but charged these students the out-of-state tuition rate. Currently, there are no federal or state laws that prohibit admission of undocumented immigrants to U.S. colleges and universities. Nor does federal or state law require students to prove citizenship to enter higher education institutions. However, policies on admitting undocumented students vary from state to state.

One must begin to think how unfair this act is to anyone who wants to better themselves through education, no matter their status in this country. Is it truly a student's fault that they were brought to the United States without authorization as a child? Not only do undocumented immigrants contribute to society, but they also contribute to the tax revenue of the state, which funds the community colleges of the state. The Department of Homeland Security does not deem any federal laws to prohibit the admission of undocumented students into public educational institutions. Even with this information, the North Carolina Community College System continues to keep its doors closed.

Federal law guarantees public education for all students in grades K-12 regardless of immigration status, so wouldn't the state of North Carolina want to further the education of its high school graduates? Do we want a population where everyone has the right to an education? Or do we want to close that option off and only make it available to certain people?

My learning includes the following steps: 1) I assumed anyone could attend a community college and seek a degree, especially high school graduates; 2) I recognize my bias of being an advocate of all students, no matter their citizenship status; and 3) I recognize my bias, being of Hispanic heritage with parents whose first language is not English.

While studying how to teach culturally diverse learners, I have learned that it is necessary to give them the confidence that they can become language proficient. But also they can achieve higher education and contribute to society by being a college graduate in whatever field they choose. Well, the state of North Carolina is surely squashing the validity of this assumption and the drive to succeed of many middle and high school students who are considered unauthorized immigrants. Even though it was only eight months ago that the NCCCS made this decision, it has already affected teachers in North Carolina trying to engage and motivate the students who see no point in trying to excel, with no light at the end of the tunnel of their hard work. I also take this action personally since it impacts mainly Hispanics, who have greatly increased their numbers in North Carolina and its public schools. These undocumented children are receiving an education, making them an unused investment of the citizens and the state of North Carolina.

This new policy of the NCCCS—of not accepting undocumented immigrants—has made my job of teaching CLD students even more difficult than it was before. Being a teacher in rural North Carolina for nearly three years, I have often worked very hard to advocate that education will help students achieve goals and dreams. How can a teacher tell a student, "Work hard so you can get ready for college"? I personally have been told twice this school year by two undocumented immigrant students, "What is the point? I can't go to college." This makes the issue very evident in the immigrant community, even though this policy was just announced less than nine months ago. Not only does this issue affect students who have not performed well enough academically to gain university acceptance, this issue hits harder when the cost of attending a college or university is the main reason why a student will begin their higher education at a community college.

In regards to personal growth, this issue has enlightened me on the true reality facing immigrants in certain regions of the United States. It also has driven me to advocate for education to all regardless of citizenship status, similar to what No Child Left Behind has preached for nearly eight years. While researching this issue, it became apparent that I must become more informed, locally and nationally, on the treatment of immigrants, whether documented or not. For example, when dealing with children's education, especially when they did not make the decision to immigrate to the United States. This act of NCCCS has caused us to not just think or just talk about joining an advocacy group or groups, but to actually join and participate in an advocacy group. One such group is El Pueblo, which is a North Carolina advocacy and public policy organization dedicated to strengthening the Latino community.

Now that I have taken the steps to truly advocate beyond my classroom, I still cannot forget about the students that I always have advocated for. But now more than ever, I need to continue to inform immigrant students about the benefits of pursuing higher education and that these policies of the NCCCS will change, that there are real people who are working toward removing these barriers. These changes will come through advocacy and community education. But I also will continue to remind students that education will help them achieve goals and dreams.

Background

In North Carolina, 3,100 Latinos accounted for 1.7% of the 183,000 students enrolled at the state's public universities in 2003-2004 (Roach, 2004). While the magnitude of this difference alone is noteworthy, the inequity is alarming because the stakes are so high and the prospects for change rather bleak. A lack of education among people from culturally diverse backgrounds diminishes their social and economic status (Castellanos & Jones, 2003). According to Wainer (2002), "Given the Latino immigrants' and the children of immigrants' alienation from school, the financial barriers to college, and the lure of immediate income from manual labor jobs, many are opting for low-skill professions with little hope of career advancement and further education" (p. 13). What is the likelihood that educational opportunities for Latinos will improve? Although that is an open question, change does not appear to be imminent because educators in southern school districts are not currently prepared to address the demographic changes in their student populations (O'Neal, Ringler, & Rodriguez, 2008; Wainer, 2002).

Educating the Next Generation of Latino Students

As students become more experienced, they begin to pose questions and comment critically about issues. In essence, they socially negotiate the meaning of complex issues. As learners come to understand their universe, they benefit immensely from reflection and cooperative learning. There are many questions that remain without answers. Are we aligning student characteristics, particularly their language and culture, with academic achievement? Are we promoting equal access to all Latino children and youth to a quality education? Are we providing our Latino students with the necessary tools to enter institutions of higher education? There is immense work to be done on behalf of our Latino children and youth. Let's start the commitment to ensure quality education for all.

References

Castellanos, J., & Jones, L. (2003). *The majority in the minority: Expanding the representation of Latina/o faculty, administrators and students in higher education.* Sterling, VA: Stylus Publishing.

O'Neal, D. D., Ringler, M., & Rodriguez, D. (2008). Teachers' perceptions of their preparation for teaching linguistically and culturally diverse learners in rural eastern North Carolina. *Rural Educator,* 5-13.

Roach, R. (2004). Surging in the southeast: NC HBCUs expected to play significant role in facilitating college access for the increasing Latino population in the region. *Black Issues in Higher Education, 21*(16), 32-34.

Wainer, A. (2002). *The new Latino south and the challenge to public education.* Claremont, CA: The Tomas Rivera Policy Institute.

Cecilia M. Espinosa's Reflection
On Language and Culture: Becoming a Bilingual Teacher

"Cuando alguien con la autoridad de un maestro describe tu mundo y tú no estas en este, hay un momento de desequilibrio psicológico. Es como si tu te mirarías en un espejo y no vieras nada." (Adrianne Rich) ("When someone with the authority of a teacher describes your world and you are not in it, there is a moment of psychological disequilibrium. It is as if you were looking at yourself in the mirror and you couldn't see a thing.")

An important aspect of my work as a teacher educator is to help prepare bilingual/biliterate teachers. Most of the teachers/prospective teachers who come to this course have a Latino background. Many were raised in the Dominican Republic, Puerto Rico, Peru, Ecuador, El Salvador, and Mexico. These were teachers who came to the United States later during their adolescent years or as young adults. Others were raised in the United States (New York, Arizona, New Mexico, Connecticut, California, etc.), but for many of them, their parents are immigrants to the United States, and as a result often spent their childhoods going back and forth between two countries, and consequently grew up in bilingual/biliterate households. Each semester, I find that they come to my biliteracy class filled with questions about how to best support emergent bilingual children in school. Given the current mandates of the NCLB law, many of them feel the daily pressures of extreme accountability and the narrowing of the curriculum. Some of them teach in settings where being bilingual/biliterate isn't necessarily considered a strength. My goals for this course are to help them see that it matters tremendously that children have opportunities to see themselves reflected in the curriculum. I want them, for example, to examine the role of the native language in biliteracy development. My aim is to help them develop a pedagogy that acknowledges that all children come to their classes with a tremendous amount of "funds of knowledge" (Mercado, 2005; Moll et al., 1992). I want them to consider seriously the idea that as bilingual teachers, our job is to build on the strengths bilingual children bring with them (Carini, 2001). I strongly believe that given this era of accountability, standardization, and monolingualism, such a stance becomes a much-needed pedagogy of resistance.

We begin this process by examining our own life stories about our experiences with different educational settings as speakers of a language other than English. My purpose is to help them reflect individually and collectively on what it was like for them to enter a new culture, a new language, new ways of thinking. For this assignment, the students receive a set of questions that lead them to write a reflective piece in narrative form. The students are asked to share this assignment in class the following week. On one of these days, Rosa, one of the teachers/prospective teachers, shared an excerpt of her piece in class:

> "Reading poetry in Spanish helped me get a better sense of who I am. I don't ever want the children in my class to feel like I did. I don't want them to feel that speaking two languages and having two cultures was something bad. They need to be proud of and love their culture, their history, who they are, who their ancestors were, who they will become. I was embarrassed of who I was and what I brought to school when I was young. I don't want them to ever give up this strength that they have now. I don't want them to have to wait until college to hear stories that strengthen their sense of identity. I became a bilingual teacher to help kids see their culture and who they are. Teaching in a dual-language setting has been very empowering for me as a teacher. I have been able to search back into my culture, to find literature I could bring into my class that reflects who the children are. I think it has been positive for all of us to learn in two languages. We should never sacrifice one language at the expense of the other. Now I know how important it is for me to share my life and the literature of my people with my students."

As Rosa shared her reflective entry in class, many others also commented on the difficulties they had when entering school and experienced "learning" in a language they could hardly understand. Adriana, another student, shared her feelings of embarrassment and humiliation because although she was already 10 years old, she was sent back to a 1st-grade class in spite of the fact that she was already a reader and writer in her native language. In the eyes of the teachers and school administrators, she wasn't ready to be with her age-mates because she didn't know any English. No one took the time to find out what she knew in her native language. It took many months for her to be moved to another grade level. For Adriana, this is still a very painful memory. As the other students share similar experiences, we begin to unpack the importance of developing literacy in the children's native language.

As the weeks go by, we continue the conversation regarding the importance of learning to read and write in one's native language through academic readings, classroom discussions, and experiences in the field. These help us strengthen our "theoretical" stance. We learn, for example, that children come to school having learned their communities' and families' ways of using language. These might differ from the school's ways of using language (Au, 1993; Gee, 1996; Heath, 1983). We learn that if language is a major vehicle for content learning (Lemke, 1990), then "What students talk, read, and write about matters" (Faltis & Hudelson, 1998, p. 101). We also learn that research shows there is ample evidence that it is easier to learn to read and write in a language one understands; and that what one learns about reading and writing in one language can be transferred to the second language (Edelsky, 1982, 1986; Freeman & Freeman, 2006; Hudelson, 1987, 2000). We also learn that as teachers, we can be proactive in developing an environment that supports bilingualism/biliteracy (Genesee, 2008; Jones & Lorenzo-Hubert, 2008).

In order to connect the power of our own personal stories with those from a larger community of writers, we read from the work of Judith Ortiz Cofer (1996), *An Island Like You*, and Sandra Cisneros, *The House on Mango Street* (1994/2006) and *Woman Hollering Creek and Other Stories* (1991). During one of our classroom discussions of Cofer's short story "*Una Hora con el Abuelo* / An Hour With Abuelo," Lina, one of the teachers, shared with us that this was the first time she read a story in which she could see images of herself reflected in the story. Her eyes filled with tears as she shared her experience. She said, "Now I understand why children need to hear stories that reflect who they are. In reading this story, I was able to travel back to Puerto Rico. I could see the streets, the buildings, the people."

As the weeks unfold, we begin our journey of examining children's literature in which Hispanics/Latinos are depicted. In doing this, we take McCarthy's (1998) position that culture isn't static; it is always shifting. In our search for relevant stories, we look, for example, for children's stories that are a "reply" to the official story or that, in some ways, fill in the missing gaps of the official story from multiple perspectives: females, children, immigrant families, etc. According to McCarthy, it is critical that we as educators challenge ourselves to understand the perspective of the world "through the gaze of the subaltern" (p. 156). We bring to share in class such books as: *La Mariposa* (1998) by Jimenez, *America Is Her Name* (1997) by Rodriguez, *Tomas and the Library Lady* (2000) by Mora, *The Rainbow Tulip* by Mora, (1999), *The Red Comb* (1998) by Pico, *My Name Is Jorge on Both Sides of the River* (1999) by Medina, etc. We read aloud many of these stories. In our discussions, we talk about the ways in which these stories challenge the stereotypical images that often appear about Latinos in the media. I also ask them to study the collection of books available in their classroom libraries. Do they represent the diversity of the Latino experience (Gangi, 2008)? My purpose in having these conversations with the students is to help them see that we can be very purposeful and proactive about the stories we choose to share in class.

As teachers, we have the power to position the mirror children see of themselves in strategic ways (McCarty & Watahomigie, 1998). It matters that as bilingual teachers, we take the time to reflect on our own life experiences, and that we strive to present to the children we work with stories that can assert who they are and what they bring, while at the same time help them envision new possibilities of what it means to become bilingual/biliterate.

References

Au, K. (1993). *Literacy instruction in multicultural settings.* Ft. Worth, TX: Harcourt Brace, Jovanovich.

Carini, P. (2001). *Starting strong: A different look at children, schools, and standards.* New York, NY: Teachers College Press.

Cisneros, S. (1991). *Woman hollering creek and other stories.* New York, NY: Random House.

Cisneros, S. (2006). *The house on Mango Street.* New York, NY: Alfred A. Knopf. (Original work published 1994)

Cofer, J. O. (1996). *An island like you: Stories of the barrio.* New York, NY: Puffin Books.

Edelsky, C. (1982). Writing in a bilingual program: The relation of L1 and L2 texts. *TESOL Quarterly, 16,* 211-228.

Edelsky, C. (1986). *Writing in a bilingual program: Habia una vez.* Norwood, NJ: Ablex Publishing.

Faltis, C., & Hudelson, S. (1998). *Bilingual education in elementary and secondary school communities: Toward understanding and caring.* Boston, MA: Allyn & Bacon.

Freeman, Y., & Freeman, D. (2006). *Teaching reading and writing in Spanish and English.* Portsmouth, NH: Heinemann.

Gangi, J. M. (2008). The unbearable whiteness of literacy instruction: Realizing the implications of the proficient reader research. *Multicultural Review, 17*(1), 30-35.

Gee, J. P. (1996). *Social linguistics and literacies: Ideology in discourses.* London, England: Routledge-Falmer.

Genesee, F. (2008). Early dual language learning. *Zero to Three,* 17-23.

Heath, S. (1993). *Ways with words.* New York, NY: Cambridge University Press.

Hudelson, S. (1987). The role of native language literacy in the education of language

minority children. *Language Arts, 64*, 827-841.
Hudelson, S. J. (2000). Developing a framework for writing in dual language settings. In J. Villamil Tinajero & R. A. DeVillar (Eds.), *The power of two languages.* New York, NY: McGraw-Hill.
Jimenez, F. (1998). *La mariposa.* New York, NY: Houghton Mifflin.
Jones, W., & Lorenzo-Hubert, I. (2008). The relationship between language and culture. *Zero to Three,* 11-16.
Lemke, J. (1990). *Talking science: Language, learning, and values.* New York, NY: Ablex.
McCarthy, C. (1998). *The uses of culture.* New York, NY: Routledge.
McCarty, T. L., & Watahomigie, L. J. (1998). Language and literacy in American Indian and Alaskan native communities. In B. Pérez (Ed.), *Sociocultural contexts of language and literacy* (pp. 69-98). Mahwah, NJ: Lawrence Erlbaum.
Medina, J. (1999). *My name is Jorge on both sides of the river.* Honesdale, PA: Wordsong/ Boyds Mills Press.
Mercado, C. (2005). Seeing what's there: Language and literacy funds of knowledge in New York Puerto Rican homes. In A. C. Zentella (Ed.), *Building on strength: Language and literacy in Latino families and communites* (pp. 134-147). New York, NY: Teachers College Press.
Moll, L., Amanti, C., Neff, D., & González, N. (1992). Funds of knowledge for teaching: Using a qualitative approach to connect homes and classrooms. *Theory Into Practice, 31*, 132-141.
Mora, P. (1999). *The rainbow tulip.* New York, NY: Viking.
Mora, P. (2000). *Tomas and the library lady.* New York, NY: Alfred A. Knopf.
Pico, F. (1994). *The red comb.* Mahwah, NJ: Bridgewater Books.
Rodriguez, L. (1997). *America is her name.* Willimantic, CT: Curbstone Press.

A Dual-Language Teacher: Maren Roedenbeck's Story

I am a 2nd-grade teacher in Florida. I am very proud to say that I work at a school that follows a dual language program. That means that our students receive instruction in two languages—in our case, English and Spanish. From the moment that students enter our school for kindergarten, they have two teachers: they spend half the day with one teacher learning in one language, and the other half of the day with another teacher learning in a second language. They receive instruction in reading, language arts, science, and math in English, and reading, language arts, and social studies in Spanish. When I was first hired as a teacher, I was told I would do the Spanish portion of the day or, if there were an odd number of classes, I would be self-contained, which meant I would teach both portions of the day. My students would not switch classrooms, only languages. As I drove home, I thought of my father and how he always insisted I maintain my home language, Spanish.

I was born in Lima, Peru, but moved to the United States when I was 8 years old. My family left Peru in March, which was the beginning of the school year in there. We had spent the summer at the beach. It would be the last summer we spent in Peru. When we arrived in Miami, my sisters and I were ready to start school. The only problem was that schools in Miami did not follow the same schedule. They were ending the school year, not beginning it. My parents had a choice: we could start school and repeat the grade (because we would only have had two months in school), or skip the next few months and start in September.

My sisters and I did not start school right away. Instead, we went to summer camp to start practicing our English. We also spent a lot of time with our cousins, who were born in the United States, so they always spoke in English.

I don't remember learning to speak English. I can't remember when I spoke Spanish exclusively, but I know I did because I went to school in Peru. I was there until 2nd grade. I do remember, in camp, being asked if I wanted watermelon, but I didn't know what that was. They tried to translate, but it did not help until I saw the fruit. In school that September, I started 3rd grade (luckily, back then, there was not the pressure that there is now). I attended ESOL in a small room. In my regular class I understood what was being said, but I did not speak in class. I even remember the teacher telling the other students that I did not understand what was being said. I only spent one year in ESOL because I started speaking in English soon after getting to Miami.

Growing up, I always spoke in English to my parents and they would answer in Spanish. This caused much concern for my parents. It was very important to them that my sisters and I maintain our home language. My father was especially adamant about this because of what happened to his family's home language. My great-grandfather immigrated to Peru from Europe. His work took him there from Germany before the First World War. When he settled in Peru he insisted that his children learn to speak German. My grandfather, who was born in Peru, hated being forced to learn and speak German. When he became a father, he did not force his children to learn German, so my father never learned the language. Although he could understand what was being said, he never became a fluent speaker. He understood how easily and quickly a language could be lost. He always regretted that he could not speak German and could not teach us to speak it.

My father would often speak to us at the dinner table about the importance of knowing languages. I was a kid, so although I heard what he said, I did not feel as strongly about language as he did or as I do now. For almost 20 years after coming to the United States, I spoke English to everyone, except to my grandmother, and even though I had learned to read in Spanish, I did not pick up a Spanish book at all.

When I was hired to work at Dr. Carlos J. Finlay Elementary, I was told I would be teaching the Spanish portion of the day. I was a little concerned and insecure about my ability to teach in Spanish because I had not read a book in Spanish in almost 20 years. But I also knew that I was able to read in Spanish and I felt that if I prepared by reading everything in advance, I could do it. Later, because of the number of students in 2nd grade, mine became a self-contained classroom. I taught in both English and Spanish.

I was and still am extremely pleased to work at a school where students learn in both languages. I am very proud and boast often of how our students learn in both languages from the time they are in kindergarten to the time they are in 5th grade. They leave Dr. Carlos Finlay Elementary speaking, reading, and writing in two languages. I cannot adequately express how delighted I am about that.

Of course, my 2nd-graders don't see the benefits of studying both languages and are not as enthusiastic about it as I am. I hear them when they talk to each other and know that they would rather speak in English all day long. Every time I make them speak in Spanish they do it, but usually give me a face beforehand. I completely understand how they feel because I felt that way once, too, and when I was their age, no one could make me understand how grateful I would be later in life that I could speak two languages.

The fact that my students don't understand how important it is yet doesn't keep me from trying to make them understand, just like it didn't stop my parents from trying to make me understand. I am satisfied with the fact that whether they appreciate it now or not, my students are gaining the base for a second language because they learn to read in two languages. I know from my own experience that once you learn to read in a language, you don't forget how to read it, even if you haven't read anything in that language in almost 20 years. Once you decide to start again, you can, and all you have to do to improve is practice. My students have that base, they know how to read, and even if they neglect one of the languages they speak now, they can easily regain it by picking up a book later in life.

Now that I have several nieces, the topic of language often comes up at family gatherings. My sisters, cousins, and I have lived longer in the United States than we lived in

Peru. We all consider English our stronger language. Still, we do not want the next generation of our family to lose the Spanish language. Our conversations revolve around what is the best way to ensure that we maintain the language. It may not be enough for us just to try to teach Spanish because most of our conversations are in English. Where we at least had our grandmother, whom we had to speak to in Spanish, my nieces don't really have that, since their grandmothers do speak and understand English. My real concern is that my generation will be the last in our family to speak Spanish. Only the future will tell.

Childhood Memories: Growing Up in a Mexican American Community

Sylvia Y. Sánchez

I was born in San Antonio, Texas, but most importantly, I was born into a family of Mexican heritage who lived in a poor, segregated barrio. My family has significantly influenced my current political world view as well as the personal and professional decisions I make every day. On a daily basis, I rely on their guidance and wisdom to make choices, even when I am not aware I am doing so. Is it possible to be so tightly linked to your family and to their history? I think it is. As an early childhood educator, I know so.

For most of my early childhood, I lived across the street from my grandparents. In other words, I lived across the street from the center of our family's universe. My grandparents' home was the center of a powerful centrifugal force that pulled us together and socialized us as a family. All of my aunts, uncles, and cousins lived no more than five miles away from where my grandparents lived. This closeness was significant to my upbringing and to the care I received as a child, but this proximity also gave me access to the power of their stories. I was the grandchild who was mesmerized when listening to their stories of survival as immigrants, as a family living in poverty, as workers on the picket line, and as members of a religious community that did not fit into the larger community. From their stories, I gathered an understanding of my history and heritage, how I was to contribute to the next generation, and why family is such a powerful source of strength.

From the time of my birth to the age of 6, I lived surrounded by a large, extended family. Because my father was in the military at the time, and my mother was the youngest in her family of 11, there was never a doubt in my grandparents' minds that the whole family was responsible for my mother and her two children. During those years, my mother attended school and went to work. During the day, I was primarily taken care of by my grandparents. Until I went to kindergarten, I do not believe I was ever out of sight of one of my family members. I never played with anyone outside of my family's backyard. Most of my playmates were family members or children of very close family friends who were considered like family members. We would call them tío/tía (uncle/aunt) out of respect, and also because we didn't know that they were not blood relatives. Most of these family friends were from the Mexican Presbyterian church, the other important socializing institution that influenced me as a young child and impacted my daily life.

From My Protestant View, Catholics Had All the Fun

As Protestants, our family stood out like sore thumbs in our predominantly Catholic Mexican community. When I was in elementary school, the children who were Catholic were taken out on Wednesday afternoon by nuns who came to the school to walk the children to catechism classes. Guess who was the one child left in the classroom? Early on, I was aware that my family did not fit in. During the school year, the local Catholic church had bingo events, dances, street pageants, festivals with lively music, and other fun activities. My church was founded by my grandparents. Their religious version of being Presbyterian was much more fundamentalist than the view of the English-speaking Presbyterian church. We were not allowed to dance, drink, smoke, or do any of the fun things Catholics did so openly. As a young girl, the dancing restriction was particularly perplexing. I remember asking my grandfather why the Presbyterian church did not allow dancing. His explanation left me even more confused. He said that dancing was evil because when you danced, you perspired, and the perspiration of the two dancers mixed. That was it. Needless to say, I did not buy it. I was a good dancer and enjoyed going to dances as a young girl. My grandfather never knew that, or so I thought.

Being Presbyterian made me a double religious minority. I was a religious minority in my predominantly Catholic Mexican American cultural community, and I was a cultural minority in the larger predominantly white and English-speaking Presbyterian denomination. As a family, we were Mexican Presbyterians because of my grandfather. He was converted while still living in Mexico. My grandmother told me that she was against this conversion and considered it heresy. She would burn any religious material my grandfather would bring home, especially the Bible, since she believed that only priests had the authority and understanding to read the Bible. In his gentle and patient way, he slowly converted her. When they immigrated to the United States during the Mexican Revolution, they settled in San Marcos, Texas, and joined the Mexican Presbyterian Church of San Marcos. This church was the first Mexican Presbyterian Church established by a U.S. Presbytery, but it was the second Spanish-speaking Presbyterian church in Texas. The first Spanish-speaking church was established in Brownsville, Texas, by missionaries from the Presbytery of Mexico. I always found this an interesting fact since most of us know about missionaries going to Latin American to convert and establish churches, but it was news for me to hear that Mexican missionaries crossed the U.S. border to convert those living in Texas. In 1908, the Texas-Mexican Presbytery was established with 17 Mexican Presbyterian churches and four ordained ministers, and it functioned for 50 years in Texas.

We attended church every Sunday with my grandparents. Most of the elders in the church were males and most were my uncles. I dutifully sat with my grandmother during the long service in Spanish. I think her main focus during that time was to make sure I did not sleep soundly through the whole service. She would pinch my arm to keep me awake. It was a struggle for me to keep from closing my eyes. However, because reading the Bible in Spanish was part of this experience, I acquired biliteracy skills at a very young age. Most of my third-generation friends spoke Spanish, but did not read it. I spoke and read formal complex Spanish language at a young age. I needed my Spanish literacy skills for a meaningful purpose; I had to read aloud in Spanish to my grandmother. She was illiterate and only spoke Spanish. She could never pass the citizenship exam. She struggled to learn to write her name. As I continued with my schooling, I was a source of pride for her, as were all her grandchildren. I knew early on that I had a role to play in the education of the next generation.

English-only Segregated Schools

As a child, not only did I attend segregated churches, I also attended segregated schools. I lived in a predominantly Mexican neighborhood. Among us lived a few black families and one or two white families. This was rare, since Texas was legally segregated at the time. We may have been neighbors, but when the school bell rang, we went our separate ways—blacks to their schools across town, whites to theirs also across town, and me to the Mexican school one block away. All the children in my elementary school were Spanish-speaking, poor, and of Mexican heritage. We were not allowed to speak in Spanish within the school property. At that time, it was against state law to speak any language other than English in a public building. Children violating this law in elementary school could suffer corporal punishment. I have a very vivid memory of a line of boys standing outside the principal's office, waiting to be spanked with a big wooden paddle. For most of the day, we were silenced either because of our fear of being caught and paddled, or because of being denied access to our home language, the only language we spoke. In essence, we were mute until around 4th grade, when we felt fully comfortable with using the English language. Until then, we spent our school days in a very quiet and oppressive classroom environment. All the teachers in the segregated Mexican schools I attended were white and spoke only English. This was different from the experience of children attending the segregated "Negro schools"; all their teachers were black and spoke the children's language. I did not have a teacher of Mexican heritage until I was in college. I knew early on that there was nothing wrong with my home language because it was the language of my family, community, and church. Their continued use of the home language permitted me to find pride in being bilingual even when the state and larger English-speaking society viewed it as a deficiency. Others were not as fortunate.

At a certain time in the year, large numbers of the children in my classroom disappeared. Their houses were boarded up and they left town. These children entered school after the beginning of the school year and left before the school year ended. The teachers never spoke about them. It was as if they were invisible and had never existed. They were simply gone from one day to the next. We had no idea what happened to them. It was years later when I was a high school student that I found out where they went for part of the year. I attended a Presbyterian high school and did volunteer work with children living in migrant labor camps in south Texas. It was through that experience that I finally figured out what happened to all those young children who disappeared every year in elementary school and, eventually, completely disappeared by dropping out before they reached secondary school. They were migrant children who, together with their families, followed the crops up north every year. Needless to say, out of the 20 or so children who started elementary school with me, I know of only five or six who graduated from high school. I know of one, other than me, who attended college. I remember my classmates' bright and eager-to-learn young faces. Our teachers could have made a positive difference in the lives of these children. Instead, in my school community, too many children and families suffered from oppressive linguistic policies and the benign neglect of their learning needs. As a teacher educator and a bilingual education specialist, I intentionally include the voices of disenfranchised communities into my university classroom. I am particularly haunted by the faces of the young boys waiting to be paddled for speaking the only language they knew. No child should have to be ashamed or hurt because of the language they speak. Although those restrictive language laws have been challenged in court, there is still strong opposition to speaking languages other than English in schools and in the general society. My personal experiences with linguistic oppression and poor, racially segregated schools have influenced me to advocate for more just and equitable treatment and schooling for language-minority children and their families, including migrant children.

Conclusion

Through my reflection on the stories shared here, I am cognizant that the love and security that I experienced in those early years when I was surrounded by many family members helped me face difficult circumstances later in life. The continuity of family care I experienced on a daily basis nurtured my development as a child, and also impacted my current perceptions of the role of family in the lives of young children. It affected how I define family. However, I am also keenly aware that being Protestant also influenced who I am today. The issue of being a cultural and religious minority resonates for me. I am willing to go against the grain on an issue because of this early experience. I do not hesitate to give a minority opinion or raise my voice in opposition to a perceived injustice. I think I embraced the word "protest" found in the word Protestant. In reflection, I think my family and church experience have helped me find my voice.

However, I also acknowledge that I gained much from the early biliteracy experiences that were part of the church practices. I benefited from being biliterate in very concrete ways throughout my life. Not only could I read in Spanish to my grandmother and, in a small way, demonstrate the respect she so rightly deserved as the matriarchal leader in our family, but in high school I was enrolled in a Spanish literature that was taught at the college level. I read many of the Spanish classics while in this class, which enriched my overall language and literacy skills and made me feel fully competent and capable to achieve more. As a doctoral student, I was awarded a fellowship to study in a prestigious university in Mexico. Again, without the strong biliteracy foundation, I could not have achieved and excelled academically. Although I am no longer as closely associated with an organized church as I was as a young child, I acknowledge that the role that a church family plays can be instrumental to the well-being of a vulnerable child. In conclusion, I may have been born to a poor family living in a poor community, but the rich experiences that my family and community provided helped me to survive and thrive. Both have been powerful forces in my life.

Interview With Dr. Ricardo R. Fernández, President of Lehman College of the City University of New York

"Supporting Latino youth in their quest for higher education"

Q: Do you feel there is a crisis in Latino education, and how does it parallel dilemmas faced by other groups? What policies/programs are in place that create a "college-going culture" to ensure success for Latino college-bound students? How early do these need to be in place—middle school? Elementary school? Preschool?

A: There is a trend whereby early childhood and childhood students are doing okay, but at middle schools they do worse. Programs like "GEAR UP"—Gaining Early Awareness and Readiness for Undergraduate Programs—provide the support needed in middle school through 12th grade. "GEAR UP" is a federally funded program designed to provide academic preparation programs and mentoring for students, as well as professional development activities for educators, and college access information for students and parents. Parents need to become a part of the support system to learn how they can help their children succeed.

Q: A national survey of Latinos by the Kaiser Family Foundation (2004) surveyed a representative sample of 3,421 adults. Findings included perceived reasons that Latino students are not doing as well as their peers. These include:

- Too many Latino parents neglect to push their kids to work hard (53%)
- The school is often too quick to label Latino kids as having behavior or learning problems (51%)
- Too many white teachers do not know how to deal with Latino kids because they come from different cultures (47%)

A: There is definitely a crisis. Latino high school students have the highest dropout rate. Here at Lehman College, there are more female students than male. They also have better retention rates on the undergraduate level. Of these women, Lehman has a higher rate of Latinas enrolled within the university. The City University of New York has developed a program for underprivileged undergraduate male students (African American and Latino) called the Black Male Initiative Urban Male Initiative Program, which helps African American and Latino males as well as other students. At Lehman, the program is called the Urban Male Leadership Program, but it also serves a number of female students. This program is available in New York State for City University of New York students at both community and senior colleges.

Another organization that offers support is the Hispanic Association of Colleges and

Universities (HACU). HACU is an advocacy organization aimed at promoting success for Hispanic students in higher education.

Q: It is a well-known fact the Latinos in urban areas have a high dropout rate in high school and college as well, especially at the four-year institutions. To what extent do you feel the Latino dropout problem at the college level is institutionalized?

A: Many students in higher education (about 40%) take 6 years to graduate from senior colleges. The average student takes 10-12 credits a semester at Lehman. Most students work part-time and attend school, thus making this the standard as a full load. Many stop attending ("stop out") for various reasons, such as a personal crisis or money issues. . . . There is a crisis in the schools and I am very surprised with the recent Kaiser Family Foundation study, which found that Latino parents neglect to push their kids to work hard (53%). On the contrary, I find that Latino parents always have high aspirations for their children. Keep in mind that in many cases, parents are not high school graduates themselves, and they have had a hard life where the opportunity to go to college was not available to them. The most prominent problem is that Latino parents cannot share with their children what needs to be done on the college level. I would recommend instituting a model outreach program for helping parents in these circumstances. The program should provide students and their parents with a concrete idea and experiences of what college is and entails. Programs could then prepare parents to become mentors for their children throughout their middle and high school years as they prepare for college.

Dr. Fernández also suggests another organization that he is affiliated with that provides support for parents: The Intercultural Development Research Association (IDRA) (wwww.idra.org). IDRA is a nonprofit organization committed to respecting the knowledge and skills of individuals and building upon the strengths of the students and parents in their schools. So once again, the key dynamic is creating a partnership between parents and the school to ensure success for their children.

Chapter 6: Special Education Stories

Maria's Reflection: Dominican Naturalized Citizen (translated)

As an immigrant in this country, it was very hard to advocate for my daughter. I could express my concerns over her language development. I did have an interpreter, but I felt that she was not saying what I was saying concerning my daughter's language development and her lack of attention. You know, as an immigrant you don't trust anyone, but I had to trust the interpreter to say my words and get help for my daughter. After a few months of meetings and translated sessions, my daughter did get services. They started first in Spanish and then changed to English. She's in the 4th grade now and receives her therapy in the classroom. I think she is okay, but the therapist and the school personnel feel that she needs more help.

Chapter 7: Reflections About Stereotypes

Juan Morales-Flores' Reflections: Self Perceptions About Stereotypes

I had worked as an elementary school teacher for three years in the Metropolitan Area in

Puerto Rico, from where I am originally, before moving to State College, Pennsylvania. Right at my arrival to State College, I applied and was accepted to the master's program in curriculum and instruction at the main campus of the Pennsylvania State University (PSU), located in that same town, State College. Immediately, I started looking for jobs to support myself. At the beginning of my first semester at PSU, I interviewed for and was offered a job at a child development center on campus. The center was a fantastic place in terms of their philosophy, practices, and procedures, in addition to the masterful lead and support provided by both the director and the assistant director of the center. I had room to grow.

Part of my tasks was to develop activities appropriate to the age group of my students, who were infants and toddlers. I was able to not only experience the information being studied in my courses in relation to child development and about curriculum and instruction in early childhood education, but also to learn through those experiences about the American culture. I learned about traditions, children's games, nursery rhymes, pop culture, etc. I was, in some aspects, experiencing for the first time what my students were also experiencing for their first time. We were learning together! Add to that situation the element of gender. I am a male. My gender, I feel, added a whole new dimension to my experience at the center, that of the administrators, colleagues/staff, but above all to the experiences of the children who were under our care, and their parents.

In that nurturing and supportive setting, I started to become aware of the reasons for which being a male Hispanic made every experience so different for me, my students, and perhaps, most of all, for their parents. The population at Penn State University was at that time (in the 1980s) overwhelmingly European American. It was very rare to see African Americans in town or on campus, and the number of other minorities was very small. I remember noticing mainly, in terms of minorities, people from Asian countries. I was a young male working in a child development center, and, in terms of my appearance, although I have light skin, I used to wear my hair in a big curly afro, and had a beard and mustache. Add to that a heavy Spanish accent, and you get the picture. The rest of the teachers at the center were European American females. The children at the center were all European American (mainly blond/light brown hair and light-colored eyes). There were two children from India (a boy and a girl) and a Chinese boy.

There is a particular experience that I will never be able to forget. Each head teacher at the child care center was assigned to be the primary caregiver for one of the infants. As a head teacher, I was assigned to take care of a healthy, beautiful, 6-month-old blond/blue-eyed boy who physically resembled his parents. The parents were originally from Central Pennsylvania, which is where the town of State College is located, and they had lived all their lives in the area. Part of my responsibilities was to greet the mother in the morning, when she brought her baby, her only child, to the center and to ease the transition. At the beginning of that morning routine, and for some time after, that I remember as being a bit too long, the boy would cry every morning as he was being given to me by his mother. As a result, the mother's eyes would get watery . . . with tears eventually rolling down her cheeks. Although I knew that this was (and continues to be) a common scene at day care centers and elementary schools all over the world, I could not help but think how this mother must have been feeling. She was leaving her only child with a young Hispanic male, with some of the physical characteristics of what has been associated, in this country, with being a rebel, a bohemian, or at times even a terrorist. Just thinking about how she must have been feeling made me, every morning, also teary-eyed (to say the least). At the end, the three of us were basically crying. The situation continued like this for some time. Eventually, the boy got used to being with me at the center. Perhaps, also, the trust of the mother in my ability for taking care of her child increased, and the crying disappeared. At times, it seemed to me that the mother was more upset when the crying stopped. The boy would make such a smooth transition, that it seemed like he did not "care" as much about her leaving.

During the periodic parent-teacher conferences, I got to share my observations about the child's developmental progress with the parents. It was not until after the first of these meetings that I felt assured that both of them were comfortable with me being their precious child's caregiver.

A Puerto Rican American's Reflection: Grace Ibanez-Friedman

I was about 15, and was with my father walking toward the boardwalk of Rockaway Beach in New York City where we were spending a few days of vacation time. The sun was very hot, and I was looking forward to joining my sisters and mother on the beach for the afternoon. For reasons I don't recall, my father and I paused and sat on one of the benches near the boardwalk. Out of the corner of my eye I saw a mother with a toddler. The mother had let go, and the child went tottering toward my direction. As she reached my bench, she began to trip forward. I immediately reached out to grab the child before she fell on the hard concrete. The mother came running and shouted out to me, "Don't touch her, I don't want her touched by a Puerto Rican." My father said nothing: my humiliation was complete.

Carlos Lopez Leiva: Realizations of My Own Skin

I was born in Guatemala. There, I am considered a "Ladino" or "Mestizo" (a mixture of European and Native American people). In the United States of America, I am considered Hispanic or Latino. The Latino population in the United States is just as diverse as in Latin America. The diversity in Latin America resides in the multiple combinations that have evolved over time by the mixture of different cultures, races, ethnic groups, and people. Thus, not all Latinos are Mestizos—some are Native American, some are African American, some are European American, and some are Asian American. By "American," I do not mean originally from the United States only, but from the Americas, the American continents; nonetheless, still many Latinos have been born in the United States. Simultaneously, this diversity is also reflected through languages, and many Latinas/os may be monolingual, bilingual, or speak more than two languages. Some may speak neither Spanish nor English, maybe K'iché—like in my hometown.

In Guatemala, there are 24 ethnic groups: 21 from Mayan descent, 1 from the Xinca indigenous group, 1 Garifuna, and 1 Ladino. Though not rich, I grew up in Quetzaltenango as part of the dominant society (i.e., "Ladinos"). I did not have a racialized experience and overt discrimination as many indigenous people do. As a child and a teenager during the 1980s, I witnessed the oppression experienced by my indigenous friends, who were often discriminated against based on either the way they spoke Spanish, dressed, smelled, or looked. I have to recognize that, as a child, I gave in to some of the "games" of joking and making fun of other kids in relation to race. I became aware of its consequences, little by little, through bonding with my indigenous friends. I learned to despise these stereotypes and discriminatory processes and wanted to stop them. But often people from the dominant group ("Ladinos") seemed more: more powerful and more self-confident. Under their racist actions, my friends simply acquiesced and looked down. I hated that silence. I knew there was something wrong about this, but it seemed that it was a regular everyday occurrence that just "happened," and at times I even unthinkingly agreed with the stereotypes.

As a teacher in the 1990s, I noticed similar patterns evolving among my students. At times these were not as overt, but eventually they became evident through conflicts among children. Despite my interventions to ameliorate these differences, they still remained. In light of the Civil War and the discussions concerning the peace agreements, I learned that much of these discrepancies were rooted in our history. Often, our history texts at school would portray the colonization process as a "civilizing" one rather than an invasion.

Over time, I learned that my students and I could engage in a deconstructive process of history and self in order to challenge these colonizing actions, strategies, and ideologies. Barrera (1979) describes colonialism as a relationship of domination based on racial lines, whereby a dominant group makes the only leading paradigm for the relationship out of its own interests and benefits. As a result, to show and remain in power, the Spaniards created a paradigmatic system that undervalued indigenous values, costumes, and traditions and placed them in a lower category. For example, towns' names were changed by Spaniards. My town's original name was "Re-She-lajuj-noj" (or Xelajú) but was changed to "Quetzaltenango," the current official name. An indigenous Guatemalan woman, Rigoberta Menchú, a recipient of the Nobel Peace Prize, describes colonization: "El pueblo indígena ha sido como el sol que poco a poco ha salido desde abajo . . . del mundo de opresión y explotación, del mundo oculto y clandestino, del mundo de abajo en el que han vivido" (Claudillo Felix, 1998, p. 117). ["Indigenous people have been like the sun that has, little by little, risen from below . . . from the world of oppression and exploitation, from the hidden and clandestine world, from the underworld where they have lived."]

Despite all these previous experiences, I finally started to get a better sense, or at least partly, of what it means to have a racialized experience. In the early 2000s, I came to the United States. As I arrived, I immediately started noticing all the different adjectives or "social identities" bestowed upon me. I officially became not only an "alien" or immigrant, but also a Hispanic (this term for me has a European connotation) and not a Latino. By looking as I do, some people have considered me and made me feel "different"—though we all are—and, at times, through glances, reactions, and/or avoidances, have also marked me as a "dangerous" person, such as a mugger or a thief. This picture becomes even more complicated, as I speak my second language, English, with an accent. The reactions have ranged from simply not being able to understand what I say, to questioning the validity of or simply ignoring my claims based on how they sound in my voice.

It has been through these negative experiences, through my own skin, that I have come to better understand the pain and the fear of exclusion. Being on both sides forced me to stand against approaches that I considered unjust, as well as to live and face unjust actions, not only against me but also to those like me. In fact, it has been more than unjust; it is real and it hurts. To remedy this, we might need more than a simple deconstructive process that leaves people living together but in different real places. Although we may know that these inequities do not derive directly from the personal but from historical patterns from both sides, we still hold certain positions, at times privileged and at others subjugated. Thus, we need a process of becoming aware of our skins, in which our efforts focus not on regretting and lamenting being at different places, but rather on seeing the potential and possibilities of a dual emancipation wherein we open ourselves to learn, accept, share, love, and build on our differences toward the equitable common goals and actions of living and being together.

References

Barrera, M. (1979). *Race and class in the southwest: A theory of racial inequality.* Notre Dame, IN: University of Notre Dame Press.

Claudillo Felix, G. A. (1998). Aproximación al discurso de Rigoberta Menchú [Approximation to Rigoberta Menchu's discourse]. *Espiral, Estudios sobre Estado y Sociedad, 5*(13), 111-141.

When I Was a Native American: A Second-generation Puerto Rican, Terry Louise Sebastian

My title reflects an experience I had back in 1994 when I came to terms with my ethnicity. I am a second-generation Puerto Rican, born in New York City and raised for the early part of my childhood in Spanish Harlem. After teaching in New York City for 16 years, I decided to teach in Little Wound High School on a Lakota reservation in South Dakota. Living on an Indian reservation is like living in another country, literally. Different issues, problems, and lifestyles. Once a month, I drove 88 miles off the reservation to Rapid City to do my shopping. I encountered a serious issue when shopping at a local merchant. I noticed that I was being watched closely and followed. It made me feel quite uncomfortable, being stalked in that way. Once back on the reservation, I shared my experience with a colleague. She informed me that since I looked like a Native American, I was treated as one. In all my years being raised in Spanish Harlem and in the Bronx, I never had encountered an experience as I did in South Dakota. I learned what it was like to be in another person's shoes. This experience truly sensitized me to the racism, insensitivity, and humiliation of being a Native American.

Chapter 8: Reflections of Celebrations, Traditions, Foods, and Fiestas

Margarita's Reflection: I Was Always Hungry

When I arrived to the United States in 1982, I had no idea of the amount of hunger I would feel when I started working. I will never forget the pain I experienced on the first day at work in the Lorel factory. I usually had a breakfast of crackers, cheese, and two cups of coffee. My day began at 6 a.m. By my first break at 10:45, I was hungry. I had another cup of coffee and then went back to work. We had a 12 noon break for lunch. I was told to be back in 45 minutes. I panicked. How could I go home to have my *almuerzo*? My cousin said, "You will get used to it. The *almuerzo* here is at 6 p.m." It took me six months to get used to having a snack for my lunch period.

Michelle Rose Banks: An African American Director's Experience With a Mexican Holiday

I have worked at a Head Start program in the Bronx for the past 12 years. In the last five years, a significant number of Mexican families have moved into a predominantly African American neighborhood. A couple of years ago, our center's picture day was on September 16th. Our staff was shocked when eight Mexican children came dressed up in velvet suits and mini ball gowns. Their parents said they were celebrating Mexican Independence Day and they were so happy that the children would be photographed in the ethnic garb. I learned that Mexican's Independence from Spain is September 16th, not May 5th! Cinco de Mayo celebrates the Mexican army's victory over the French in 1682.

American versus Mexican Practices in Honoring the Dead: Linda K. Parkyn

It is 1963, and I am 10 years old. We are in the car on the way to the cemetery and I am surrounded in the backseat by geraniums. It is Memorial Day, and we are going to plant geraniums on the graves of my grandparents. I remember this day every year of my childhood. My Mom does the planting. My Dad does not have a planting job; he is there only to carry the geraniums and fetch the water. My mother is silent. She digs deep into the Pennsylvania soil, and she remembers those who have come before her. When finished, the three of us stand respectfully for a few minutes and then we leave. We eventually moved from our home near these gravesites, but every summer of my childhood we took the long car ride back to do our ritual one more time.

Many years have passed since my annual cemetery car rides with Mom and Dad. This year, I am on the bus in Aguascalientes, Mexico, and I am surrounded by the Mexican flower that most resembles marigolds. The flowers are bigger and brighter than marigolds, but they are still orange and smelly. It is November 1, Day of the Dead in Mexico, and everyone is jostling each other on the bus ride to the town cemetery. In this cemetery, everybody has a job. It is bustling with activity! Little boys run up to the people who got off the bus. The children carry tin cans tied with string across their shoulders. They yell frantically, vying for business: "Agua, un peso!" Mariachis stroll the cemetery, willing to sing *Abuelo*'s favorite song before he died for a small fee. Women carry brooms and mops from home and scrub the tombstones with soap and water until they glisten in the afternoon sun. Little children scramble over the cool marble and hold up pictures of loved one who have died. Aunts and uncles tell stories about the deceased and everybody laughs. Senoras sell *pozole*, the Mexican version of chicken soup, with a bit of chile in it to help you remember that you are alive and kicking! Shiny new vases with Bible verses on them are for sale to hold all the calla lilies, wreaths, and smelly marigolds that everyone uses to decorate.

Everyone is preparing for nightfall. All the people are singing and telling stories about those who have come before them to live and die on this earth. Long into the Aguascalientes evening, families sit on warm blankets, eat the favorite foods of their ancestors, and, yes, even talk to those who have come and gone before them. November 2 is the festival of the dead, a time to remember, to bring the favorite food and drink of those you love and see no more. It is especially a time to tell the stories of their loved ones to the next generation. It is a time to assure themselves that those whom they love have gone to a better place.

All week leading up to the Day of the Dead, altars are erected in public places in memory of those who have died. The university where I was teaching had a contest for the best altar fashioned by students in each academic department. Some departments erected altars to a famous person in the discipline, some to a former colleague who had recently passed, and some to a family member of a current student who died.

Downtown, the public library erected their altar to Emiliano Zapata, the revolutionary leader. Each high school dedicated one to a person in the town square and businesses chose a person to memorialize in their front entrances. My local grocery store erected one to a manager who had died that year. A business nearby dedicated one to Marilyn Monroe and decorated the altar in scarves. In 2001, after the September 11 terrorist attacks in the United States, the Mexican government erected a memorial altar to all who died in the World Trade Center. In the week leading up to the Day of the Dead, I saw over 300 altars throughout the city.

These altars are playful; they are not morbid at all. Many of them reflect the personality of the deceased and they are full of life! One special one had a skeleton wearing the suit coat and glasses of the deceased. Another had the Rollerblades of the man who had died next to his picture. Rollerblades were his main mode of transportation, and the altar explained that he died in a traffic accident. Altars reflect who people were in life. They tell the story of the deceased. The altars help family stories to live. If the deceased was a guitar player, his instrument and his music are on the altar. Along with candles, food, and flowers, altars tell the story of someone who is missed. There are usually three levels to an altar, representing the past, the present, and the future life of the memorialized. Along with the big altars in public places and in town squares, everyone has small ones in their homes.

Calavera (little skulls) markets spring up overnight in the streets surrounding the city cemeteries for the week prior to Day of the Dead. Street vendors sell little fruit candies in the shape of foods that people enjoyed, and sugared skulls to paint your name across the forehead in different colors of icing are bought and exchanged among friends. Mexicans, according to Octavio Paz, "play with death." They are not afraid of it—they see the death of a loved one as a life to be celebrated and remembered. Everyone eats *pan de muertos* (special bread baked with dried fruit into it), and they especially cook the tamales or the tacos that a deceased person enjoyed.

And so the festival of the dead brings souls back to life for one night each year. The smelly marigolds keep the evil spirits at bay, and the spirits of our loved ones come to visit for awhile. All of this made me ponder a bit about how much we cover death up in our U.S. culture, and how we might learn to play with it a bit more.

My mother died recently, and I thought once more, on the anniversary of Day of the Dead, November 1 and 2, about those geraniums in the hard Pennsylvania soil. I built an altar in our home in memory of my Mom. I placed her knitting needles and her cookie cutters next to her picture, along with a nameplate from the back door of our old house. In true Mexican spirit, as I played with her memory, I felt a peace about her death that I had not experienced before.

Peace to the memory of those who have come and gone before us.

Cuban-Chilean American Reflection: Annette Macari
Growing Up Organic

A few months back, one of my daughters, Cristina, had a special project to do for her class. She had to interview a modern "pilgrim" from her family; someone who had immigrated to the United States. She chose my mother, her *abuelita*, who had come from Cuba to the United States in the late 1950s. Something my mother said during the interview struck me as funny but so true. When Cristina (my daughter) asked her to describe what the food in Cuba was like compared to the United States, Abuelita remarked, "We only ate organic food in Cuba." She then went on to explain that the food consisted of local products that went from the farm directly to the table. Coffee beans were roasted in the oven that morning, and the smell of the roasting was better than anything you could find at the grocery store now.

When I moved to Miami, a door to my cultural heritage was opened, although I didn't realize that until much later. Suddenly, I was trying foods from my mother's homeland that I had not had before. I was lucky to spend my youth in Miami, which had diversity of Latin food and easy access to ingredients. My mother was making more Cuban dishes at home and every corner had some type of Hispanic food. The holidays were different in that now, I was having roast pig with black beans and white rice for Christmas Eve. The desserts were fantastic and unlike anything I had before living in Miami. I grew to a young adult loving these foods and traditions. Yet I never knew the impact that this culture and cuisine would have on me until I moved away from home and didn't have access to those familiar foods anymore.

I caught a glimpse when I left to attend a university in Louisiana. Although I missed the food at home, I was living in New Orleans. I had a new type of food to discover and that kept my pangs at bay. I also had vacations and holidays, not to mention an entire summer, to return home. You could eat voraciously when you came home on break just to get your fill before going away again. It was later, in my early 30s, that it really hit home.

I was a mom to two children then and maintaining my own household. I was cooking various foods for my family and we still had easy access to any Cuban food that I wanted. My ingredients were not organic—they came out of a can or bottle in the grocery store. If I needed *sofrito* for my recipe, I could buy it made already. My black beans came out of a can already spiced up. If I didn't feel like cooking, there were restaurants that we could call and order out. It was easy.

My husband's company wanted us to relocate to the Midwest and as it was a good opportunity, we left. Suddenly, I was at a loss. For some of the meals I was used to preparing, I had trouble finding ingredients. At first, I asked my mother to send me care packages.

Then, I was on a quest to find these foods near where I lived. I found a store that had select items from the Goya brand that were placed in the "international" aisle. I laughed at that. In Miami, rice was with the rice, beans were in the vegetable aisle, and Mojo was with the condiments. I still couldn't have plantain chips, though, and forget about any tropical fruit other than a mango.

Never had I missed Cuban food so much. It was in my soul and I didn't know it. The only thing left to do was to learn to make it myself. I started going through my Cuban cookbook that I bought before leaving Miami and making those familiar foods myself. I learned to make black beans from scratch. I make my own sofrito now. There is still much to learn, but I am enjoying it so much. I am also teaching my children about these wonderful Cuban foods and helping them to grow to love the culture—the organic way.

Appendix B
Print/Video/Web Resources

This appendix presents print and video resources for educators and care providers when working with Latino/Hispanic families. It is a compilation of print resources for all age levels that we have come upon in preparing this manuscript.

First is a list of annotated bibliographies on children's and adult books that highlight positive images of Hispanic children and their families, as recommended by the School of Communication and Information, Rutgers, The State University of New Jersey, and by Colorín Colorado's website at www.colorincolorado.org/read/forkids/recommended?startnum=21&theme=print.

Annotated Bibliography of Children's Books

Ada, Alma Flor. (1997). *The Lizard and the Sun / La Largartija y el Sol.* New York, NY: Doubleday Dell.

This Mexican folktale describes how the persevering Lizard searches for the sun, which has disappeared for days. Children learn about how important the sun is for all living creatures.

Ada, Alma Flor. (1998). *Under the Royal Palms: A Childhood in Cuba (Bajo las palmas reales).* New York, NY: Atheneum.

The author's memoir about her childhood in Cuba is compelling and stimulates the imagination of what life in Cuba might have been like as seen through the eyes of a child.

Ada, Alma Flor. (2002). *I Love Saturdays y Domingos.* New York, NY: Atheneum.

A young girl who spends weekends with her grandparents alternates her languages to speak to each set of grandparents. Saturday is English day, when she speaks English with Grandpa and Grandma. On Sundays, *los Domingos*, she speaks Spanish with *Abeulito* and *Abeulita*. Written in English, with Spanish vocabulary interspersed throughout the text.

Argueta, Manilo. (1990). *Magic Dogs of the Volcanoes / Los Perros Magicos de Los Volcanes.* San Francisco, CA: Children's Book Press.

A Salvadoran folktale about magical dogs that live in volcanoes and watch over the neighboring villages.

Altman, Linda Jacobs. (1993). *Amelia's Road.* New York, NY: Lee and Low.

Amelia, a migrant child, longs to have a place to call home. Readers learn of the struggles when moving from place to place and being able to keep only those personal items that will fit in a car.

Ancona, George. (1997). *Mayeros: A Yucatec Maya Family.* New York, NY: Morrow.

This book depicts the history, culture, and life of Mayan Indians in the Yucatan Peninsula. Several generations of Mayans are presented via photographs and text.

Ancona, George. (1994). *Piñata Maker / El Piñatero.* New York, NY: Harcourt Brace.

This book depicts a piñata maker in a Mexican town that celebrates fiestas with masks, piñatas, puppets, etc. Colorful illustrations with English and Spanish text.

Anzaldua, Gloria. (1993). *Friends From the Other Side/Amigos del Otro Lado.* San Francisco, CA: Children's Book Press.

Prietita, a young Mexican American girl, takes care of Joaquin, a newly arrived Mexican immigrant, as he faces the challenges of life in Texas after crossing the Rio Grande with his mother in search of a new life.

Brusca, Maria Cristina. (1991). *On the Pampas.* New York, NY: Holt.

This is the story of an Argentine girl named Brusca and her adventures at her grandparents' ranch on the Argentine pampas. Brusca participates in the daily life of *gauchos* (Latin American cowboys) as they herd cattle, tend to the horses, etc. Beautifully illustrated.

Cameron, Ann. (1998). *The Most Beautiful Place in the World.* New York, NY: Knopf.

This is the story of young Juan from Guatemala, who lives with his grandmother and makes his living by shining shoes. His eagerness to go to school prompts him to teach himself how to read. Readers get a sense of the lives of poverty-stricken children in Guatemala.

Castaneda, Carlos. (1993). *Abuela's Weave.* New York, NY: Lee and Low.

The relationship of a grandmother teaching her granddaughter the art of weaving, in Guatemala, is beautifully depicted in this book. Strong family relationships are presented metaphorically as the *abuela* instructs her granddaughter to thread the yarn close together, just like family. The color illustrations represent rural Guatemala.

Cowley, Joy. (1998). *Big Moon Tortilla.* Honesdale, PA: Boyds Mills Press.

Set in the Papago reservation in southern Arizona on the Mexican border, this story recounts Marta's run of bad luck (e.g., her dog chews her homework and her glasses break). Her grandmother comes to the rescue, repairing her glasses and making comforting tortillas. Watercolor illustrations capture the desert and sunsets.

Delacre, Lulu. (2008). *Rafi and Rosi: Carnival!* New York, NY: Rayo Publishing.

Rafi and Rosi are charming and mischievous *coquis* (tree frogs) who live in Puerto Rico. The three stories presented here depict their adventures during carnivals and parades. Available in Spanish as well.

Dorros, Arthur. (1995). *Isla.* New York, NY: Dutton Books.

Young Rosalba's imagination grows, inspired by the beautiful stories her grandmother tells of the tropical island where she grew up.

Dorros, Arthur. (1999). *Abuela.* New York, NY: Dutton.

Rosalba imagines that she and her *abuela* can fly. Their bird's-eye view includes docks, an airport, tourist attractions, and her father's office. The book includes dialogue in English and Spanish, with a useful glossary of definitions and colloquial language.

Galindo, Mary Sue. (2000). *Icy Watermelon/Sandia Fria.* Houston, TX: Piñata Books.

On Sunday family get-togethers, the grandchildren listen to their grandparents' and parents' stories about their relationships. They learn that if it weren't for watermelons, their grandparents would not have met and married.

Garay, Luis. (1997). *Pedrito's Day.* New York, NY: Orchard Publications.

The story portrays a day in Pedrito's life as he rides his bike, plays soccer, and excels in school. While on an errand to get change for his aunt, he loses the money and experiences a dilemma; should he lie about how he lost the money or should he tell the truth?

Jimenez, Francisco. (1998). *La Mariposa.* Boston, MA: Houghton Mifflin.

Young Francisco is excited to be going to school, but soon experiences embarrassment and frustration as he enters a classroom where only English is spoken. He finds comfort in watching a caterpillar in the process of becoming a butterfly, paralleling his own transformation and adjustment.

Jimenez, Francisco. (2000). *The Christmas Gift/El Regalo de Navidad.* Boston, MA:

Houghton Mifflin.
This holiday story centers on Panchito, a boy growing up in a family of migrant farm workers in California. Panchito wants a red ball for Christmas, but his parents cannot afford to buy it. He learns that Christmas is not just about gift giving, but about the greatest gift of all—family.

Lomas Garza, Carmen. (1996). *In My Family/En Mi Familia*. San Francisco, CA: Children's Book Press.
Carmen Garza Lomas shares memories of her childhood in Kingsville, Texas, a border town. She describes her favorite foods and family celebrations in this colorful, warm story, written in both English and Spanish.

Montex, Marisa. (2000). *Juan Bobo Goes to Work*. New York, NY: HarperCollins.
Bobo causes minor catastrophes with everything he does, yet his innocence and honest dismay are clear. Eventually, one of his mishaps brings good fortune!

Mora, Pat. (1992). *A Birthday Basket for Tia*. New York, NY: Macmillan.
Cecilia plans a surprise gift for her great-aunt's 90th birthday. Her plans are affected by her playful and curious cat, Chica. Beautifully illustrated.

Mora, Pat. (1999). *The Rainbow Tulip*. New York, NY: Viking Press.
In this book, Stella and her brothers speak Spanish at home, but English at school. Living in two cultures, Stella finds a way to wear her Mexican skirt to honor her heritage. She then realizes that her Mexican skirt is more similar to, than different from, skirts worn by the other girls at school. Spanish words are included within the text.

Moreton, Daniel. (1997). *La Cucaracha Martina: A Caribbean Folktale/La Cucaracha Martina: Un Cuento Folklorico del Caribe*. New York, NY: Turtle Publishing.
Beautiful cockroach Martina rejects all offers of marriage made with harsh city sounds, until she hears the beautiful noise of a cricket. The author/illustrator was inspired when writing this book by memories of tales told by his Cuban grandmother.

Perez, Amada Irma. (2000). *My Very Own Room/Mi Propio Cuartito*. San Francisco, CA: Children's Book Press.
An 8-year-old Mexican American girl longs for a room of her own, where she can have privacy from her five brothers. The whole family becomes involved in creating a special place for her. While cherishing her new area, the young girl also expresses much joy in her family bonds.

Reiser, Lynn. (1998). *Tortillas and Lullabies/Tortillas y Canciones*. New York, NY: Greenwillow.
In this story, a young girl's tale about how her mother, grandmother, and great grandmother make tortillas provides a look at Central American folk art. The rhythmic text includes both Spanish and English.

Rohmer, Harriet. (1993). *Uncle Nacho's Hat*. San Francisco, CA: Children's Book Press.
In this Nicaraguan tale, Uncle Nacho is very fond of his old hat, even if it is rather ragged. When he receives a new hat, he throws the old one away, but it keeps returning to him.

Stanton, Karen, and Moreno, Rene King. (2007). *Papi's Gift*. Honesdale PA: Boyds Mills Press. Graciella's father, a migrant worker, makes his living working on various farms. He calls every Sunday and tells Graciella that for her seventh birthday he is sending her a special gift. The gift gets lost, causing Graciella to miss her father even more. A touching story with lovely illustrations.

Soto, Gary. (1997). *Too Many Tamales*. New York, NY: Putnam.
Maria tries on her mother's wedding ring while she's making tamales for Christmas dinner. She loses the ring and is convinced that it is in one of the tamales. She and her cousins decide to solve the problem by eating the tamales in search of the ring.

Van Laan, Nancy. (1996). *La Boda: A Mexican Wedding Celebration*. Boston, MA: Little Brown.
Maria's grandmother teaches her about Mexican traditions and rituals celebrated at a

Zapotec Indian wedding. The text is interspersed with Spanish vocabulary throughout.
Van Laan, Nancy. (1998). *The Magic Bean Tree: A Legend From Argentina*. Boston, MA: Houghton Mifflin Books.
This is a pourquoi tale from the Quechua culture about the first tree in the world. The carob tree tells young Topec how to bring needed rain to the land. When he and his people do so, the tree rewards them by dropping beans, which then take root as new trees throughout the land.
Viesti, Joe and Hall, Diane. (1997). *Celebrate in Central America*. New York, NY: Lothrup, Lee & Shepard.
Holidays celebrated in Guatemala, Belize, Panama, El Salvador, Honduras, Nicaragua, and Costa Rica are described.
Zamorano, Ana. (1996). *Let's Eat!* Illus. by Julie Vivas. New York, NY: Scholastic.
Traditional Spanish dishes provide a framework for the depiction of day-to-day life for a loving family.

Annotated Bibliography of Adult Books

The following section lists books recommended to sensitize adult readers to some aspects of Latino culture (e.g., family, immigration, and cultural ways).

Nonfiction

Aliotta, Jerome J. (1991). *The Puerto Ricans*. Introductory essay by Daniel Patrick Moynihan. New York, NY: Chelsea House Publishers. ISBN: 0-87754-897-8. 110 pp. Grade 5-7. Discusses the history, culture, and religion of Puerto Ricans, their place in American society, and the problems they face as an ethnic group in North America. Photographs, bibliography, and index are included.
Arnold, Sandra Martin. (1993). *Alicia Alonso: First Lady of the Ballet*. New York, NY: Walker and Company. ISBN: 0-8027-8242-6. 100 pp. Grade 4-6. This is the story of a Cuban ballerina who founded her own ballet school and company, performed with the Ballet Russe, and continued to dance even after she lost her sight. Includes photographs, bibliography, and index.
Bandon, Alexandra. (1993). *Mexican Americans. (Footsteps to America.)* New York, NY: Macmillan. ISBN: 0-02-768142-4. 110 pp. Grade 4-6. An account of immigration to the United States by Mexicans, focusing on recent history, with first-person narratives. Includes photographs, bibliography, and index.
Catalano, Julie. (1988). *The Mexican Americans*. Introductory essay by Daniel Patrick Moynihan. New York, NY: Chelsea House Publishers. ISBN: 0-87754-857-9. 95 pp. Grade 5-7. Presents the history, culture, and religion of Mexican Americans, and discusses factors prompting their emigration and affecting their acceptance as an ethnic group in North America. Photographs, bibliography, and index included.
Cedeno, Maria E. (1993). *Cesar Chavez: Labor Leader*. Brookfield, CT: The Millbrook Press. ISBN: 1-56294-280-8. 32 pp. Grade 3-4. This publication traces the accomplishments of the famed labor leader, who fought to improve the lives of Mexican American farm workers in California.
de Ruiz, Dana Catharine, and Richard Larios. (1993). *La Causa: The Migrant Farmworkers' Story*. Illustrated by Rudy Gutierrez. (*Stories of America*, Alex Haley, general editor.) Austin, TX: Steck-Vaughn. ISBN: 0-8114-7231-0. 92 pp. Grade 3-5. This book describes the efforts of Cesar Chavez and Dolores Huerta during the 1960s to organize migrant workers in California into a union, which became the United Farm Workers.
Fernandez-Shaw, Carlos M. (1991). *The Hispanic Presence in North America From 1492 to Today*. Translated by Alfonso Bertodano Stourton and others. New York, NY: Facts on File. ISBN: 0-8160-2133-3. 375 pp. Grade 6-10. A general historical overview, begin-

ning with colonization and a discussion of Hispanic culture, is followed by a state-by-state study of the history and influence of Hispanics in the United States. Photographs, listings of media, associations, selected readings, and index are included. A valuable reference tool.

Garver, Susan, and Paula McGuire. (1981). *Coming to North America: From Mexico, Cuba, and Puerto Rico.* New York, NY: Delacorte Press. ISBN: 0-440-01459-X. 161 pp. Grade 5-6. Explores the immigrant experiences of Mexicans, Cubans, and Puerto Ricans in the United States through personal accounts, histories, and photographs. Includes bibliography, a history of U.S. immigration laws, and an index.

Gilbert, Thomas W. (1991). *Roberto Clemente.* New York, NY: Chelsea House. ISBN: 0-7910-1240-9. 111 pp. Grade 5-7. Biography of the baseball hero, from his birth in Puerto Rico to his career with the Pittsburgh Pirates. Includes photographs, index, bibliography, chronology, and career statistics.

Lankerford, Mary D. (1994). *Quinceañera: A Latina's Journey to Womanhood.* Photographs by Jesse Herrera. Brookfield, CT: The Millbrook Press. ISBN: 1-56294-363-4. 47 pp. Grade 2-4. Photographs and narration describe the preparation for and celebration of a young girl's *quinceañera*, a rite of passage at age 15 for Latinas.

http://latino.sscnet.ucla.edu/Latino_Bibliography.html

Latino Memoirs: Biographies and Autobiographies

Rosay, Rosalina. (2007). *Journey of Hope, Memoirs of a Mexican Girl: Autobiography - Illegal Immigrant From Guanajuato Mexico to Los Angeles California in the 1970's.* New York, NY: AR Publishing Company.
Rosay shares her journey from poverty in Mexico to her unauthorized entry to America, in the name of pursuing a better education and life.

Alvarez, Julia. (1992). *How the Garcia Girls Lost Their Accents.* New York, NY: Plume.
This is a story of four sisters who acculturate to American life after having to flee from the Dominican Republic. As they adjust to American ways, they suffer embarrassment when friends meet their parents, hurt and offense when they are called "spics," and identity confusion when they visit their homeland.

Allende, Isabel. (2008). *The Sum of Our Days: A Memoir (P.S.).* New York, NY: Harper Perennial.
Allende shares a family memoir based on her idea that her deceased daughter Paula would want to know what has happened to the family since her death. This biographically based novel describes how a family survived death and drug addiction with love.

Santiago, Esmeralda. (1993). *When I Was Puerto Rican.* Reading, MA: Addison-Wesley.
Santiago shares her experiences growing up in rural Puerto Rico and details her life's journey from rural Puerto Rico to Brooklyn. The books reflects her disconnect with transitioning from her Spanish-speaking Puerto Rico to English-speaking Brooklyn.

Fiction: Novels for Adult Readers

Anaya, Rudolfo. (1999). *Bless Me, Ultima.* New York, NY: Grand Central Publishing.
This novel, set in a small eastern New Mexico town during the 1940s, tells the story of young Antonio Márez and the local *curandera* who comes to live with his family. Antonio's greatest conflict is choosing between his parents' opposing wishes for his future.

Diaz, Junot. (2008). *The Brief Wondrous Life of Oscar Wao.* New York, NY: Riverhead.
Oscar is a sweet but disastrously overweight ghetto nerd who dreams of becoming the Dominican J.R.R. Tolkien and, most of all, finding love. But Oscar may never get what he wants. Blame the *fukú*—a curse that has haunted Oscar's family for generations, following them on their epic journey from Santo Domingo in the Dominican Republic to the United States.

Cisneros, Sandra. (2002). *Caramelo.* New York, NY: Knopf.
In this sweeping saga of the Reyes family, young Lala takes the reader on the migrations of her people between the United States and Mexico.

Cisneros, Carlos. (2008). *The Case Runner.* Houston, TX: Arte Público Press.
Alejandro "Alex" del Fuerte, fresh out of law school, is returning home to South Texas, ready to open his solo practice, humble as it may be. But when he meets Porfirio "Pilo" Medina, who just crossed the border in search of his wife and son, Alex is suddenly dragged into a world of wrongdoings and political payoffs rarely covered in law school.

Castillo, Ana. (2008). *The Guardians.* New York, NY: Random House.
In this powerful tale, Regina, a virgin-widow in her 50s living in rural New Mexico, cares for her unusually disciplined teenage nephew, Gabo, who believes he's destined for the priesthood. Gabo's father often crosses the border to visit, but this time something has gone wrong; given the gruesome fate of Gabo's mother, there is cause for alarm.

Chávez, Denise. (1994). *Face of an Angel.* New York, NY: Farrar, Straus, and Giroux.
Set in southern New Mexico, this novel relates the story of Soveida Dosamantes, a waitress in a Mexican food restaurant. Through the cast of characters, the reader is provided insightful portraits of the Hispanic working-class in the American Southwest.

Lagasse, Mary Helen. (2004). *The Fifth Sun.* Willimantic, CT: Curbstone Press.
A young Mexican woman, Mercedes, leaves her village to work as a housemaid in New Orleans, Louisiana. This fast-paced novel chronicles her adventures in New Orleans, her marriage, her struggle to raise her children, her deportation, and her attempt to re-cross the river and be reunited with her children.

Férre, Rosario. (1995). *The House on the Lagoon.* New York, NY: Farrar, Straus and Giroux.
The history of severe economic and racial divisions in the Puerto Rican culture is reflected via a wealthy Puerto Rican's woman desire to become a novelist, much to her husband's dismay.

Cisneros, Sandra. (2009). *The House on Mango Street.* New York, NY: Vintage.
A classic and classroom staple, this coming-of-age novel is told in character sketches and vignettes by 11-year-old Esperanza Cordero. Life in the oppressive Hispanic quarter of Chicago is revealed in gritty detail through the young girl's eyes.

Saldaña, Jr., René. (2001). *The Jumping Tree.* New York, NY: Delacorte.
American-born Rey and his family maintain close ties with their Mexican relatives, who live just across the border, yet have very different opportunities. Rey's family, though poor, struggles and survives through their kind and honest efforts, religious beliefs, and hard work.

Print Resources for Teachers

Ada, Alma Flor. (2002). *A magical encounter: Latino children's literature in the classroom* (2nd ed.). Boston, MA: Allyn & Bacon.

Cisneros, H. G. (Ed.). (2009). *Latinos and the nation's future.* Houston, TX: Arte Público Press.

Day, F. A. (2003). *Latina and Latino voices in literature: Lives and works, updated and expanded.* Westport, CT: Greenwood Press.

Eggers-Piérola, C. (2005). *Connections & commitments: Reflecting Latino values in early childhood programs.* Portsmouth, NH: Heinemann Press.

Menard, V. (2004). *The Latino holiday book: From cinco de mayo to dia de los muertos—the celebrations and traditions of Hispanic-Americans.* New York, NY: Marlowe & Company.

O'Brien, S., with Arce, R. M. (2009). *Latino in America.* New York, NY: Celebra Trade, a division of Penguin Group.

Ramos, J. (2009). *Tierra de todos: Nuestro momento para crear una nación de iguales.* New York, NY: Random House. (*A country for all: An immigrant manifesto,* English edition.)
Suarez-Orozco, M., & Paez, M. (2002). *Latinos: Remaking America.* Berkeley, CA: University of California Press.
Valverde, L. A. (Ed.). *The Latino student's guide to college success.* Westport, CT: Greenwood.
York, S. (2002). *Picture books by Latino writers: A guide for librarians, teachers, parents, and students.* Santa Barbara, CA: Linworth Publishing.
Zertuche Trevino, R. (Ed.). (2006). *The Pura Belpre awards: Celebrating Latino authors and illustrators.* Chicago, IL: American Library Association.

Videos and Curriculum Resources for Educators

Latino Artistic Expression: An Educational Guide for Teachers
Based on the PBS Documentary "Visiones: Latinos Arts and Culture" produced by the National Association of Latino Arts and Culture (for grades K – 12)
www.patmora.com/pdf_files/latinoteacherresourceguide.pdf
National Latino Children's Literature Conference
www.latinochildlitconf.org (bi-annual conference, next to be held in 2012)
National Public Radio's (NPR) Latino USA
www.latinousa.org/
Smithsonian Education: Hispanic Heritage Teaching Resources
http://smithsonianeducation.org/educators/resource_library/hispanic_resources.html
StoryCorps Historias: Cuenta tu historia
http://storycorps.org/historias-en/
Al Otro Lado: To the Other Side
www.pbs.org/pov/alotrolado/lesson_plan.php
This lesson plan is designed for use with the film *Al Otro Lado (To the Other Side).* This 60-minute film provides a window into issues along the border between the United States and Mexico. A young Mexican man named Magdiel faces an economic crisis in his fishing town. He is unable to make it as a fisherman, so he considers whether to immigrate to the U.S. without authorization or to traffic drugs like many of his friends.

Hispanic/Latino Films, Videos, and DVDs

Documentaries/Docudramas
American Experience: A Class Apart
Studio: PBS; DVD Release Date: April 21, 2009; Run Time: 60 minutes

American Harvest Documentary
Studio: White Hot Films; DVD Release Date: 2008; Run Time: 100 minutes

Balseros
Studio: New Video Group; DVD Release Date: July 26, 2005; Run Time: 120 minutes

Biculturalism and Acculturation Among Latinos
Studio: Films for Humanities and Sciences; Release Date: 1991; Run Time: 28 minutes

Border War: The Battle Over Illegal Immigration
Studio: Genius Entertainment; DVD Release Date: October 10, 2006; Run Time: 95 minutes

The Changing Role of Hispanic Women
Studio: Films for Humanities and Sciences; Release Date: 1995; Run Time: 44 minutes

Children in No Man's Land
Studio: New Day Films; DVD Release Date: October 2008; Run Time: 39 minutes

Crossing Our Borders
Studio: New Day Films; DVD Release Date: November 12, 2010; Run Time: 55 minutes

CUBA MIA: Portrait of an All-Woman Orchestra
Studio: Arkadia DVD; DVD Release Date: September 16, 2005; Run Time: 86 minutes

De Nadie (I Belong to No One)
Studio: Laguna Films; DVD Release Date: January 16, 2007; Run Time: 80 minutes

Each Mind Is a World - Cada Cabeza es un Mundo
Studio: Hispanic Education and Media Group, Inc.; VHS Release Date: July 1, 2001; Run Time: 43 minutes

Farmingville
Studio: New Video Group; DVD Release Date: November 2, 2004; Run Time: 78 minutes

Hispanic Americans: One or Many Cultures?
Studio: Films for Humanities and Sciences; Release Date: 1995; Run Time: 45 minutes

A History of Hispanic Achievement in America
Studio: Ambrose Video Publishing, Inc.; DVD Release Date: September 13, 2006; Run Time: 216 minutes

Hispanic Americans: The Second Generation
Studio: Films for Humanities and Sciences; Release Date: 1995; Run Time: 44 minutes

Hispanic Culture—The Sights & Sounds of Modern Mexico
Studio: Fideo Knowledge, Inc.; DVD Release Date: August 1, 2004; Run Time: 25 minutes

Hispanic Culture—The Sights and Sounds of Puerto Rico
Studio: Video Knowledge, Inc.; DVD Release Date: August 1, 2004; Run Time: 26 minutes

Hispanic Culture—The Sights and Sounds of South America
Studio: Video Knowledge, Inc.; DVD Release Date: August 1, 2004; Run Time: 25 minutes

Hispanic Education at the Crossroads
Studio: Films for Humanities and Sciences; Release Date: 1996; Run Time: 45 minutes

If the Mango Tree Could Speak
Studio: New Day Films; Release Date: 1993; Run Time: 58 minutes

La Caminata
Studio: New Day Films; Release Date: 2009; Run Time: 15 minutes

Latinos Now: A National Conversation
Studio: PBS; DVD Release date: 2006; Run Time: 30 minutes

Leaders: Hispanic Excell
Studio: Homevision; VHS Release, Date: June 6, 2000; Run Time: 35 minutes

Los Trabajadores / The Workers
Studio: New Day Films; Release Date: 2002; Run Time: 15 minutes

Maid in America
Studio: New Day Films; DVD Release Date: 2003; Run Time: 58 minutes

National Geographic—Wetback: The Undocumented Documentary
Studio: Nat'l Geographic Video; DVD Release Date: February 6, 2007; Run Time: 90 minutes

Next Door Neighbors: Hablamos Español
Studio: PBS; DVD Release Date: 2009; Run Time: 29 minutes

The Latino Factor: A New Documentary About Immigration
Studio: Produced by Marcos Nelson Suárez; DVD Release Date: 2006; Run Time: 45 minutes

The Other Side of Immigration
Studio: Roy Germano Films; DVD Release Date: October 25, 2010; Run Time: 55 minutes

When Worlds Collide: The Untold Story of the Americas After Columbus
Studio: PBS; DVD Release Date: 2010; Run Time: 90 minutes

Unsung Heroes: Hispanics and the Medal of Honor
Studio: A&E Home Video; DVD Release Date: June 24, 2008; Run Time: 50 minutes

Yo Soy Boricua, Pa'Que Tu Lo Sepas! (I Am Puerto Rican, So You Know It!)
Studio: Magnolia Home Entertainment; DVD Release Date: September 29, 2009; Run Time: 86 minutes

Entertainment

A Day Without a Mexican (2004)
Studio: Televisa Cine; DVD Release Date: May 14th, 2004; Run Time: 97 minutes

American Family—The Complete First Season (2002)
Studio: 20th Century Fox; DVD Release Date: April 29, 2003; Run Time: 99 minutes

Amexicano (2007)
Studio: Maya Entertainment; DVD Release Date: January 13, 2009; Run Time: 84 minutes

Al Otro Lado (2004)
Studio: Uni Cine; DVD Release Date: March 6, 2007; Run Time: 90 minutes

Arts & Entertainment (Hispanic Magazine's Guide to Hispanic Excellence) (2000)
Studio: Homevision; VHS Release, Date: June 6, 2000; Run Time: 35 minutes

El Norte (1983)
Studio: Criterion; DVD Release Date: January 20, 2009; Run Time: 140 minutes

La Quinceañera
Studio: Customflix; DVD Release Date: May 7, 2007; Run time: 40 minutes

Real Women Have Curves (2002)
Studio: HBO Home Video; VHS Release Date: April 22, 2003; Run Time: 86 minutes

Sweet 15 (2004)
Studio: All Things Family; DVD Release Date: December 21, 2004; Run Time: 120 minutes

Tortilla Soup (2002)
Studio: Sony Pictures; DVD Release Date: January 15, 2002; Run Time: 102 minutes

Under the Same Moon (2007)
Studio: 20th Century Fox; DVD Release Date: June 17, 2008; Run Time: 106 minutes

Appendix C
Latino Music by Ethnicity

The following links provide music from the various Hispanic groups. Some are classic melodies recognized by each group and others are universal songs for Latino children. Enjoy!

Mexican/Azteca
www.youtube.com/watch?v=jgPhQOhY-SM
www.youtube.com/watch?v=Ev-vExGNbSk&feature=PlayList&p=6A31B8B0E8349728&playnext=1&playnext_from=PL&index=8
www.youtube.com/watch?v=-IiI0AzqYlU

Mexican Children's Music
www.youtube.com/watch?v=ksx4XmO96Yo
www.youtube.com/watch?v=CXBnRE_Rbgg

Danza Azteca
www.youtube.com/watch?v=-1Zcz94sfE4

Danza del Peru
www.youtube.com/watch?v=3E9807Uxi1Q
www.youtube.com/watch?v=KLKimfCydNo&feature=PlayList&p=0BF30BC87D968E26&playnext=1&playnext_from=PL&index=32

Peruvian Music
www.youtube.com/watch?v=3xOqfCTi534
www.youtube.com/watch?v=clIfpTr21HY

Children's Peruvian Music
www.youtube.com/watch?v=8ZFZcsLqCdQ
www.youtube.com/watch?v=f07ClZR37WE
www.youtube.com/watch?v=O9jRlvOJK9s

Puerto Rican Music
www.youtube.com/watch?v=bYBynOjF4vo
www.youtube.com/watch?v=_VYJ9bOzRnE&feature=PlayList&p=1824CDD912711E7E&playnext=1&playnext_from=PL&index=48
www.youtube.com/watch?v=VS1kMM32kWg
www.youtube.com/watch?v=Mv1ZsSrE03o
www.youtube.com/watch?v=kAr1K2-skoA
www.youtube.com/watch?v=_0U5wxcyJug
www.youtube.com/watch?v=3If2U2Ao9q4

Children's Puerto Rican Music
www.youtube.com/watch?v=pLX6OiBrllc
www.youtube.com/watch?v=_4y6PEWhGmE&feature=related
www.youtube.com/watch?v=F61K0f7OZeY&feature=related
www.youtube.com/watch?v=ttu81UiJNuA&feature=related

Cuban Music
www.youtube.com/watch?v=sk7bbF4uQ0U
www.youtube.com/watch?v=lArGoRhFr4E&feature=rec-LGOUT-real_rn-HM
www.youtube.com/watch?v=Y_ShCX_JAbg
www.youtube.com/watch?v=QbKAhX9ySmo

Children's Cuban Music
www.youtube.com/watch?v=vtnTC0yPD1w&feature=PlayList&p=DEFD9766D75EEE31&playnext=1&playnext_from=PL&index=5
www.youtube.com/watch?v=be0z0AM6XuU&feature=PlayList&p=2625EF1E1A58ED5F&playnext_from=PL&playnext=1&index=26

Colombian Music
www.youtube.com/watch?v=KE0geFpJ0uM
www.youtube.com/watch?v=yQ0EoBR7GZ4
www.youtube.com/watch?v=DXLmNXJxoKA

Children's Colombian Music
http://www.youtube.com/watch?v=4aGk2vUUiK0
http://www.youtube.com/watch?v=cGgK0U0EHiU

Dominican Music
www.youtube.com/watch?v=gkq4Mc531Ls&feature=PlayList&p=BF4F2B40652F8D6B&playnext_from=PL&playnext=1&index=1
www.youtube.com/watch?v=09ztWyNGOSw
www.youtube.com/watch?v=Oj_rAcygKsk&feature=PlayList&p=C3CE427A00FEDA5E&playnext_from=PL&playnext=1&index=6
www.youtube.com/watch?v=hLKs6hx8H-A&feature=related

Children's Dominican Music
www.youtube.com/watch?v=drx6Ya4AKkI
www.youtube.com/watch?v=qMaJ1_eZDos&feature=channel
www.youtube.com/watch?v=LTwtX3drCeA&feature=related
www.youtube.com/watch?v=uOWKQAksrj0&feature=related

Brazilian Music
www.youtube.com/watch?v=y0wt-NSv2ao&feature=PlayList&p=A7BB17A50C32E7C9&playnext_from=PL&playnext=1&index=9
www.youtube.com/watch?v=nlyxphWDBw4
www.youtube.com/watch?v=psLmZ2apAlE&feature=related
www.youtube.com/watch?v=VyA2qZm1lt4

Children's Brazilian Music
www.youtube.com/watch?v=tiuErzIQkhg
www.youtube.com/watch?v=sSahy_HhQDM&feature=related
www.youtube.com/watch?v=XqyghWTLrOs&feature=related

Appendix D
Legal Rulings Concerning Bilingual Education

Lau vs. Nichols

In 1974, the class-action case of Lau vs. Nichols highlighted some of the issues regarding bilingual education. The case was originally brought against the San Francisco school district on the grounds that many Chinese students were not receiving a quality education because of their limited English skills. The lower California courts had ruled that the Chinese students were receiving equal education. In 1974, however, the Supreme Court ruled that equivalent school materials did not constitute equal education. Key language from the 1974 Supreme Court decision of Lau vs. Nichols reads as follows:

> There is no equality of treatment by providing students with the same facilities, textbooks, teachers and curriculum, for students who do not understand English are effectively foreclosed from any meaningful education.
>
> Basic English skills are at the very core of what public schools teach. Imposition of a requirement that, before a child can effectively participate in the educational program, he must already have acquired those basic skills is to make a mockery of public education.

This decision required schools to take "affirmative steps" in helping students learning English as a second language to access curriculum. Students would no longer be required to sit in "English-only" classrooms.

The Mid-Atlantic Equity Consortium (www.maec.org/lyons/4.html) provides a wonderful summary of some of the actions taken to meet the needs of English language learners in the United States, including a list of what is commonly referred to as the Lau Remedies or Lau Guidelines. These guidelines (created in 1975 by the Education Commissioner of the Department of Health, Education and Welfare—HEW) were sent as a memo to all school officials and made public for all who had an interest in the education of English language learners (ELLs), yet were never officially documented in the Federal Register. The document was very specific about methods, procedures, and approved approaches for working with ELL children, and included guidelines for:

- Identifying and evaluating national origin minority students' English language skills
- Determining appropriate instructional treatments
- Deciding when ELL children were ready for mainstream classrooms
- Determining the professional standards to be met by teachers of language-minority children.

"The Lau Remedies redirected school districts to provide strong versions of bilingual education for language minority students to enable them to become bilingual, biliterate, and bicultural" (Ovando, 2003, p. 10). The nation was attempting to address federal mandates at the state and local levels in order to receive the funding necessary to support programs for language minority students.

Civil Rights Language Minority Regulations

Civil Rights Language Minority Regulations published in 1980 included four important components for school districts to address when working with language minority students: identification, assessment, services, and exit procedures. The component that had the greatest effect on school systems was more than likely the "services" section, which specified that bilingual instruction would have to be provided by "qualified teachers." Districts were required to monitor their teachers as well as the credentialing requirements to meet these regulations. Immediate disagreement arose as to how these services would be provided and by whom, and led to a series of cases that ultimately had a major impact on bilingual education.

Key Court Cases in the 1980s That Affected ELLs

1981
- Castaneda vs. Pickard (Texas State Court)
  Helped to set the standard for the courts in evaluating programs that provided LEP (limited English proficiency) services. Only required that "appropriate action to overcome language barriers" be taken.

1981
- Idaho vs. Migrant Council (Idaho State Court)
  Established the legal responsibility of the State Department of Education to monitor implementation of programs for LEP students.

1983
- Keyes (Denver) vs. School District Number 1 (Colorado and Supreme Courts)
  Used the Castaneda vs. Pickard decision to evaluate the district program for LEP students.

1987
- Illinois vs. Gomez (Illinois State Court)
  Established that it was the state's responsibility to establish/enforce minimums for implementation of language remediation programs. Requirements were set for moving students from LEP to FEP (fluent English proficiency) status.

1987
- Teresa P. vs. Berkeley Unified (California State Court)
  Used Castaneda vs. Pickard decision to evaluate the district program offerings for LEP students.

The Florida Consent Decree: A State's Framework for Implementation

In stark contrast to English-only advocates are those who champion the cause of using the school systems to support families with the transition from a home language to English. In Florida, for example, it became necessary to obtain a Consent Decree in order to ensure the civil rights of the growing number of English language learners. The interpretation of the following laws and court cases were considered when preparing the consent decree:

- Title VI and VII Civil Rights Act of 1964
- Office of Civil Rights Memorandum (Standards for Title VI Compliance) of May 25, 1970
- Requirements based on the Supreme Court decision in *Lau v. Nichols*, 1974
- Equal Education Opportunities Act of 1974
- Requirements of the Vocational Education Guidelines, 1979
- Requirements based on the Fifth Circuit court decision in *Castañeda v. Pickard*, 1981
- Requirements based on the Supreme Court decision in *Plyler v. Doe*, 1982
- Americans with Disabilities Education Act (PL 94-142)
- Florida Education Equity Act, 1984
- Section 504 of the Rehabilitation Act of 1973

There are six major sections to the Consent Decree in the State of Florida: (www.fldoe.org/aala/edpage2.asp)

Section I: Identification and Assessment Synopsis: All students with limited English proficiency must be properly identified and assessed to ensure the provision of appropriate services. The Consent Decree details the procedures for placement of students in the English for Speakers of Other Languages (ESOL) program, their exit from the program, and the monitoring of students who have been exited.

Section II: Equal Access to Appropriate Programming Synopsis: All ELL students enrolled in Florida public schools are entitled to programming, which is appropriate to their level of English proficiency, their level of academic achievement, and any special needs they may have. ELL students shall have equal access to appropriate English language instruction, as well as instruction in basic subject areas, which is understandable to the students given their level of English proficiency, and equal and comparable in amount, scope, sequence and quality to that provided to English language learner (or non-ELL) students.

Section III: Equal Access to Appropriate Categorical and Other Programs for ELL Students Synopsis: ELL students are entitled to equal access to all programs appropriate to their academic needs, such as compensatory, exceptional, adult, vocational or early childhood education, as well as dropout prevention and other support services, without regard to their level of English proficiency.

Section IV: Personnel Synopsis: This section details the certificate coverage and inservice training teachers must have in order to be qualified to instruct ESOL students. Teachers may obtain the necessary training through university coursework or through school district provided inservice training. The Consent Decree details specific requirements for ESOL certification and inservice training and sets standards for personnel delivering ESOL instruction.

Section V: Monitoring Issues Synopsis: The Florida Department of Education is charged with the monitoring of local school districts to ensure compliance with the provisions of the Consent Decree pursuant to federal and state law and regulations including Section 229.565, Florida Statutes (Educational Evaluation Procedures) and Section 228.2001, Florida Statutes (Florida Educational Equity Act). This monitoring is carried out by the Office of Academic Achievement through Language Acquisition (AALA), Division of Public Schools, Florida Department of Education.

Section VI: Outcome Measures Synopsis: The Florida Department of Education is required to develop an evaluation system to address equal access and program effectiveness. This evaluation system is to collect and analyze data regarding the progress of ELL students and include comparisons between the LEP population and the non-ELL population regarding retention rates, graduation rates, dropout rates, grade point averages and state assessment scores.

In some large, urban school districts, like Miami-Dade County, which has a high concentration of ELLs, the school system requires that all teachers meet the mandate within a few years of becoming employed with the district. In other, smaller and more homogeneous districts, this is not necessary, because very few students will need the services of these specially trained educators. The federal policy is interpreted at the state level, and then each school system (district) meets the mandate as regulated by their state for the necessary funding.

Aside from establishing teacher credentials, schools must monitor the number of students requiring ESOL services. Therefore, systems are in place to screen students upon entry into the system, determining their English language level and the level of service necessary to support English language learning. Typically, younger children tend to "exit" the system very quickly (Riley, 2000). They pick up the English language very naturally and require less support each year. In order to exit the system, students must pass the established criteria. Then, they are moved to a non-ESOL placement. Many levels of placement and services are provided through many models. For example, a school district might have a kindergarten classroom of all ESOL level 3 students—it depends on the concentration of ELLs in any given district. Schools are quite proud when students exit the system. If the services are no longer needed, however, the funding to provide those services is discontinued. Rachel Moran (1998) notes that

> The battle over the allocation of discretion to structure the curriculum for linguistic minority students has reflected three distinctive approaches:
>
> 1. constraining the discretion of state and local educators in order to remedy past abuses;
> 2. enabling state and local educators to exercise their discretion more satisfactorily; and
> 3. limiting the discretion of bilingual educators who promote bilingualism and biculturalism. (p. 614)

References by Chapter

Foreword References

Callejo Pérez, D., Fain, S. M., & Slater, J. J. (Eds.). (2004). *Pedagogy of place: Understanding place as a social aspect of education.* New York, NY: Peter Lang Publishing.

Dewey, J. (1997). *Democracy and education.* New York, NY: Free Press. (Original work published 1916)

DuBois, W. E. B. (2003). *The souls of black folk.* New York, NY: Simon and Schuster. (Original work published 1903)

McLaren, P., & Hammer, R. (1996). Media knowledges, warrior citizenry, and postmodern literacies. In H. A. Giroux, C. Lankshear, P. McLaren, & M. Peters (Eds.), *Counternarratives: Cultural studies and critical pedagogies in postmodern spaces* (pp. 81-116). New York, NY: Routledge.

Public Law 107-110. (2001). *No Child Left Behind Act.* Retrieved from http://www2.ed.gov/policy/elsec/leg/esea02/index.html

Sepulveda, J. (2004). *The life and times of Willie Velasquez: Su voto es su voz.* Houston, TX: Arte Publico Press.

Introduction References

U.S. Census Bureau. (2010). Retrieved from www.census.gov/

The Jones Act. (1917). Retrieved from www.loc.gov/rr/hispanic/1898/jonesact.html.

Perez, C. (2006). *Living by dichos: Advice from a mother to a daughter.* New York, NY: Atria Books.

Webster's New Collegiate Dictionary. (1995). Springfield, MA: Merriam-Webster.

Chapter 1 References

Bureau of Labor Statistics. (October, 2010). *Economic new release: Employment situation summary.* Retrieved from www.bls.gov/new.release/empsit.nr0.htm

DeNavas-Walt, C., Proctor, B. D., & Smith, J. C. (2010). *Income, poverty, and health insurance coverage in the United States: 2009.* Washington, DC: U.S. Census Bureau. Retrieved from www.census.gov/prod/2010pubs/p60-238.pdf

Ennis, S. R., Rios-Vargas, M., & Albert, N. G. (2010). *The Hispanic population: 2010. 2010 Census brief issues May 2011 (#C2010BR-04).* Retrieved from www.census.gov/prod/cen2010/briefs/c2010br-04.pdf

Escovar, P. L., & Lazarus, P. J. (1982). Cross-cultural childrearing practices: Implications for school psychologists. *School Psychology International, 3,* 143-148.

Harwood, R. L., & Miller, J. G. (1991). Perceptions of attachment behavior: A comparison of Anglo and Puerto Rican mothers. *Merrill-Palmer Quarterly, 37*(4), 583-601.

Hispanic Scholarship Fund. (2001). *Revelations and recommendations: The 2000 HSF Hispanic education study.* San Francisco, CA: Author, with funding from Lilly Endowment Inc.

Holman, L. J. (1997). Meeting the needs of Hispanic immigrants. *Educational Leadership, 54*(7), 37-38.

Landale, N. S., & Oropresa, R. S. (2001). Migration, social support and perinatal health: An origin-destination analysis of Puerto Rican women. *Journal of Health and Social Behavior, 42*, 166-183.

Livingston, G., & Parker, K. (September 9, 2010). *Since the start of the great recession: More children raised by grandparents.* Washington, DC: Pew Research Center's Social and Demographic Trends Project. Retrieved from http://pewsocialtrends.org

Logan, A. (2009). *Minorities struggle in the labor market: Minorities and the labor market in the recession by the numbers.* Retrieved from www.americanprogress.org/issues/2009/02/btn_minorities.html

Lopez, M. H., Taylor, P., & Morin, R. (2010, October). *Illegal immigration backlash worries, divides Latinos.* Retrieved from http://pewresearch.org/pubs/1781/survey-hispanics-unathorized-immigration-policy-discrimination-deportation-politics

Martinez, R., Nielsen, A. L., & Lee, M. T. (2003). Reconsidering the Marielito legacy: Race/ethnicity, nativity, and homicide motives. *Social Science Quarterly, 84*(2), 397-411.

New Velázquez Spanish and English Dictionary, The. (1999). El Monte, CA: New Win Publishing, Inc.

Novas, H. (2003). *Everything you need to know about Latino history.* New York, NY: Plume.

Passel, J. S. (2006). *The size and characteristics of the unauthorized migrant population in the U.S.* Retrieved from http://pewhispanic.org/files/reports/61.pdf

Pérez, P. A, & McDonough, P. M. (2008). Understanding Latina and Latino college choice: A social capital and chain migration analysis. *Journal of Hispanic Higher Education,* 7(3), 249-265.

Roberts, S. (November 17, 2007). In U.S. name count, Garcias are catching up with Joneses. *The New York Times.* Retrieved from www.nytimes.com/2007/11/17/us/17surnames.html?ref+us#

Suro, R. (1998). *Strangers among us: How Latino immigration is transforming America.* New York, NY: Alfred A. Knopf.

Swail, S., Cabrera, A., & Lee, C. (2003). *Latino youth and the pathway to college.* Washington, DC: Pew Hispanic Study Center. Retrieved from www.pewhispanic.org

Tashakkori, A., & Ochoa, S. H. (1999). *Education of Hispanics in the United States: Politics, policies, and outcomes.* New York, NY: AMS Press.

Taylor, P., Passel, J., Fry, R., Morin, R., Wang, W., Velasco, G., & Dockterman, D. (March 18, 2010). *The return of the multi-generational family household.* Washington, DC: Pew Research Center's Social and Demographic Trends Project. Retrieved from http://pwesocialtrends.org

The Miami Herald. November 17, 2007. Retrieved from http://Themiamiherald.com

U.S. Census Bureau. (2003). *The Hispanic population in the United States: March 2002.* Washington, DC: U.S. Department of Commerce.

U.S. Census Bureau. (2008). *American community survey.* Retrieved from http://factfinder.census.gov/servlet/STTable?_bm=y&-geo_id=01000US&-qr_name=ACS_2008_3YR_G00_S1201&-ds_name=ACS_2008_3YR_G00_&-redoLog=false

U.S. Department of Education. (2009). *High school dropout and completion rates in the United States: 2007.* Washington, DC: National Center for Education Statistics. Retrieved from http://nces.ed.gov/

U.S. Immigration Online. (2007). *1882 Chinese Exclusion Act.* Retrieved from http://library.uwb.edu/guides/USimmigration/1882_chinese_exclusion_act.html

Chapter 2 References

Applewhite, S. L. (1995). Curanderismo: Demystifying the health beliefs and practices of elderly Mexican Americans. *Health and Social Work, 20,* 247-253.

American Lung Association: Search Lung USA. Retrieved from www.lungusa.org/site/apps/s/

Bearison, D., Minian, N., & Granowetter, L. (2002). Medical management of asthma and

folkmedicine in a Hispanic community. *Journal of Pediatric Psychology, 27*(4), 385-392.
Campos, C. (2007). Addressing cultural barriers to the successful use of insulin in Hispanics with type-2 diabetes. *Southern Medical Journal, 100*(8), 812-820.
Carter-Pokras, O. D. (November 18th, 2006). *How to achieve culturally linguistic competent healthcare.* Proceedings tri-caucus health summit: The power of many. Transcript provided by the Kaiser Network. Retrieved from www.Kaisernetwork.org
Centers for Disease Control and Prevention. (2003). Deaths: Leading causes for 2001. *National Vital Statistics Report, 52*(9), 1-86.
Dutton, M. A., Orloff, L. E., & Aguilar Hass, G. (2000). Characteristics of help-seeking behaviors, resources and service needs of battered immigrant Latinas: Legal and policy implications. *Georgetown Journal on Poverty Law and Policy, 7*(2), 245-305.
Flores, G., Abreu, M., Chaisson, C., Meyers, A., Ramesh, C., Fernandez, H., Francisco, P., Diaz, B., Milena, A., & Santos-Guerro, I. (2005). Randomized control trial of the effectiveness of community based case management in insuring uninsured Latino children. *Pediatrics, 116*(6), 1433-1441.
Flores, G., Barton, M. L., Mayo, S. J. , Zukerman, B. Abreu, M., Medina, L., & Hardt, E. J. (2003). Errors in medical interpretation and their potential clinical consequences in pediatrics encounters. *Pediatrics, 111*(1), 6-14.
Garcia, H., Sierra, A., & Balam, G. (1999). *Wind in the blood: Mayan healing and Chinese medicine.* Berkeley, CA: North Atlantic Books.
Gary, T. L., Venkat Narayan, K. M., Gregg, E. W., Beckles, G. L. A., & Saaddine, J. B. (2003). Racial/ethnic differences in the healthcare experience (coverage, utilization, and satisfaction) of U.S. adults with diabetes. *Ethnicity & Disease, 13*(1), 47-54.
Hispanic Health Council. (2006). *A profile of Latino health in Connecticut: The case for change in policy and practice.* Hartford, CT: Author.
Johnson, R. M. (2006). Lost in translation. *Oncology Nursing Forum, 33*(5), 853.
Kaiser Daily Health Policy Report. (2002a). *Study examines coverage for uninsured Latino children.* Retrieved from http://kaisernetwork.org/daily_reports/print_report.cfm?DR_ID+34596&dr_cat=3
Kaiser Daily Health Policy Report. (2002b). *Health needs of Latino children overlooked and misunderstood.* Retrieved from www.kaiserhealthnews.org/Daily-Reports/2002/July/03/dr00012044.aspx?referrer=search
Kaiser Daily Health Policy Report. (2006). *Latino Children in U.S. more likely to be obese by age three than blacks, whites.* Retrieved from www.kaisernetwork.org/daily_reports/rep_index.cfm?hint=3&DR_ID=37771
March, K. L., & Gong, W. (2005). Providing pharmaceutical care to Hispanic patients. *American Journal of Health System Pharmacy*, *62*, 210-213.
Martinez, C. (1997, November). *Among family.* U.S. Department of Health and Human Services National Symposium on la violencia domestica: An emerging dialogue among Latinos, Washington, D.C.
Murguia, A., Peterson, R. A., & Zea, C. M. (2003). Use and implications of ethnomedical health care approaches among Central American immigrants. *Health and Social Work, 28*(1), 43-53.
Murphy, J. M. (1993). *Santeria: African spirits in American.* Boston, MA: Beacon Press.
Perez, S. M. (2000). *U.S. Latino children: A status report.* Washington, DC: National Council of La Raza. (ERIC Document Reproduction Service No. ED 451 294)
Rios-Ellis, B. (2005). *Critical disparities in Latino mental health: Transforming research into action* (white paper). Washington, DC: National Council of La Raza.
Smart, J. F., & Smart, D. W. (1995). Acculturative stress of Hispanics: Loss and challenge. *Journal of Counseling and Development, 73,* 390-396.
Suro, R. (1999). *Strangers among us: Latino lives in a changing America.* New York, NY: Vintage Books.

Trotter, R. (2001). Curanderismo: A picture of Mexican-American folk healing. *Journal of Alternative and Contemporary Medicine, 7*(2), 129-131.

Chapter 3 References

Bowen, P. D. (2010). Early U.S. Latina/o, African-American Muslim connections: Paths to conversion. *The Muslim World, 100*(4), 390-413.

Buddhism in Latin America. (2006). Retrieved from www.mandalamagazine.org/archives/mandala-issues-for-2006/august/buddhism-in-latin-america/

Cortez, J. D. (2000). *The osha: Secrets of the Yoruba-Lucumi santeria religion in the United States and the Americas.* Brooklyn, NY: Athelia Henrietta Press.

De la Vega, G. (1871). First part of the royal commentaries of the Yncas. Translated by Sir Clements Markham. *Hakluyt Society Publications, Vol. II*, 155-167. Retrieved from www.sacred-texts.com/nam/inca03htm

Family in Islam, The. (n.d.). Retrieved from www.islam-guide.com/frm-ch3-14.htm

Frerichs, C. (2003). Hispanic ministry in the northwest. *Message Magazine Online, 51*(2), 1.

Green, L. (2003). *Latino Methodists learn value in social principles.* Retrieved from www.wfn.org/2003/11/msg00110.html

Latino religion in the U.S.: Demographic shifts and trends. Retrieved from www.facsnet.org/issues/faith/esponosa.php

McIntosh, K. (2005). *The Latino religious experience: People of faith and vision.* Philadelphia, PA: Mason Crest Publishers.

Miranda, J., & Carrasco, R. (1994). *On the social significance of five million Latino Protestants.* Hispanic Association of Bicultural Ministries. Retrieved from www.urbanonramps.com/rc/fivemillion.htm

Murray, B. (2006). *Latino religion in the U.S.: Demographic shifts and trends "Pentecostalization" takes hold among Latinos; Catholic Church remains strong.* Retrieved from www.facsnet.org/index.php?option=com_content&view=article&id=180:latino-religion-trends-1-06&catid=75:archives&Itemid=100003

Navas, Y. (2000). *It's all in the frijoles.* New York, NY: Simon and Schuster.

Novas, H. (2003). *Everything you want to know about Latino history.* New York, NY: Plume Books.

Perez y Mena, A. I. (1998). Cuban santería, Haitian vodun, Puerto Rican spiritualism: A multiculturalist inquiry into syncretism. *Journal for the Scientific Study of Religion, 37*(1), 15-27.

Pew Hispanic Center/Pew Forum on Religion and Public Life. (2007). *Changing faiths: Latinos and the transformation of American religion.* Retrieved from http://pewhispanic.org/files/reports/75.pdf

Ramirez, M. (2005). *Family focus attracts minorities to faith with past steeped in racism.* Retrieved from www.rickhoss.com/reference/mormon253.html

Ventura, M. G. (March 12th, 2005). Latter day church increasingly drawing in Latinos in the U.S. *Desert News.* Retrieved from http://desertnews.com.article/content/05036351558,00.html

Viscidi, L. (June 2003). Latino Muslims a growing presence in America. *Washington Report on Middle East Affairs, XXII*(5), 56-59. Retrieved from http://hispanicmuslims.com/articles/latinogrowth.html

What is Buddism? (n.d.). Retrieved from www.fwbo.org/buddhism.html

What Mormons believe. (2007). Retrieved from www.whatmormonsbelieve.org/mormon_books.html

What Presbyterians believe. (May, 2009). Retrieved from www.pcusa.org/today/believe/believe.htm

Zubizarreta, R. (Summer 2003). El latinismo y sus bellos colores: Voices of Latina and

Latino Buddhists. *Turning Wheel: The Journal of Socially Engaged Buddhism,* 18-25.

Chapter 4 References

Adams, M., Coltrane, S., & Parke, R. D. (2007). Cross-ethnic applicability of the gender-based attitudes toward marriage and child rearing scales. *Sex Roles: A Journal of Research, 56*(5-6), 325-339.

Arciniega, M., Anderson, T., Tovar-Blank, Z., & Tracey, T. (January, 2008). Toward a fuller conception of machismo: Development of a traditional machismo and caballerismo scale. *Journal of Counseling Psychology, 55*(1), 19-33.

Brotanek, J. M., Halterman, J. S., Auinger, P., Flores, G., & Weitzman, M. (2005). Iron deficiency, prolonged bottle feeding, and racial/ethnic disparities in young children. *Archives of Pediatric Adolescent Medicine, 159*, 1038-1042.

Bunik, M., Clark, L., Zimmer, L. M., Jimenez, L. M., O'Connor, M. E., Crane, L. A., & Kempe, A. (2006). Early infant feeding decisions in low-income Latinas. *Breastfeeding Medicine: Journal of the Academy of Breastfeeding, 1*(4), 225-235.

Clutter, A. W., & Zubieta, A. C. (2009). *Understanding the Latino culture.* Ohio State University Fact Sheet: Family and Consumer Sciences. Retrieved from http://ohioline.osu.edu/hyg-fact/5000/pdf/5237.pdf

Cofer, J. O. (2001). *Palomita* (poem). In P. Mora & P. Parrgen (Eds.), *Love for mama! A tribute to mothers.* New York, NY: Lee and Low Books.

Contreras, J. (2004). Parenting behaviors among mainland Puerto Rican adolescent mothers: The role of grandmother and partner involvement. *Journal of Research on Adolescence, 14*(3), 341-368.

Crean, H. F. (June, 2008). Conflict in the Latino parent-youth dyad: The role of emotional support from the opposite parent. *Journal of Family Psychology, 23*(2), 484-493.

Cuevas De Caissie, R. M. (2005, November 17). Hispanic culture: A hispanic thanksgiving. *Havana Journal.* Retrieved from http://havanajournal.com/cuban_americans/entry/hispanic_culture_a_hispanic_thanksgiving/

DeBord, K., & Ferrer, M. (2000). *Working with Latino parents/families.* Retrieved from http://www1.cyfernet.org/prog/fam/latinofam.html

Fontes, L. A. (2002). Child discipline and physical abuse in immigrant Latino families: Reducing violence and misunderstandings. *Journal of Counseling & Development, 80*(1), 31-40.

Guilamo-Ramos, V. G., Dittus, P., Jaccard, J., Johnson, M., Bouris, A., & Acosta, N. (2007). Parenting practices among Dominican and Puerto Rican mothers. *Social Work, 52*(1), 17-29.

Halgunseth, L. C., Ispa, J. M., & Rudy, D. (2006). Parental control in Latino families: An integrated review of literature. *Child Development, 77*(5), 1282-1297.

Kersey, M., Lipton, R., Quinn, M. T., & Lantos, J. T. (2010). Overweight in Latino preschoolers: Do parental health beliefs matter? *American Journal of Health Behaviors, 34*(3), 340-348. Retrieved from www.ncbi.nlm.nih.gov/pmc/articles/PMC2804943/pdf/nihms167131.pdf

Mennella, J. A., Ziegler, P., Briefel, R., & Novak, T. (January, 2006). Feeding infants and toddlers study: The types of foods fed to Hispanic infants and toddlers. *Journal of the American Dietetic Association, 106*(1), 96-106.

Meyers., R. G. (1994). Childrearing practices in Latin America. *United Nations Children's Fund (UNICEF). The Consultant Group on Early Childhood Care and Development Notebook, 15*, 1-20.

Nava, R. G. (2000). A multi-dimensional multi-level perspective of holistic education: An integrated model. *Holistic Education Network of Tasmania, Australia.* Retrieved from www.hent.org/world/rgn/integration.htm

Perez, C. (2006). *Living by dichos: Advice from a mother to a daughter.* New York, NY: Atria Books.

Pérez-Escamilla, R. (1993). Breastfeeding patterns in nine Latin American and Caribbean countries. *Bulletin of Pan American Health Organization, 27*(1), 32-42.

Queralt, M. (1984). Understanding Cuban immigrants: A cultural perspective. *Social Work Journal, 29*(2), 115-121.

Rodriguez, G. G. (1999). *Raising nuestros niños in a bicultural world.* New York, NY: Simon & Schuster.

Schulze, P. A., Harwood, R. L., Schoelmerich, A., & Leyendecker, B. (2002). The cultural structuring of parenting and universal developmental tasks. *Parenting: Science and Practice, 2*, 151-178.

Tacon, A. M., & Caldera, Y. M. (2001). Attachment and parental correlates in late adolescent Mexican American women. *Hispanic Journal of Behavioral Sciences, 23*(1), 71-87.

Vazquez, C. (2004). *Parenting with pride—Latino style.* New York, NY: HarperCollins.

Vazquez, C. (2005). Entendiendo el tratamiento bilingue y bicultural. Understanding bilingual and bicultural treatment. *Salud Mental. Mental Health Education, Advocacy and Resources: Serving the Latino Community, 1*(3), 2-32.

Whiteside-Mansell, L., Bradley, R. H., & McKelvey, L. (2009). Parenting and preschool child development: Examination of three low-income U.S. cultural groups. *Journal of Child and Family Studies, 18*, 48-60.

Chapter 5 References

Brown, S. E. (June 22, 2009). Sotomayor and our future. *Inside Higher Ed.* Retrieved from www.insidehighered.com/views/2009/06/22/brown

Carnegie Corporation of New York. (1994). *Meeting the needs of our youngest children.* Retrieved from www.carnegie.org/starting_points/index.html.

Cochran-Smith, M. (2003). Standing at the crossroads: Multicultural teacher education at the beginning of the 21st century. *Multicultural Perspectives, 5*(3), 3-11.

Crawford, J. (1993). *Hold your tongue: Bilingualism and the politics of English only.* Upper Saddle River, NJ: Addison-Wesley Longman.

Dewey, J. (1897). My pedagogic creed. *School Journal, 54*, 77-80. Retrieved from http://dewey.pragmatism.org/creed.htm

Dotson-Blake, K. P., Foster, V. A., & Gressard, C. F. (2009). Ending the silence of the Mexican immigrant voice in public education: Creating culturally inclusive family-school-community partnerships. *Professional School Counseling, 12*(3), 230-239.

Duncan, A. (2009, July 28th). *Remarks to the National Council of La Raza.* www.ed.gov/news/speeches/secretary-arne-duncans-remarks-national-council-la-raza

Gandara, P. (2005). *Fragile futures: Risk and vulnerability among Latino high achievers.* Princeton, NJ: Educational Testing Service (ETS) policy report. Retrieved from www.ets.org/Media/Research/pdf/PICFRAGFUT.pdf

Henderson, Z. P. (1992). Project promotes literacy among migrant families. *Human Ecology, 20*(2), 4-12.

Hispanic Scholarship Fund. (2000). *Revelations and recommendations: The 2000 HSF Hispanic education study.* Rand Corporation. Retrieved from http://www.hsf.net/uploadedFiles/About_HSF/HSFRANDbook.pdf

Lau v. Nichols, 414 U.S. 563 (1974).

Llagas, C. (2003). *Status and trends in the education of Hispanics.* Retrieved from http://nces.ed.gov/pubsearch/pubsinfo.asp?pubid=2003008

Lopez Pedrana, A. (2009). Teachers of English language learners: Tracking personal practical knowledge, reflection, and narrative authority. In B. S. Stern (Ed.), *Curriculum and teaching dialogue* (Vol. 11, Numbers 1 & 2, pp. 175-191). Charlotte, NC: Infor-

mation Age Publishing.
Massey, D. S., & Redstone Akresh, I. (2006). Immigrant intentions and mobility in a global economy: The attitudes and behavior of recently arrived U.S. immigrants. *Social Science Quarterly, 87*(5), 954-971.
Mikow-Porto, V., Humphries, S., Egelson, P., O'Connell, D., & Teague, J. (2004). *English language learners in the southeast: Research, policy & practice*. Greensboro, NC: SERVE Regional Educational Laboratory. Retrieved from http://education.ucf.edu/mirc/Research/ELLSoutheast.pdf
Moran, R. F. (1998). The politics of discretion: Federal intervention in bilingual education. In R. Delgado & J. Stefancic (Eds.), *The Latino/a condition: A critical reader* (pp. 610-621). New York, NY: New York University Press.
National Center for Education Statistics. (2009). *High school dropout and completion rates in the United States: 2007 (NCES 2007 059)*. Retrieved from http://nces.ed.gov/pubs2009/2009064.pdf
National Center for Family Literacy. (2006). *The history of Even Start*. Retrieved from www.famlit.org/ProgramsandInitiatives/EvenStart/History.cfm
National Collaborative on Diversity in the Teaching Force. (2004). *Assessment of diversity in America's teaching force*. Washington, DC: Author. Retrieved from www.ate1.org/pubs/uploads/diversityreport.pdf
National Education Association and Minority Community Outreach, in collaboration with the National Migrant and Seasonal Head Start Association. (2010). *Working with migrant students: A national imperative for head start students and families*. Retrieved from www.nmshsaonline.org/Doc/MCO-NMSHSA.pdf
Ochoa, G. L. (2007). *Learning from Latino teachers*. San Francisco, CA: John Wiley & Sons.
Ovando, C. J. (2003). Bilingual education in the United States: Historical development and current issues. *Bilingual Research Journal, 27*, 1-24.
Perry, J. D. (1997). *Migrant education: Thirty years of success, but challenges remain*. Washington, DC: U.S. Department of Education. Retrieved from www.ed.gov
Pew Hispanic Center and Kaiser Family Foundation. (2004). *National survey of Latinos: Education*. Retrieved from http://pewhispanic.org/files/reports/25.pdf
Quijada, P., & Alvarez, L. (2006). Cultivando semillas educacionales (Cultivating Educational Seeds): Understanding the experiences of K-8 Latino/o students. In J. Castellanos, A. M. Gloria, & M. Kamimura (Eds.), *Abriendo caminos: The Latino/a pathway to the Ph.D.* Sterling, VA: Stylus.
Riley, R. W. (March 15, 2000). *Excelencia para todos—excellence for all: The progress of Hispanic education and the challenges of a new century*. Remarks as prepared for delivery by U.S. Secretary of Education Richard W. Riley at Bell Multicultural High School in Washington, D.C.
Rodriguez, J. C. (2009, December 23). A shortage of Hispanic teachers. *Albuquerque Journal*. Retrieved from www.abqjournal.com/cgibin/decision.pl?attempted=www.abqjournal.com/news/metro/232237106600newsmetro12-23-09.htm
Romanowski, M. H. (2003). Meeting the unique needs of the children of migrant workers. *Clearing House, 77*(1), 27-33.
St. Pierre, R., Gamse, B., Alamprese, J., Rimdzius, T., & Tao, F. (1998). *Even Start: Evidence from the past and a look to the future: National evaluation of the Even Start Family Literacy Program*. Washington, DC: U.S. Department of Education.
U.S. Department of Education. (2000). *The provision of an equal education opportunity to limited-English proficient students*. Office for Civil Rights. Washington, DC: Author. [Online]. Retrieved from www.ed.gov/about/offices/list/ocr/eeolep/index.html/
U.S. Department of Education. (2003). *President's advisory commission on education excellence for Hispanic Americans*. Retrieved from www.ed.gov/nes/

pressreleases/2003/04/04092003a.html.
Valdes, G. (1996). *Con respeto: Bridging the distances between culturally diverse families and schools: An ethnographic portrait.* New York, NY: Teachers College Press.
Vocke, K. S. (2007). *Where do I go from here? Meeting the unique educational needs of migrant students.* Portsmouth, NH: Heinemann.
Whittaker, C., & Salend, S. J. (1997). Voices from the field: Including migrant farm workers in the curriculum. *The Reading Teacher, 50*(6), 482-494.

Chapter 6 References

Agbenyega, S., & Jiggetts, J. (1999). Minority children and their over-representation in special education. *Education, 119*(4), 619-632.
Alvarez-McHattan, P., & Correa, V. (2005). Stigma and discrimination: Perspectives from Mexican and Puerto Rican mothers of children with special needs. *Topics in Early Childhood, 25*(3), 131-142.
Artiles, A., Rueda, R., Salazar, J. J., & Higareda, I. (2005). Within-group diversity in minority disproportionate representation: English language learners in urban school districts. *Council for Exceptional Children, 71*(3), 283-300.
Bailey, D., Skinner, D., Correa, V., Reyes-Blanes, M., Rodriguez, P., Vazquez-Montilla, E., & Skinner, M. (1999). Needs and supports reported by Latino families of young children with developmental disabilities. *American Journal on Mental Retardation, 104*(5), 437-451.
Brice, A. (2002). *The Hispanic child: Speech, language, culture and education.* Boston, MA: Allyn & Bacon.
Canfield, M. A., Brender, J., Cooper, S. P., & Greenberg, F. (1996). Hispanic origin and neural tube defects in Houston/Harris County, Texas. *American Journal of Epidemiology, 143*(1), 1-11. Retrieved from www.ahs.uic.edu/ahs/files/idhd/downloads/emerging-disabilities/latinos.htm.
Figueroa, R. (Spring, 2005). Difcultades o desabilidades de apprendizaje? *Learning Disability Quarterly, 28*, 163-167.
Gannotti, M. E., Handwerker, W. P., Groce, N. E., & Cruz, C. (2001). Sociocultural influences on disability status in Puerto Rican children. *Physical Therapy, 81*(9), 1512-1532.
Ginsberg, E. (1992). Access to health care for Hispanics. In A. Furinao (Ed.), *Health Policy and the Hispanic* (pp. 22-31). Boulder, CO: Westview Press.
Graf, N. M., Blankenship, C. J., Sanchez, G., & Carlson, R. (2007). Living on the line: Mexican and Mexican American attitudes toward disability. *Rehabilitation Counseling Bulletin, 50*(3), 153-165.
Hardin, B., Mereoiu, M., Hung, H. F., & Scott, M. R. (2009). Investigating parent and professional perspectives concerning special education services for preschool Latino children. *Early Childhood Education Journal, 37*(2), 93-102.
Hispanic women have increased risk of birth defects. (2009). *The Latino Journal.* Retrieved from www.thelatinojournal.com/2009/01/Hispanic-women-have-increased-risk-of.html
Individuals With Disabilities Education Act. (IDEA, 2004). Retrieved from http://idea.ed.gov/
Joseph-DiCaprio, J., Garwick, A. W., Kohrman, C., & Blum, R. W. (1999). Culture and the care of children with chronic conditions: Their physicians' views. *Archives of Pediatrics and Adolescent Medicine, 153*(10), 1030-1035.
Lamorey, S. (2002). The effects of culture on special education services: Evil eyes, prayer meetings, and IEPS. *Teaching Exceptional Children, 34*(5), 67-71.
Langdon, H. (2009). Providing optimal special education services to Hispanic children and their families. *Communications Disorders Quarterly, 30*(2), 83-96.

Maldonado-Duran, J. M., Munguia-Wellamn, M., Lubin, S., & Lartigue, T. (2002). Latino families in the perinatal period: Cultural issues in dealing with the healthcare system. *Great Plains Research, 12*(1), 75-100.

Mathews, T. J., & MacDorman, M. F. (2005). Infant mortality statistics from the 2005 period linked birth/infant death data set. *National Vital Statistics Report 2008, July 30, 57*(2), 1-32.

Medical genetic services in Latin America. (1999). Ninth International Congress of Human Genetics, The. Retrieved from http://whqlibdoc.who.int/hq/1998/WHO_HGN_CONS_MGS_98.4.pdf

Molina, C., Zambrana, R., & Aguirre-Molina, M. (1994). The influence of culture, class and environment on health care. In C. Molina & M. Aguirre-Molina (Eds.), *Latino health in the US: A growing challenge* (pp. 23-24). Washington, DC: American Public Health Association.

River-Bermudez, C. (1998). *The culturally unique management strategies of families of young children with special needs in Puerto Rico.* Educational Resources Information Center. (ERIC Document Production Service No. ED 419 356)

Skinner, D., Correa, V., Bailey, D. B., & Skinner, M. (2001). Role of religion in the lives of Latino families of young children with developmental delays. *American Journal on Mental Retardation, 106*(4), 297-313.

Zhao, H., & Modarresi, S. (April 2010). *Evaluating lasting effects of full-day prekindergarten program on school readiness, academic performance, and special education services.* Montgomery County Schools, Office of Accountibility, Program Evaluation Unit. Retrieved from http://montgomeryschoolsmd.org/departments/sharedaccountability/reports/2010/10.04.30%20Pre%20K%20report.pdf

Chapter 7 References

Adams, D. (2005). ABC, CBS, NBC, Fox... Univision? *The St Petersberg Times*. Retrieved from www.sptimes.com/2005/06/05/Business/ABC__CBS__NBC__Fox_Un.shtml.

Alvarez-Gonzalez, J. (2010). Structural characteristics of the 50 highest-rated television shows broadcast by Univision and Telemundo network for the Hispanic markets in the United States and Puerto Rico. *The Journal of Spanish Language Media*, University of Texas, Vol. 3.

Angeleri, S. (April 2011). *Telenovelas forming the social mind.* Retrieved from http://sandraangeleri.com/main/index.php?option=com_content&task=view&id=126&Itemid=222.

Aronson, J. (2004). The threat of stereotype. *Educational Leadership, 62*(3), 14-19.

Barrera, V., & Bielby, D. (2001). Places, faces, and other familiar things: The cultural experience of telenovela viewing among Latinos in the United States. *Journal of Popular Culture, 34*(4), 1-18.

Children Now and the National Hispanic Foundation for the Arts. (2002). *Prime time for Latinos. Report III: 2001-02 prime time television season.* Oakland, CA, and Washington, DC: Author.

Dovidio, J. F., Gluszek, A., John, M. S., Ditlmann, R., & Lagunes, P. (2010). Understanding bias toward Latinos: Discrimination, dimensions of difference and experience of exclusion. *Journal of Social Issues, 66*(1), 59-78. Retrieved from http://onlinelibrary.wiley.com/doi/10.1111/j.1540-4560.2009.01633.x/pdf

Gaztambide-Fernández, R., & Guerrero, C. (2010). *Proyecto Latino year 1: Exploratory research report to the Toronto district school district.* Retrieved from www.oise.utoronto.ca/cus/UserFiles/File/ProyectoLatinoFINAL.pdf

Gibens, G. (2009). Univision and Telemundo: Spanish language television leaders in the United States. In A. B. Albarran (Ed.), *The handbook of Spanish language media* (pp.

237-245). New York, NY: Routledge Press.
Hernandez, J. (2009). "Miss, you look like a Bratz Doll": On Chonga girls and sexual aesthetic excess. *National Women's Studies Association Journal, 21*(3), 63-90. Retrieved from http://muse.jhu.edu/login?uri=/journals/nwsa_journal/v021/21.3.hernandez.html
Isais, E. (1997). *Latinos work to change stereotypes in Hollywood.* http://dnn.epcc.edu/nwlibrary/borderlands/15_latinos_change_stereotypes.htm
Jackson, L. A. (1995). *Stereotypes, emotions, behavior, and overall attitudes toward Hispanics by Anglos. Report #10.* East Lansing, OH: Julian Samora Research Institute at the Midwest Premier Latino Research Center, Michigan State University. Retireved from http://jsri.msu.edu/Rands/research/irr/rr10/abs.html
Marin, G. (1984). Stereotyping Hispanics: The differential effect of research method, label, and degree of contact. *International Journal of Intercultural Relations, 8,* 17-27.
Market, J. (2009). Latino whiteness: The problem of being a brown for Hispanics in the United States—Perpetuating stereotypes on Univision. *Journal of Social Imagination, 45*(2), 43-61.
Mastro, D. E., & Behm-Morawitz, E. (2005). Latino representation on primetime television. *Journalism and Mass Communication Quarterly, 82*(1), 110-130.
Mendoza, J., & Reese, D. (2001). Examining multicultural picture books for the early childhood classroom: Possibilities and pitfalls. *Early Childhood Research & Practice, 3*(2), 1-38. Retrieved from http://ecrp.uiuc.edu/v3n2/mendoza.html
Mora, M. T., Villa, D. J., & Davila, A. (2006). Language shift and maintenance among the children of immigrants in the U.S.: Evidence in the Census for Spanish speakers and other language minorities. *Spanish in Context, 3*(2), 239-254.
Nilsson, N. L. (2005). How does Hispanic portrayal in children's books measure up after 40 years? The answer is "It depends." *The Reading Teacher, 58*(6), 534-548.
Perez-Stable, M. (1997). Keys to exploring Latino cultures: Folktales for children. *The Social Studies, 88*(1), 29-34.
Peterson, B., & Ramirez, M. (1971). Real, ideal-self disparity in Negro and Mexican American children. *Psychology, 8,* 22-26.
Rios, D. (2011). *Telenovelas: Dangerous and popular fare.* Retrieved from http://today.uconn.edu/blog/2011/06/telenovelas-dangerous-but-popular-fare/
Rodriguez, C. E. (1997). Promoting analytical and critical viewing. In C. E. Rodriguez (Ed.), *Images of Latinas and Latinos in the U.S. media* (pp. 240-254). Boulder, CO: Westview Press.
Rodriguez, A. L., Guido-DiBrito, F., Torres, V., & Talbot, D. (2000). Latina college students: Issues and challenges for the 21st century. *NASPA Journal, 37*(3), 511-527.
Shear, L. (2007). *Myths and truths regarding Hispanics in America.* Retrieved from www.associatedcontent.com/pop
Subervi, F., Torres, J., & Montalvo, D. (2005). *The portrayal of Latinos & Latino issues on network television news, 2004 with a retrospect to 1995 quantitative & qualitative analysis of the coverage.* Washington, DC: National Association of Hispanic Journalists.
Suro, R., & Passel, J. S. (2003). *The rise of the second generation: Changing patterns in Hispanic population growth.* Washington, DC: Pew Hispanic Center. Retrieved from http://pewhispanic.org/files/reports/22.pdf
United States Census Research Data Reports. (2002). Retrieved from www.ces.census.gov/index.php/ces/cespapers?down_key=101653
Woodrick, A. C., & Grey, M. A. (2002). *Welcoming new Iowans: A guide for Christians and churches.* Cedar Falls, IA: The University of Iowa New Iowans Program and Ecumenical Ministries of Iowa.
Young, S. (2009). *9 myths about Latinos: Dispelling stereotypes.* Retrieved from www.associatedcontent.com/pop

Chapter 8 References

Clutter, A. W., & Zubieta, A. C. (2009). *Understanding the Latino culture, family and consumer sciences.* Ohio State University Extension: No. 800-589-8292. Retrieved from *http://ohioline.osu.edu/hyg-fact/5000/pdf/5237.pdf*

Lopez-Rayo, A. (2007). *Fifteen candles: Fifteen years of taffeta, hairspray, drunk uncles and other quinceañera stories.* New York, NY: HarperCollins.

Menard, V. (2004). *The Latino holiday book: From cinco de mayo to dia de los muertos—The celebrations and traditions of Hispanic Americans.* New York, NY: Marlowe and Co. Avalon Publishing Group.

Padilla, A., & Borrero, N. (2006). Effects of acculturative stress on the Hispanic family. In P. Wong & L. Wong (Eds.), *The handbook of multicultural perspectives* (pp. 299-319). New York, NY: Springer Publications.

Rodriguez, G. (1999). *Raising nuestros niños in a bicultural world: Bringing up Latino children.* New York, NY: Simon and Schuster.